To all our friends
throughout the world who
are looking forward to the 2008
Beijing Olympics and interested
in this ancient capital!

To all our friends
throughout the world who
are looking forward to the 2008
Beijing Olympics and interested
in this ancient capital!

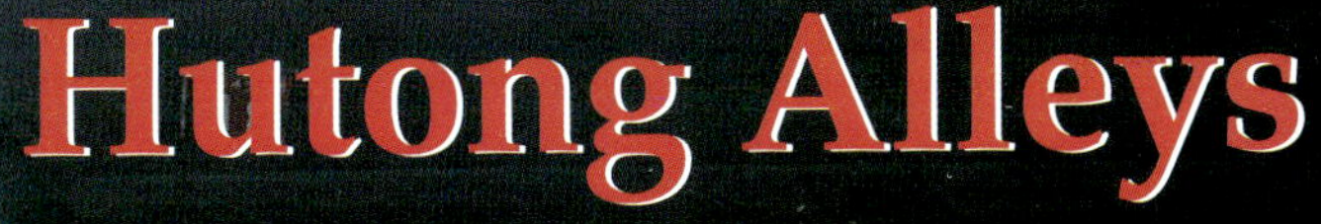

Hutong Alleys

Former Residences of Celebrities

Beijing is a place of great antiquity and mystery, with world-famous imperial palaces and gardens, as well as unique *hutong* alleys of cultural interest.

...

Many celebrities have lived in Beijing's *hutong*, which have a unique architectural style, have witnessed many historical events, are surrounded by folklore, and are now inhabited by modern Beijing people.

...

Visitors from afar will be greatly impressed by the atmosphere of the ancient capital.

Foreign Languages Press

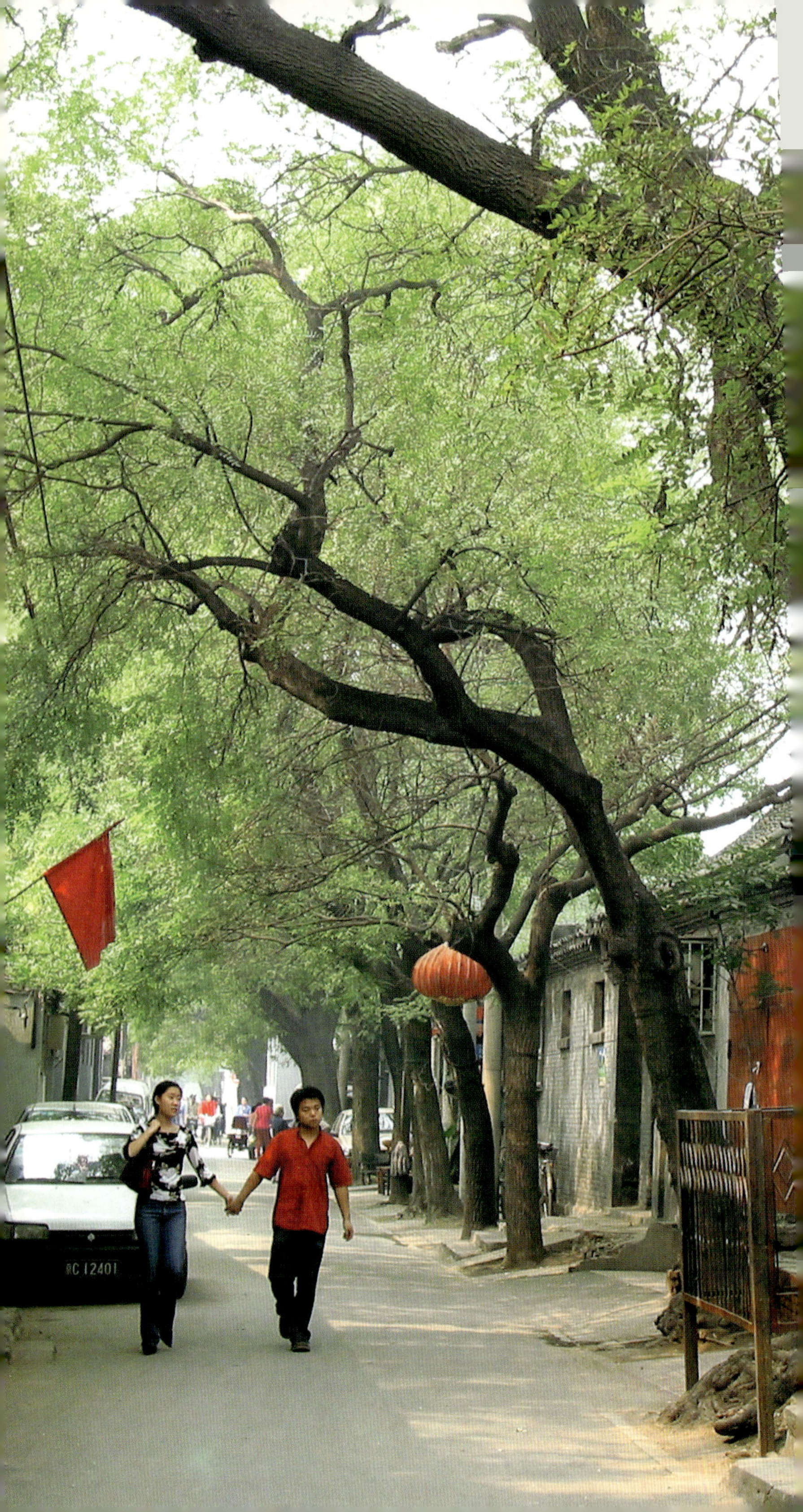

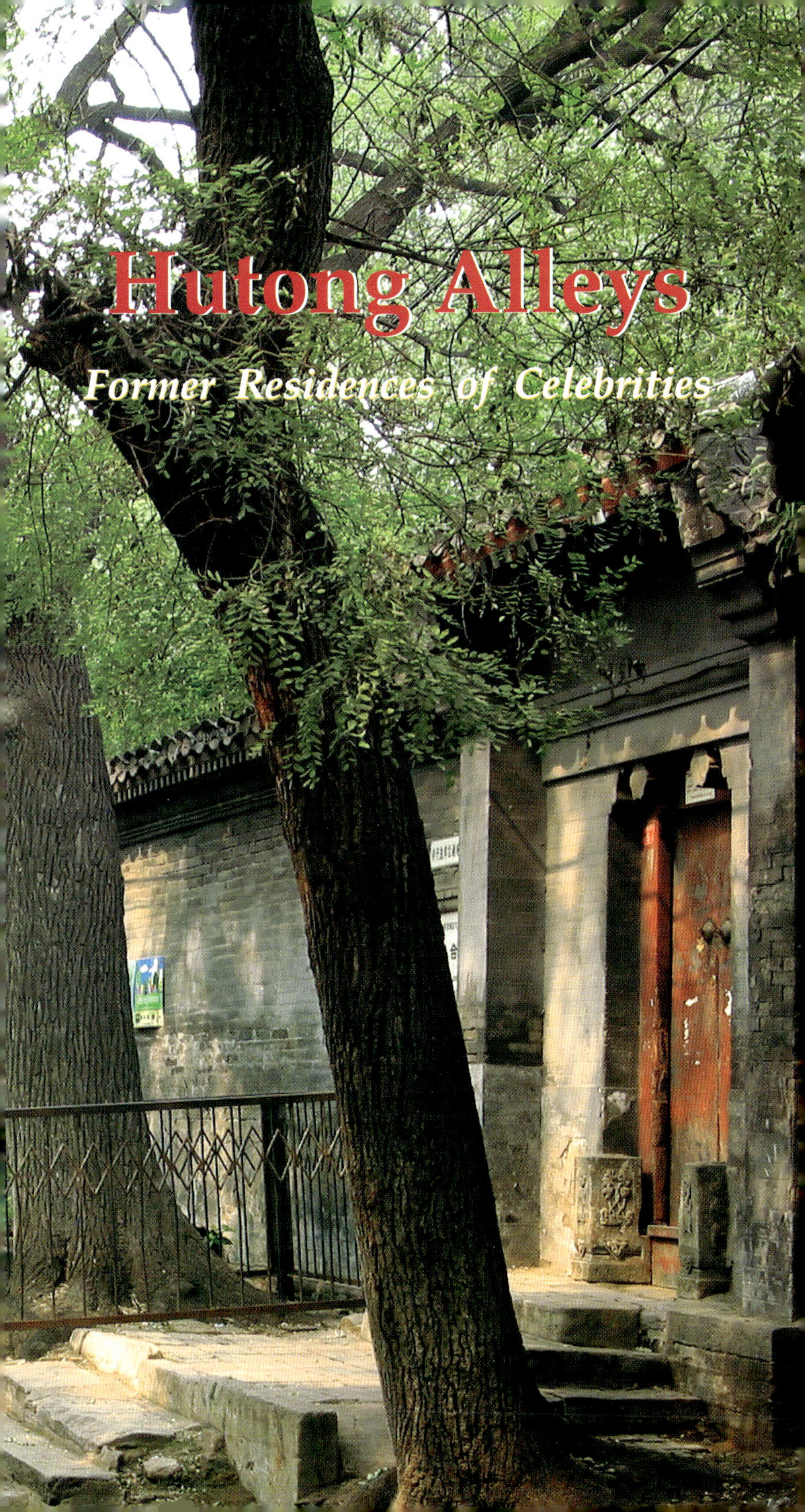

Hutong Alleys
Former Residences of Celebrities

Planned by : Xiao Xiaoming

Managing editor: Lan Peijin

Text by Li Lianxia

Photos by Wang Jianhua, Wang Wengbo, Gao Mingyi,
Yan Xiangqun, Lan Peijin, et al.

Translated by Yan Jing

English text edited by Peter Brennan, Yu Ling

Cover designed by Wu Tao

Format designed by Lan Peijin, Yuan Qing, et al.

First Edition 2005

Hutong Alleys : Former Residences of Celebrities

ISBN 7-119-03346-8

© Foreign Languages Press
Published by Foreign Languages Press
24 Baiwanzhuang Road, Beijing 100037, China
Home Page: http://www.flp.com.cn
E-mail Addresses: info@flp.com.cn
                sales@flp.com.cn
Distributed by China International Book Trading Corporation
35 Chegongzhuang Xilu, Beijing, 100044, China
P.O. Box 399, Beijing, China

Printed in the People's Republic of China

Contents

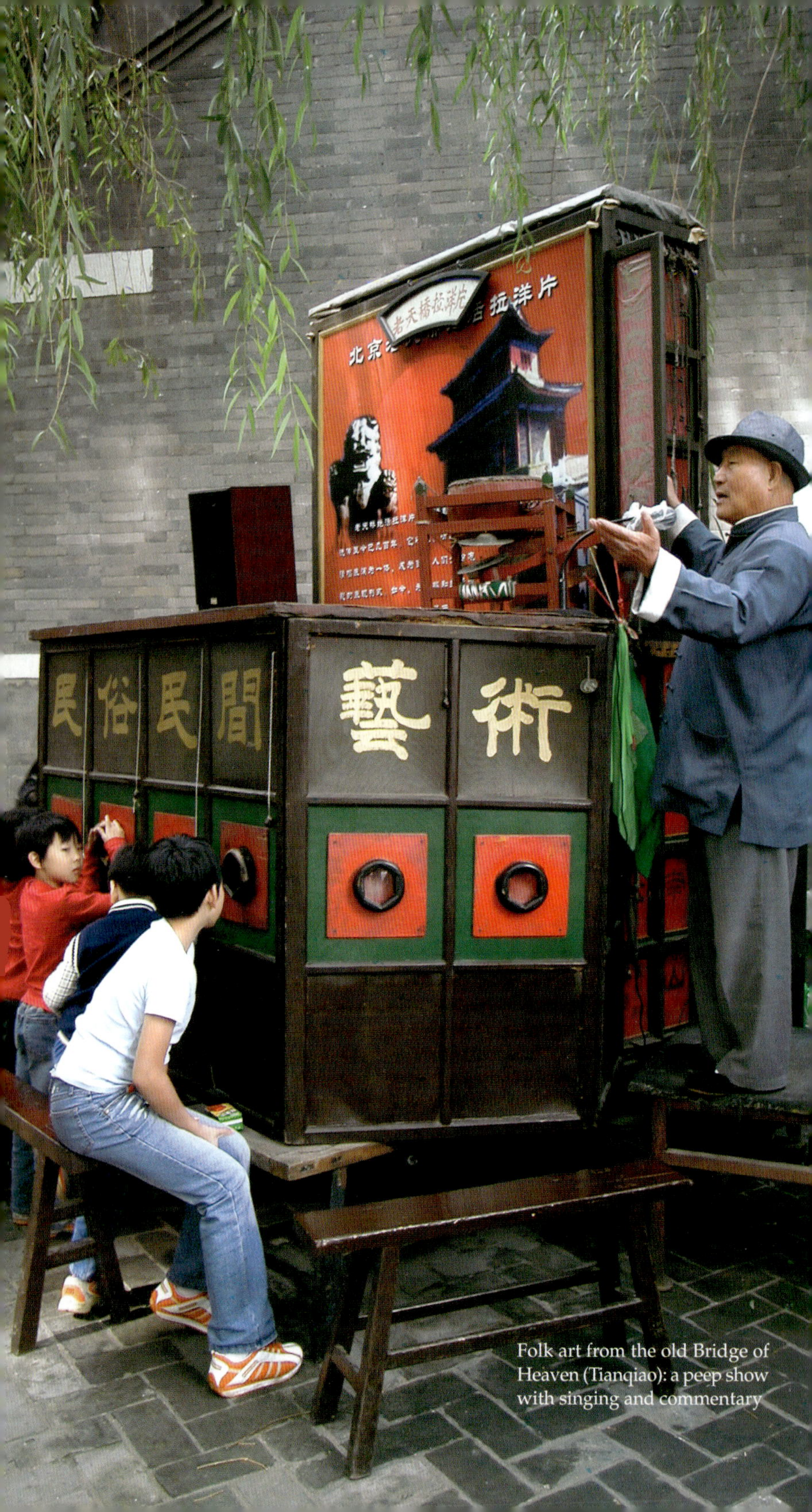

Folk art from the old Bridge of Heaven (Tianqiao): a peep show with singing and commentary

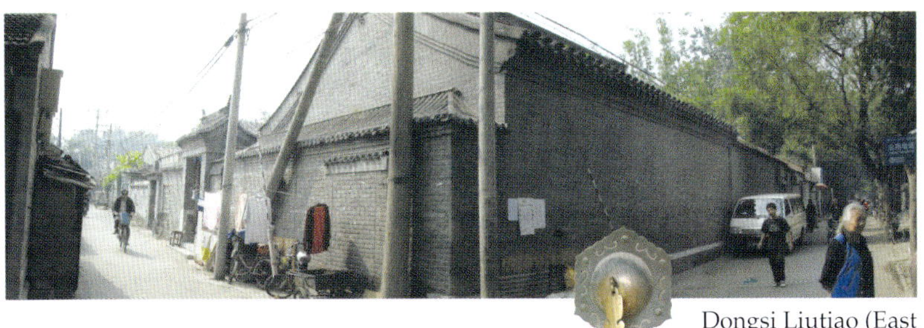

I. Beijing's Hutong Alleys

Dongsi Liutiao (East Four Sixth Lane)

Beijing is a well-known historical and cultural Chinese city as well as one of the most magnificent cultural wonders in the history of world civilization. Many world-famous specialists in city construction share the view that the city of Beijing is the greatest work of culture. Tian'anmen Square, the resplendent and magnificent Forbidden City, and the grand Great Wall are world-famous, but even the inconspicuous little *hutong* alleys also deserve careful study.

The city's *hutong* are Beijing's veins and transportation channels. They came into being after the city became the capital of the Yuan Dynasty (1271-1368). The city's appearance symbolizes the development of society. Like folk custom exhibition centers, displaying the variety of ways of living, the *hutong* record the changes in history and the look of the times and they contain the rich flavor of cultural life.

The *hutong* originated in the Yuan Dynasty but, at that time, they were not called *hutong* but *huolong* ("fire lane") or *longtong* ("open lane"). These terms referred to the gaps between buildings in the city layout, which acted as thoroughfares in normal times and to prevent the flames from spreading in the case of a fire.

So just how many *hutong* are there in

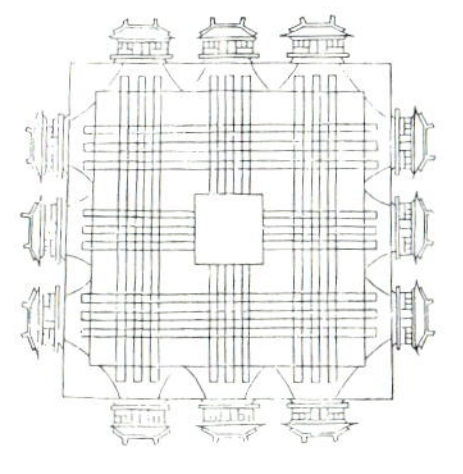

The Rites of the Zhou records that the capital is nine li in circumference, with three gates on each side. There are nine main streets from north to south, on each of which nine carriages can stand side by side. There are also nine main streets from east to west. The ancestral temple is to the left of the imperial palace, the altar to the right, the imperial court in front, and markets behind.

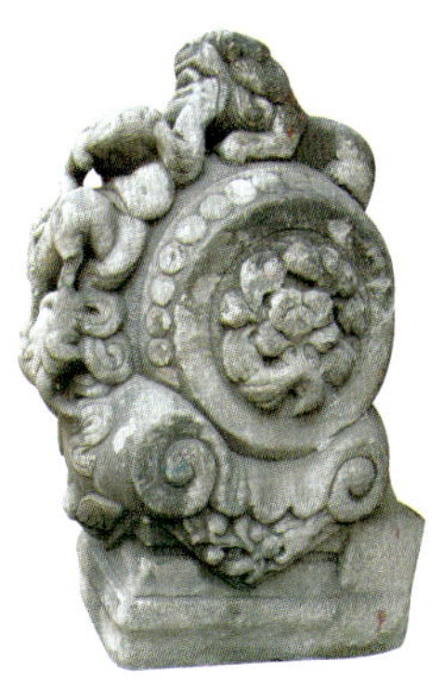

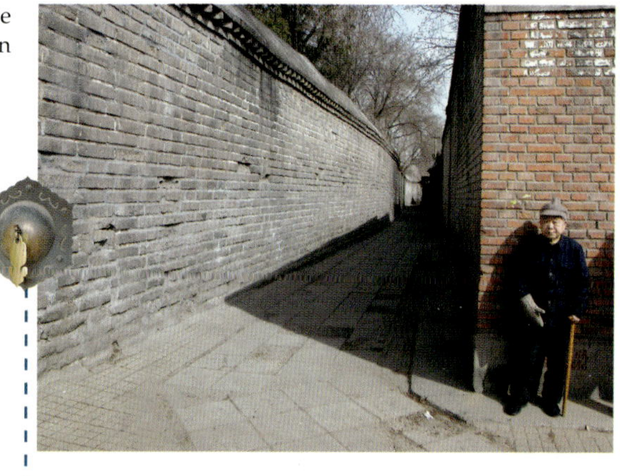

The narrow lane outside the Forbidden City's east wall

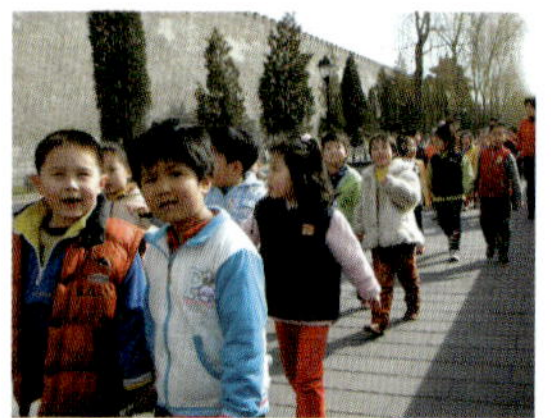

Children walk past the imperial city wall.

Diagram of the capital during the Yuan Dynasty

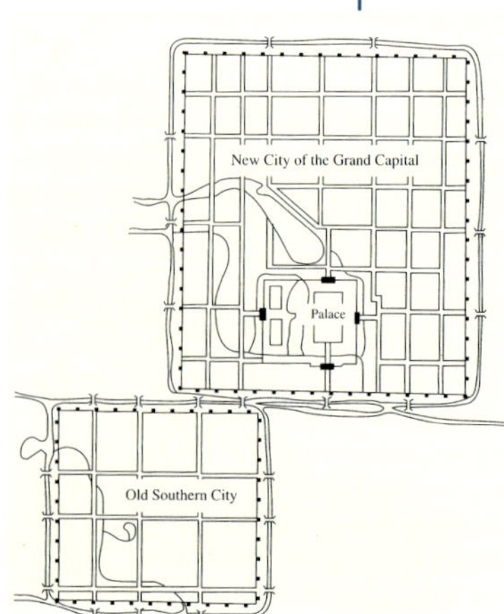

Beijing? Veteran residents say: "There are 360 major *hutong* and there are as many small ones as there are hairs on an ox." In other words, there are countless Beijing *hutong*. When the *hutong* of the Yuan Dynasty had just taken shape, they were set out in an orderly way and in a checkerboard style. However, the layout was less methodical during the Ming and Qing dynasties. There are not only *hutong* running from east to west or from north to south but also *hutong* at oblique angles, half *hutong* and dead-end *hutong*. Some big *hutong* enclose small *hutong*. In some *hutong*, pedestrians enter, turn left then right, make a circle and then emerge from another place near the entrance. With characteristic vivid humor, Beijing residents call this kind of *hutong* "arms-folded" *hutong* because they are shaped like a person's folded arms. There are also some tortuously shaped *hutong*. So, it is really not easy to count the number and figure out how many *hutong* there are in Beijing.

According to historical records, during the Yuan Dynasty, Beijing had 384 *huoxiang* (narrow strips of open

8

space between houses acting as firebreaks) and 29 *xiangtong* ("open lanes"). That is to say, there were 413 alleys and lanes altogether, of which 29 ones were lanes in a strict sense, while the 384 *huoxiang* were lanes in a broad sense.

A count made using a restored map of Beijing from the Ming Dynasty (1368-1644) shows there were altogether 629 alleys and lanes in Beijing, of which 359 were lanes in a strict sense.

The names of more than 30 *hutong* have remained unchanged for seven or eight centuries, such as Yangfang Hutong (Goat Room Lane), Luo'er Hutong (Sieve Lane), Cuihua Hutong (Jadeite Flower Lane), Yueya Hutong (Crescent Moon Lane), Toufa Hutong

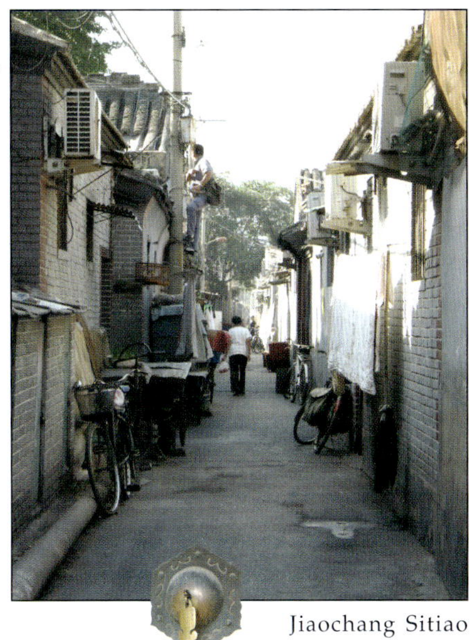
Jiaochang Sitiao (Drill Ground Fourth Lane)

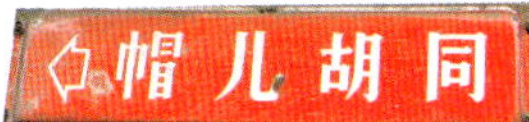

The sign of Maor Hutong (Hat Lane)

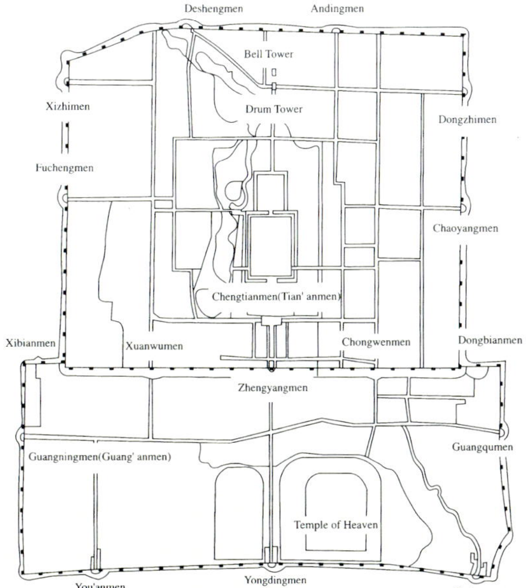
A map of Beijing during the Ming Dynasty

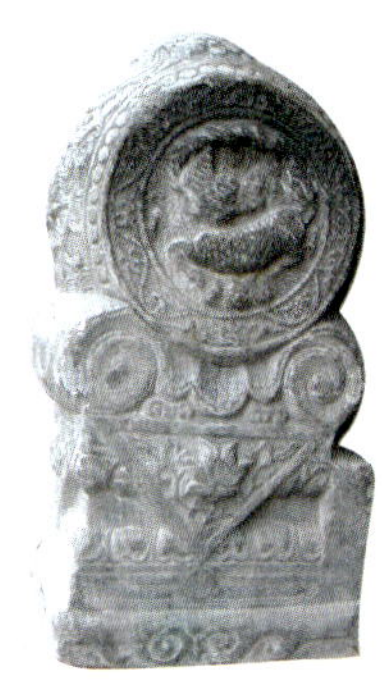

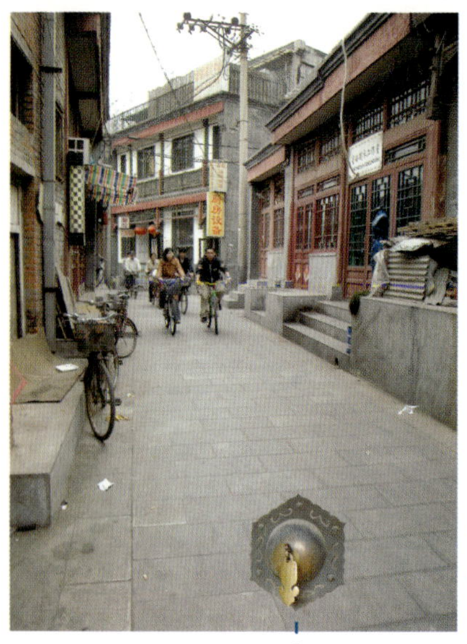

Yandai Xiejie (Tobacco-Pipe Oblique Street)

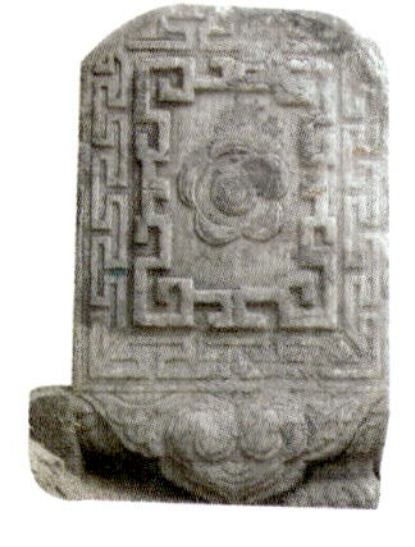

Streets and lanes from the Full Map of the Capital during Emperor Qianlong's Reign

(Hair Lane), Dengcao Hutong (Rush Lane), Shijia Hutong (Shi Family Lane), and so on.

During the Qing Dynasty (1644-1911), Beijing lanes had developed considerably compared to the Ming Dynasty. According to *Capital Lanes Annals* (*Jingshi Fangxiang Zhigao*) written by Zhu Yixin of the Qing Dynasty, there were 2,077 alleys and lanes altogether during the Qing Dynasty, of which 978 had the word *hutong* in their names.

By the year 1944, according to the *Beijing Place Names Annals* (*Beijing Diming Zhi*), Beijing had a total of 3,200 lanes, including those that did not have the word *hutong* in their names.

How many lanes does Beijing have today? The *Directory of Beijing Streets and Lanes* (*Beijing Shi Jiexiang Mingcheng Lu Huibian*) of the Beijing Public Security Bureau, compiled in August 1986, collected the names of streets, alleys, lanes and hamlets (so-called naturally

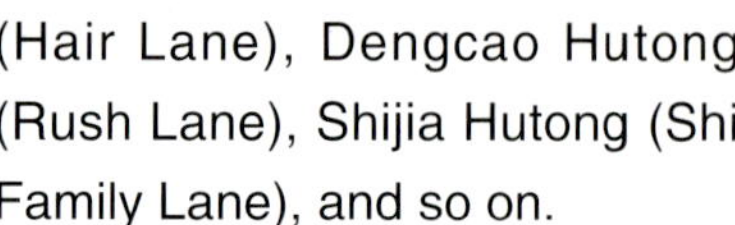

10

formed villages) from Beijing's 10 districts – Dongcheng, Xicheng, Chongwen, Xuanwu, Chaoyang, Haidian, Fengtai, Shijingshan, Mentougou, and Yanshan. According to the register, there were 6,104 streets, alleys, lanes and hamlets altogether, of which 1,316 had the word *hutong* in their names. However, building work in the capital in recent years has meant many alleys have been consigned to history.

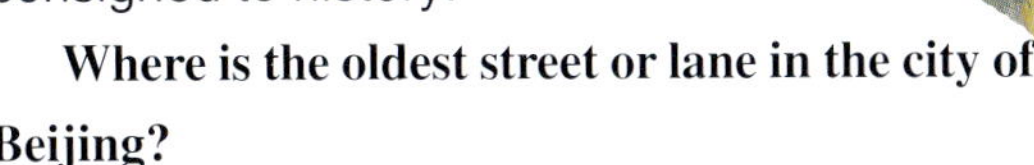

A store of long standing in Dashilan or Dazhalan Jie (Big Railings Street)

Where is the oldest street or lane in the city of Beijing?

It is located in what is now the Sanmiao Jie (Three Temple Street) area behind the Guohua shopping mall in Xuanwu District and is more than 900 years old.

The oldest oblique lane in the city of Beijing: Yandai Xie Jie (Tobacco-Pipe Oblique Street)

North of Di'anmen (Gate of Earthly Peace) and in front of the Drum Tower lies the oldest oblique street in the city of Beijing, called Yandai Xie Jie (Tobacco-Pipe Oblique Street). This street runs from northeast to southwest and is more than 300 meters long. Why was it given the name Tobacco-Pipe Oblique Street? There is a reason for that. Early in the Ming Dynasty, the street was called Dayu Ting Xie Jie (Fishing Hall Oblique Street), while it was called Gulou Xie Jie (Drum-Tower Oblique Street) during the Qing Dynasty. In those years, most of the Manchu bannermen living in the north of the city had the habit of smoking a long-stemmed Chinese pipe or water pipe, which spurred the development of the tobacco industry in Beijing.

Beijing people like to put the national flag outside their doorways to celebrate National Day on October 1 each year.

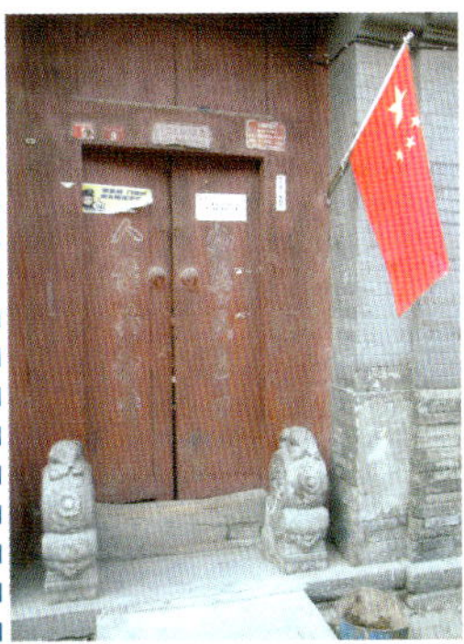

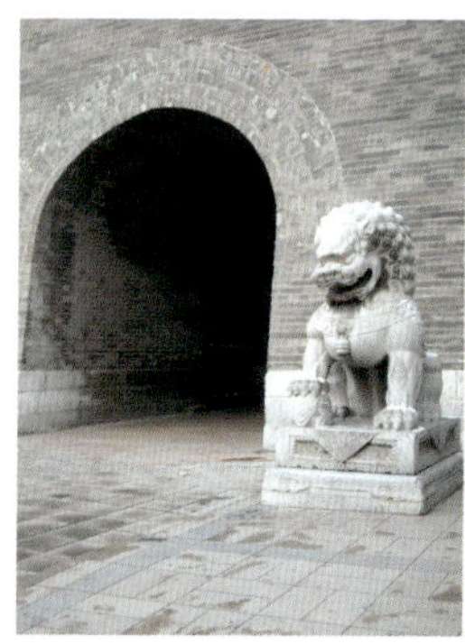

The sign of the reconstructed Wangfujing Dajie (Well in the Prince's Mansion Street). On the sign are engraved the names of many shops of long standing.

Smokers were used to smoking pipes at that time and were very particular about their pipes. Residents of the oblique street had a head for business. They understood what the market needed and opened pipe shops one after another. Therefore, the names Fishing Hall Oblique Street and Drum-Tower Oblique Street gradually disappeared, while the name Tobacco-Pipe Oblique Street became more and more popular. This is the origin of the name Tobacco-Pipe Oblique Street. But one coincidental fact is worthy of attention. The 300-meter road is shaped like the stem of a tobacco pipe, while the east entrance looks like the mouthpiece, and the western part turning south toward Yinding (Silver Ingot) Bridge looks just like a pipe bowl.

A stone lion defends the city gate.

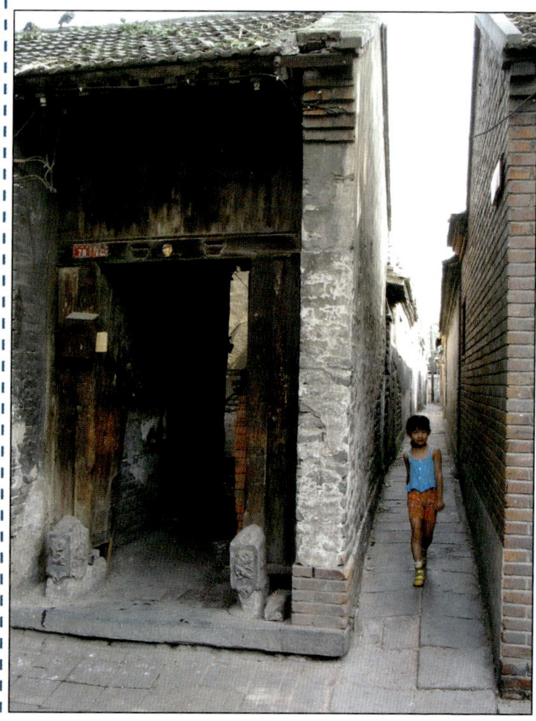

One of Beijing's narrow lanes

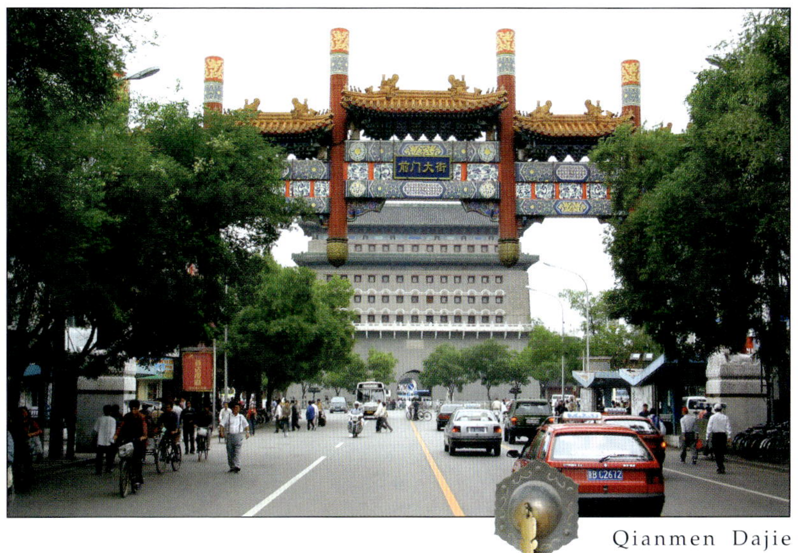

Qianmen Dajie
(Front Gate Avenue)

The most famous *hutong* in Beijing: Dashilan (Dazhalan)

A prominent characteristic of the old Beijing *hutong* in their early years was that wood or iron fences were installed at their entrances, functioning like today's popular anti-theft doors. During the Ming Dynasty, a junior officer named Wang Min presented a memorial to the emperor, saying: "There are so many streets and alleys in the capital, but only 700 policemen. When there is a burglary, we are short of hands, and the alleys will make it easy for thieves to slip away and hide. So I suggest that fences be installed at the entrances of Beijing's alleys and that they be closed at night." At that time, a curfew was imposed every night in the city, banning pedestrians from coming and going in the streets. However, it could not prevent thieves from hiding in the streets and alleys. Thus fences needed to be installed to help police officers combat theft. The emperor gave his approval as soon as he saw this memorial for the benefit of public security. As a result, fences were installed at the entrance of Beijing's

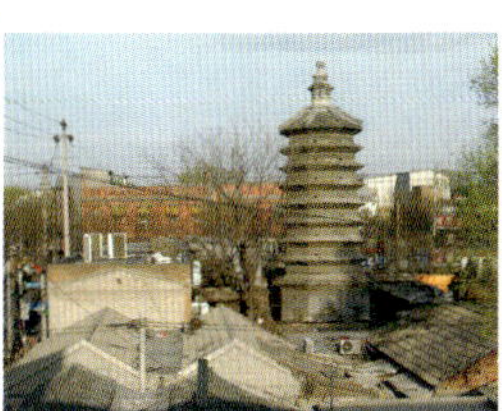

The ancient brick pagoda east of Zhuanta Hutong (Brick Tower Lane)

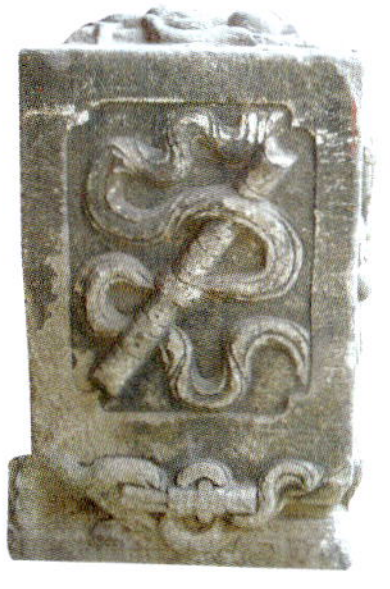

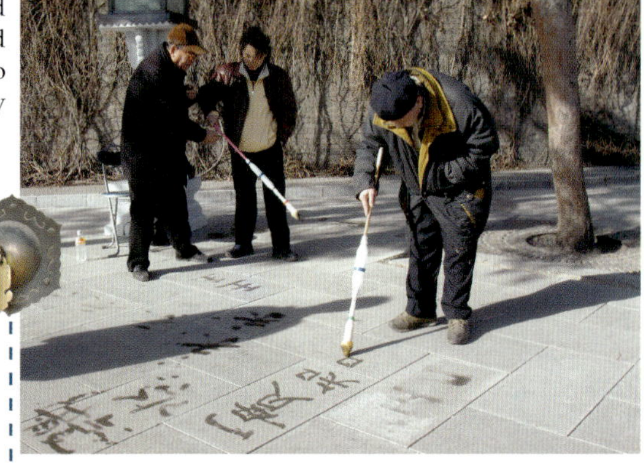

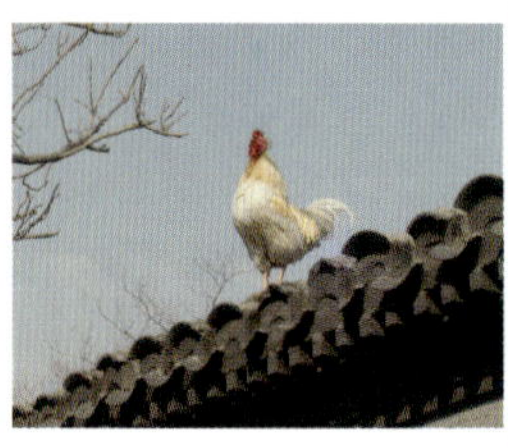

A new day in the lane begins with a wake-up call.

hutong. More and more fences were put up during the Qing Dynasty. Although they have now disappeared, there still remain many *hutong* named after fences, the most famous of which is Dashilan or Dazhalan Jie (Big Railings Street), south of Qianmen Xidajie (Front Gate West Avenue).

The longest *hutong* in the city of Beijing: Dongjiaomin Xiang and Xijiaomin Xiang (East and West Dealing-with-the-People Lanes)

The street comprising Dongjiaomin Xiang and Xijiaoming Xiang runs parellel to and south of the avenue Chang'an Jie. It stretches from Chongwenmennei Daj (Gate of Literary Virtue Inner Street) in the east to Beixinhua Jie (North New China Street) in the Hepingmen (Peace Gate) neighborhood in the west. In the Ming Dynasty, this area had a canal, where rice transported from southern China to Beijing was unloaded. The southern rice was called *jiangmi* ("river rice" or glutinous rice), so the lane was called Jiangmi Xiang (Glutinous Rice Lane). After the First Opium War (1840-42), some foreign embassies were set up in the region one after another, so the lane's name was changed from Glutinous Rice Lane to Jiaomin Xiang (Dealing-with-the-People Lane).

In front of a restaurant is a statue of an old man in a mandarin jacket carrying a birdcage.

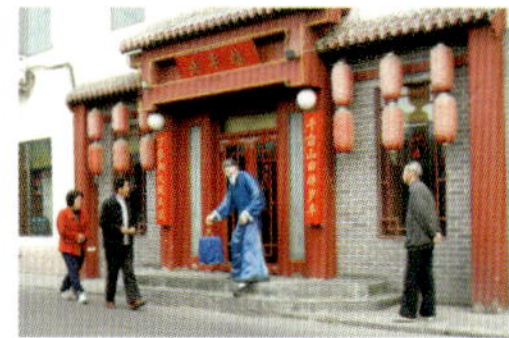

14

The shortest lane in Beijing: Yichi Dajie (One-Foot Street)

Yichi Dajie runs southeast of the east entrance of Liulichang Dongjie (Antique Street). With a length of only about a dozen meters, the route merges into Yangmeizhu Xie Jie (Red Bayberry and Bamboo Oblique Street). It is regarded as the shortest lane in Beijing.

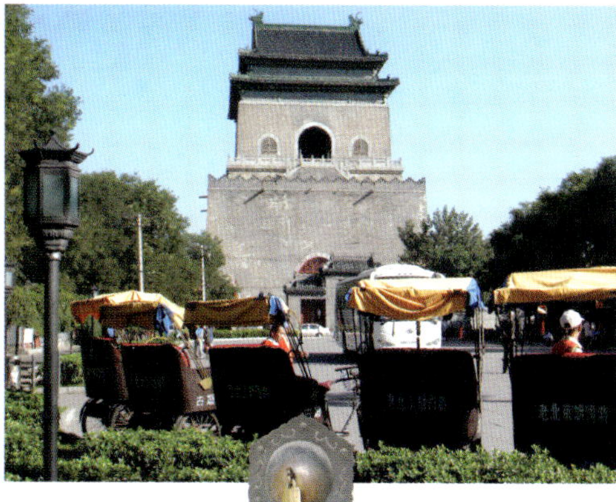
The Bell Tower

The narrowest *hutong* in Beijing: Gaoyou Hutong

Gaoyou Hutong is located in the bridge area of eastern Zhushikou (Pearl Market Entrance) in Chongwen District. Its narrowest section is only about 60 centimeters across. But it was later discovered that Xiaolaba Hutong (Little Trumpet Lane), located west of Tianqiao (Heaven Bridge) in the Yong'an Lu (Eternal Peace Road) neighborhood is only about 50 centimeters across. However, Qianshi (Banking) Hutong in the Dashilan (Dazhalan) neighborhood outside Qianmen (Front Gate) has proved to be only 40 centimeters across.

The lane with the most bends: Jiudaowan Xiang (Nine Bends Lane)

Jiudaowan Xiang, located in the Beixinqiao (North New Bridge) area of Dongcheng District, has more than 20 twists and turns. It has now been divided into five sections: Jiudaowan Beixiang, Nanxiang, Dongxiang, Xixiang and Zhongxiang (North, South, East, West and Central Nine Bends Lane).

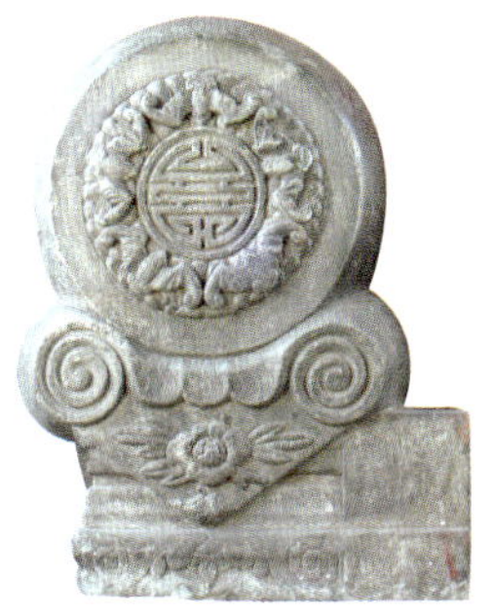

Beijing hutong names

Beijing has a great many *hutong* and they are arranged in crisscross patterns. They also have a wide variety of names, covering everything under the sun. The names can be divided into four categories: 1. *Hutong* named after people. 2. *Hutong* named after goods sold at market. 3. *Hutong* named after buildings. 4. *Hutong* named after geographical features. Some people say that Beijing's *hutong* can be compared to an encyclopedia and that they reflect not only the evolution of history but also changing fashions in society.

Hutong named after people:

Hutong such as Wenchengxiang Hutong (Prime Minister Wen Lane), Zhangzizhong Lu (Zhang Zizhong Road), Tonglinge Lu (Tong Linge Road) and so on were given their names to commemorate national heroes and patriotic generals, expressing people's admiration.

For instance, today's Sanbulao Hutong, located west of Denei Dajie (Moral Victory Gate Inner Street), was named in memory of the fa-

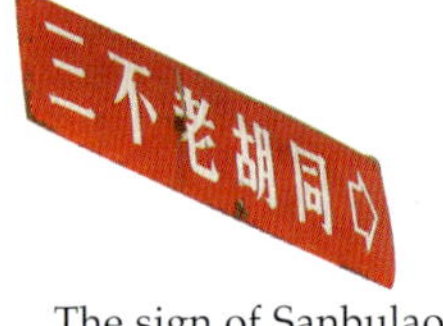

The sign of Sanbulao Hutong

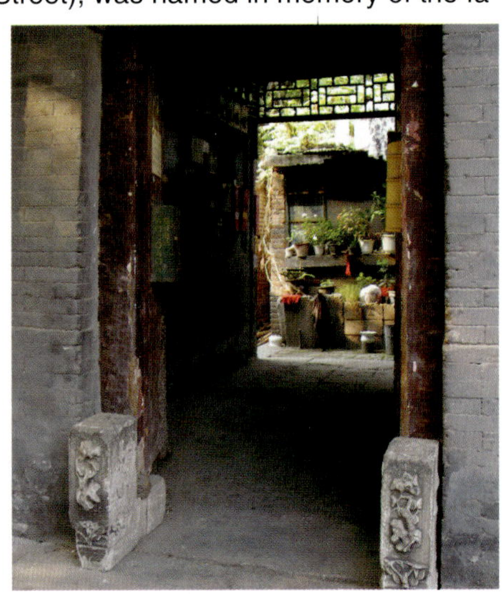

The decorative work inside the tower gate

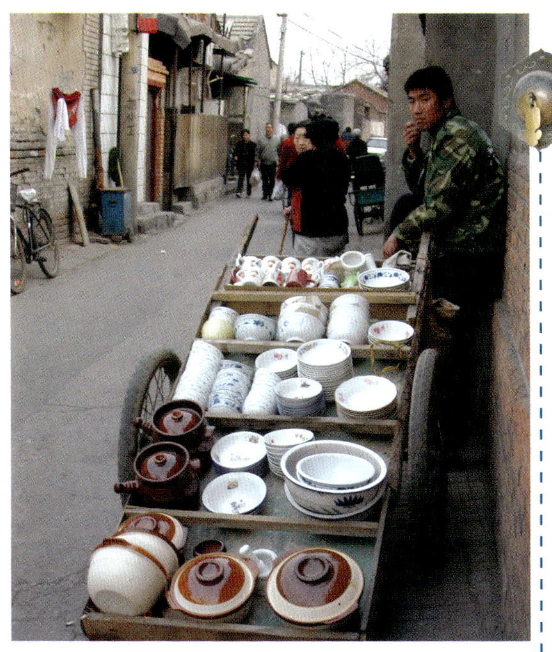

A street peddler selling everyday items from a cart

mous Ming Dynasty navigator Zheng He (Eunuch Sanbao), who had sailed across the Western Seas seven times. The street was originally called Sanbaolaoye Hutong (Lord Sanbao Lane). During the Qing Dynasty, it became Sanbolao Hutong (Venerable Sanbo Lane) and later Sanbulao Hutong (which could mean Venerable Sanbu Lane or the Lane of Three Immortals).

Located west of the Cultural Palace of Nationalities, Dashaguo and Xiaoshaguo Hutong (Big and Small Crab Apple Lanes) were not originally related to any fruit. The lane was first called Shaguoliu Hutong (Earthenware-Pot Liu Lane) because a certain person named Liu lived in the *hutong* and sold earthenware pots there. Later the name was corrupted and became Shaguoliuli Hutong (Earthenware-Pot Colored Glaze Lane), then Dashaguo and Xiaoshaguo Hutong (Big and Small Crab Apple Lanes). This just proves that Beijing *hutong* names were handed down by word of mouth.

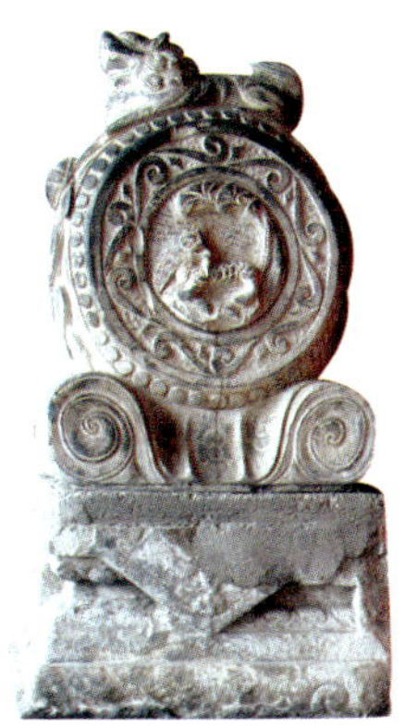

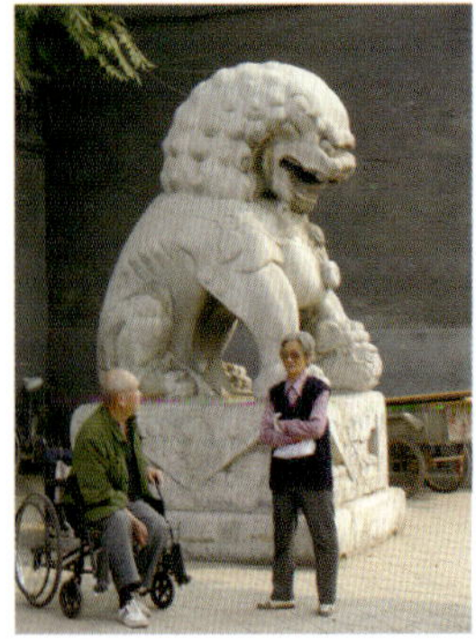
A stone lion in front of a prince's residence

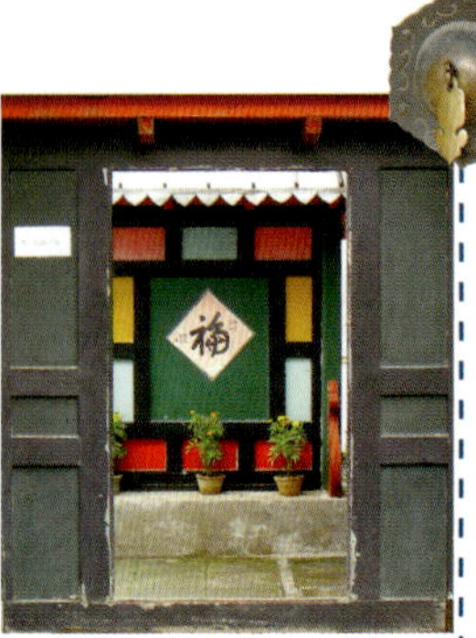
A modern-style wooden "inner screen"

Beijing *hutong* attract a lot of foreign tourists

***Hutong* named after goods sold at market:**

People need food, so there are *hutong* named after food. Hutong named after grains, flour and rice include Ganmian Hutong (Wheat-Flour Lane), Lanmian Hutong (Mushy Noodle Lane), Ximi Hutong (Fine Rice Lane), Dongjiangmi and Xijiangmi Xiang (East and West Glutinous Rice Lane) and Baimi Xie Jie (Polished Rice Oblique Street). But people do not eat only these staple foods, so there are also names such as Qiezi Hutong (Eggplant Lane), Douya Hutong (Bean Sprouts Lane), Doujiao Hutong (Fresh Kidney Beans Lane), Yangrou Hutong (Mutton Lane) and Ganyu Hutong (Dried Fish Lane). Moreover, there are Shaojiu Hutong (Spirit Lane), Chaye Hutong (Tea Leaf Lane), Guozi Hutong (Fruit Lane), Guozi Xiang (Fruit Alley), Putaoyuan Hutong (Vineyard Lane), Yingtao Hutong (Cherry Lane), and so on.

***Hutong* named after buildings:**

In Beijing's early years, the city's most eye-catching and outstanding symbols were the city gates, temples and *pailou* (decorated archways). From these, some *hutong* got their

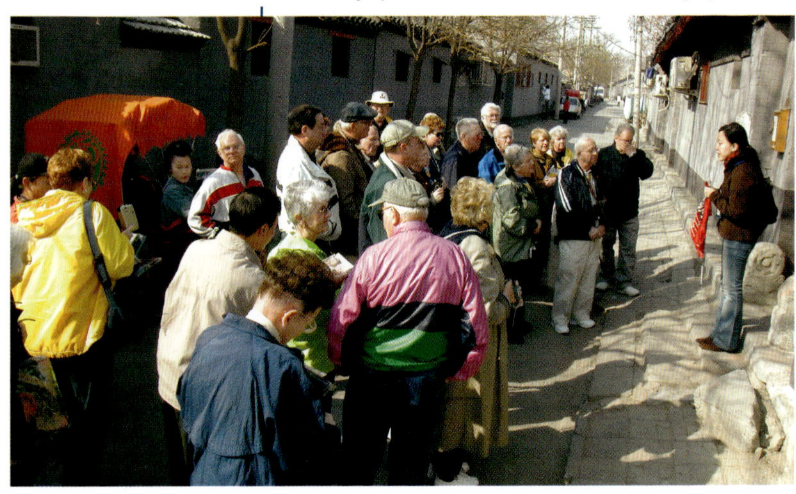

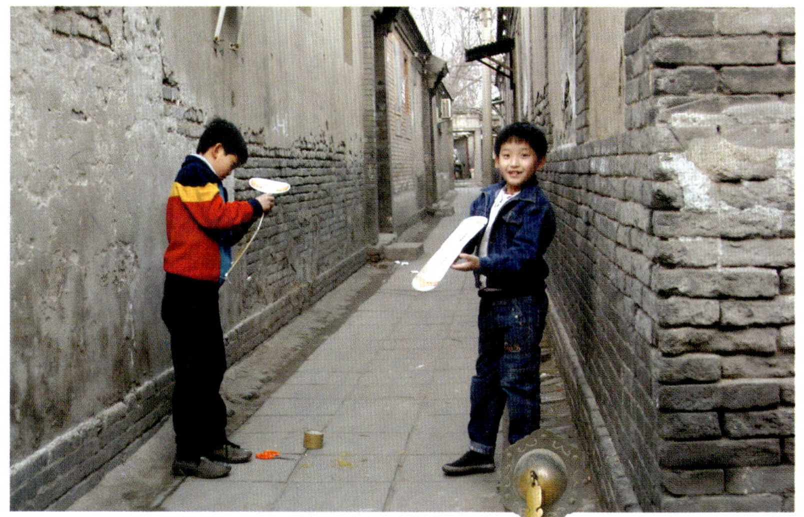

names, such as Xizhimennei and Xizhimenwai Dajie (Inner and Outer Straight West Gate Street), Qianyuan'ensi and Houyuan'ensi Hutong (Front and Back Round-Kindness Temple Lane), Dongsi (East Four) (*pailou*, decorated archways), Xidan (West Single) (*pailou*, decorated archways), and so on.

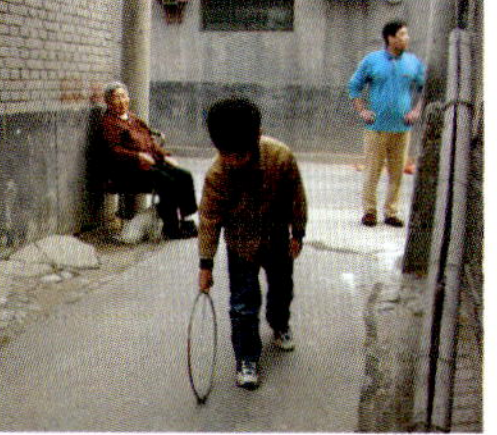

Boys playing in Beijing's lanes

Other *hutong* are named after temples, such as Longfusi Hutong (Grand Blessing Temple Lane), Dafosi Jie (Big Buddha Temple Street), Baochansi Jie (Precious Buddhist Temple Street), Huguosi Jie (Defending-the-Nation Temple Street), Zhengjuesi Hutong (Right-Consciousness Temple Lane), Guanyinsi Hutong (Goddess of Mercy Temple Lane), and so on.

Hutong named after geographical features:

At the end of the Qing Dynasty and beginning of the Republic of China, Yuan Shikai once set up his presidential office in Jurentang (Benevolence Hall) in the Zhongnanhai (Middle and South Lake) area. He then opened a door in the imperial city wall under Baoyuelou (Treasured Moon Building) at Nanhai (South Lake), which was named Xinhuamen (New

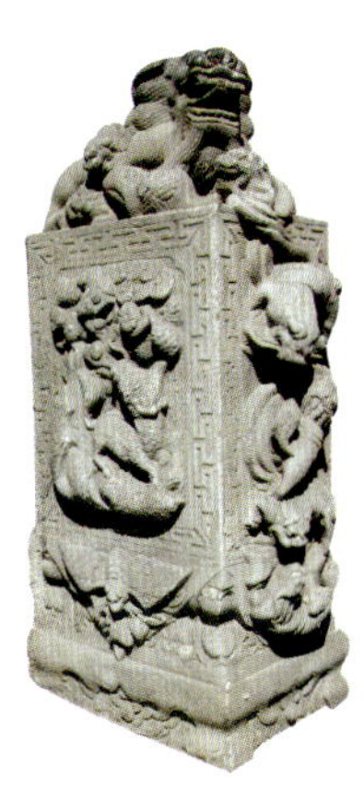

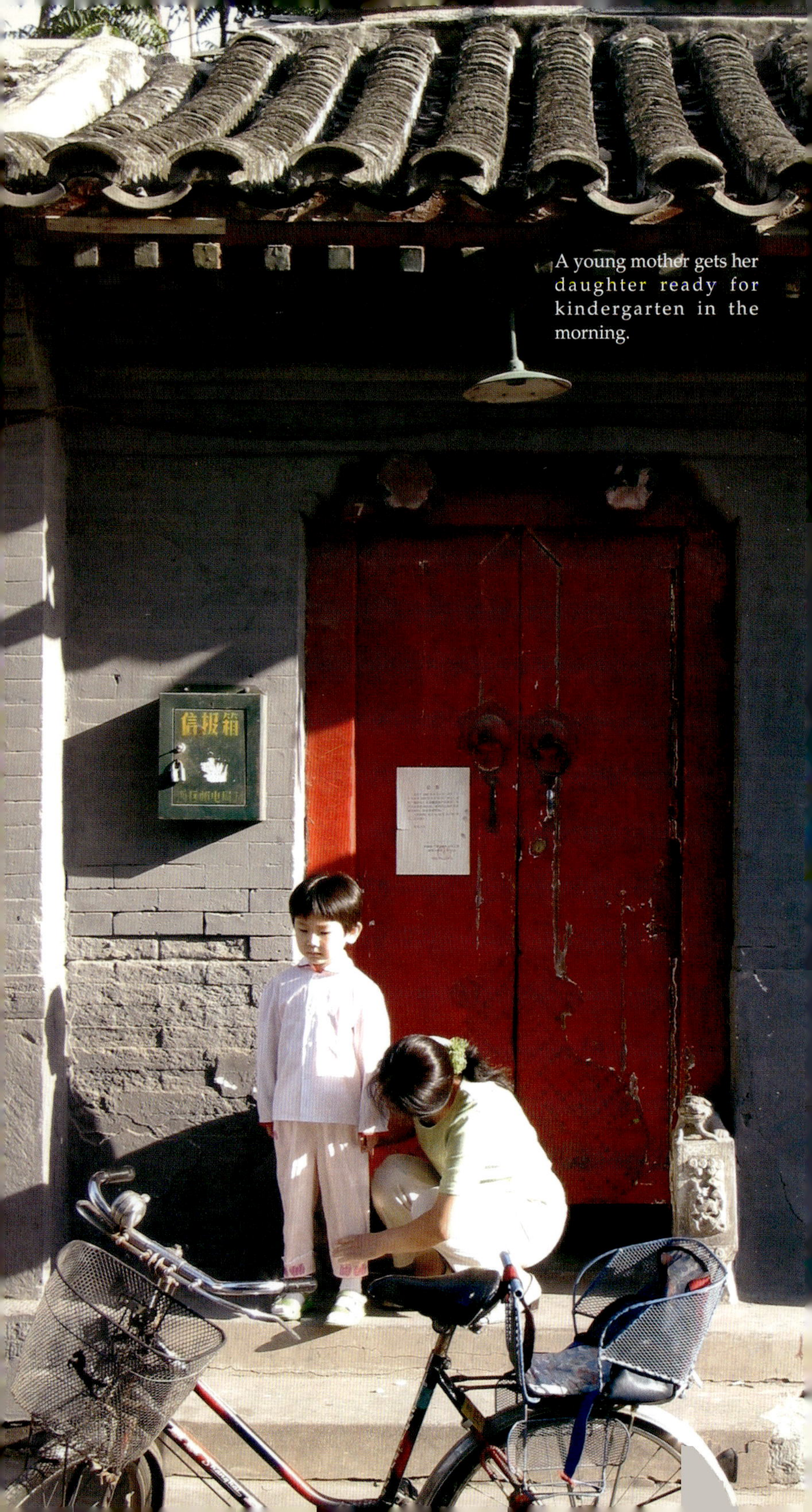

A young mother gets her daughter ready for kindergarten in the morning.

China Gate). Consequently, the western part of the avenue Chang'an Jie in front of Xinhuamen was re-named Fuqian Jie (Front Mansion Street) at that time. A street west of Zhongnanhai was renamed Fuyou Jie (Right Mansion Street), a name it has kept to this day. There are *hutong* named af-ter geographical fea-

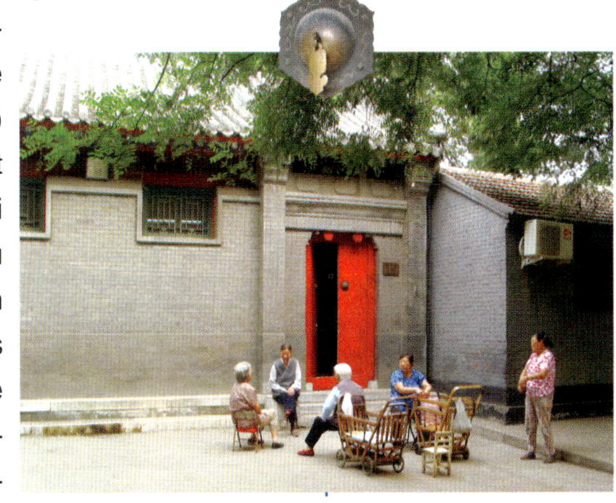

Elderly residents of Guozijian (Imperial College) enjoy chatting in the lane.

tures whose names have not changed since the Ming Dynasty, such as Songshu Hutong (Pine Tree Lane), Chunshu Hutong (Chinese Toon Tree Lane), Banjing Hutong (Broad Well Lane), and so on.

The term *hutong* is a general title represent-ing Beijing's streets and alleys. However, the *hutong* have constituted not only a key part of Beijing's traffic network but also something that props up Beijing urban life. The *hutong* conse-quently became a significant arena for Beijing's historical and cultural development and evolution. Without a doubt, the stories and leg-ends that took place in the *hutong* are indispensable.

The Story of Tongfu Jiadao (Tong Mansion Lane)

North of Dengshikou Dajie (Lantern Market Entrance Street) in Dongcheng District, there is located an old *hutong* commonly called Tongfu Jiadao (Tong Mansion Lane). In the lane stands a tall mansion, which was originally the residence of the Qing Dynasty Emperor Kangxi's in-laws Tong Guogang and Tong

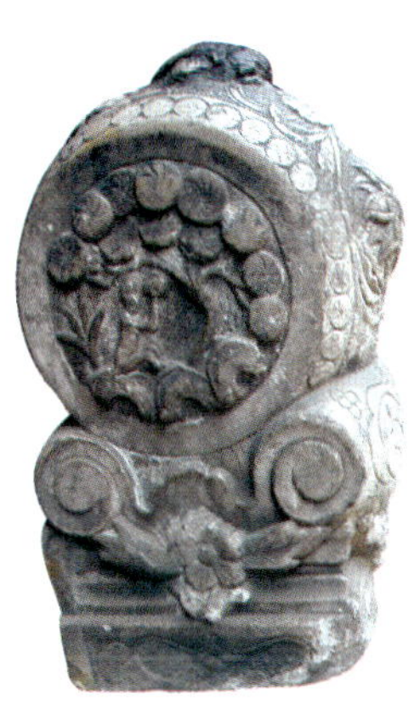

Guowei. Why is it still so renowned after more than a century? That has a great deal to do with the old mansion's architecture, particularly the huge white marble in the screen wall in front of the original mansion. The marble, loved by the people, has black and brown natural veins on it. Whenever it rains, an image of Guanyin, the Goddess of Mercy, is faintly visible above undulating hills and clouds on the stone, her bun of hair, shawl and features all revealed by the natural veins. In front of Guanyin is a lifelike incense burner with smoke curling up from it. The marvelous marble has been called the Tong Mansion Guanyin Stone for a century. After 1949, the mansion was transformed into Beijing High School No. 166. In the early years of the "cultural revolution" (1966-76), the teachers and students buried the marble underground to prevent it from being damaged. In the 1980s, the marble was brought to light again, and Tong Mansion Lane became more famous.

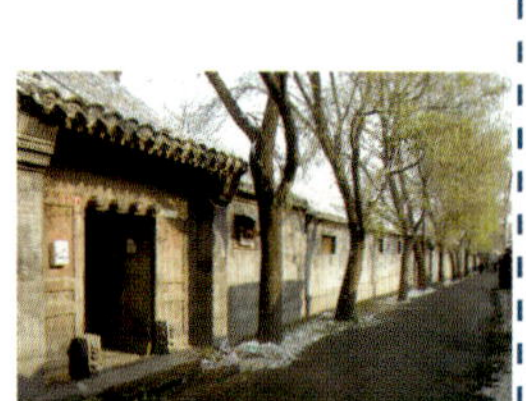
Early morning in a *hutong*

Dongjiaomin Xiang (East Dealing-with-the-People Lane)

Elderly people all know that Dongjiaomin Xiang (East Dealing-with-the-People Lane) in the Zhengyangmen (South-Facing Gate) area can be regarded as Beijing's most orderly and standard lane. In the past, Dongjiaomin Xiang was not only the site of foreign embassies but also of foreign concessions in disguised form, constituting a record of the humiliation once experienced by the Chinese people.

So, how did Dongjiaomin Xiang turn into an embassy area? Originally, the Qing Dynasty institutions for managing relations with Western nations were the Ministry of Rites and Honglusi

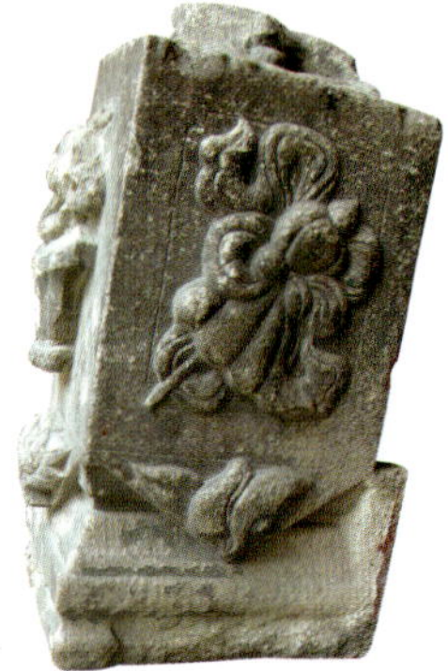

(Court of State Ceremonials), which were located in the Dongjiaomin Xiang neighborhood. Later, according to the customs of different countries, legations were set up here to receive emissaries from various countries. For instance, the Koreans would live in the legation built especially for them. Since the Opium Wars, one country after another had set up an embassy in China, and these were set up in Dongjiaomin Xiang. In June 1900, the Boxers (Yihetuan or Society of Righteousness and Harmony) burned down the embassies in Dongjiaomin Xiang. Later, the Eight Allied Powers (Austria, Britain, France, Germany, Italy, Japan, Russia and the United States) invaded Beijing and forced the Qing government to sign the Treaty of Xinchou (1901). The treaty designated Dongjiaomin Xiang as a legation section. Foreign garrisons were permitted, while Chinese people could not live there. Foreign countries then started construction work on a large scale, building embassies, barracks, hospitals, foreign firms, and churches. The original *yamen* (government offices) of the Qing government, together with its mansions, ancestral temples and residences, were all pulled down to make room. In this way, the neighborhood turned into a "country inside a country." It was not until 1949 that

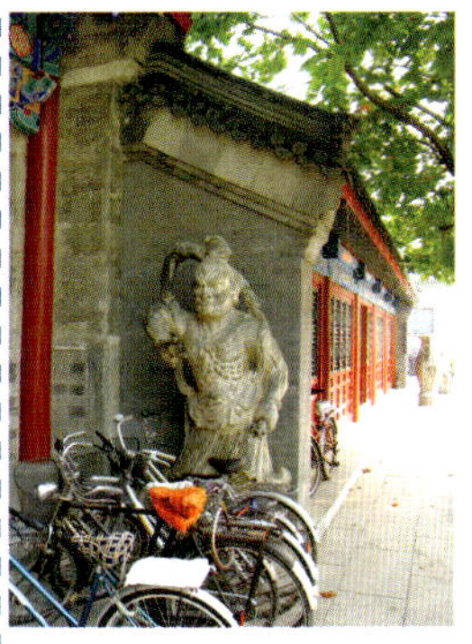

Princess Hejing's Mansion in Ping'an Dadao (Safety Avenue)

The gate at 40 Jiajia Hutong (Jia Family Lane), facing Lin Zexu's former home

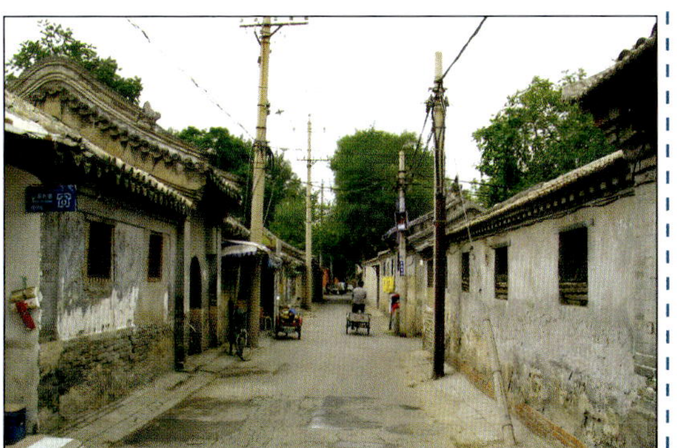

Zhuanta Hutong (Brick Tower Lane)

Dongjiaomin Xiang returned to the Chinese people.

Old Qilinbeir Hutong (Kylin Stele Lane)

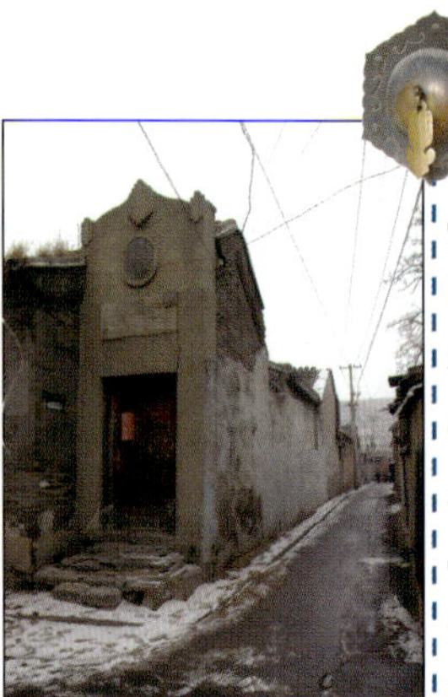

One of the peculiar gates found in Beijing's lanes

Qilinbeir Hutong (Kylin or Chinese Unicorn Stele Lane) in the Eastern District is well known in Beijing. There used to be a gigantic stone carving from the Yuan Dynasty in the lane. On front of it was an exquisite relief sculpture with simple and unsophisticated but extraordinary engraving, revealing the superb skill of ancient Chinese workers. For many centuries, people have affectionately called it Qilinbeir (Kylin Stele), so the lane was called Qilinbeir Hutong.

A beautiful legend has been spread among the elderly residents: A long time ago, an ancient well close to the Kylin Stele had such sweet water that the neighborhood's residents all flocked here to fetch water. One night, a bright moon hung high in the sky and all was quiet in the dead of night. An old resident returned from outside to see several animals keeping watch beside the well. After looking carefully, he saw that they were some mighty kylins. He kept quiet and quickly went back home, telling his neighbors: "The well in our lane is truly precious. I have just seen the kylins from the stele guarding it!" When several residents hurried to the well, the kylins had already gone. But they found the kylin relief sculpture was still on the stele. Every day, when the lane's residents passed the stele, they would stop for a moment to look at the kylins. In people's minds, the kylin is a symbol of good luck. The stele is

Kylin Stele

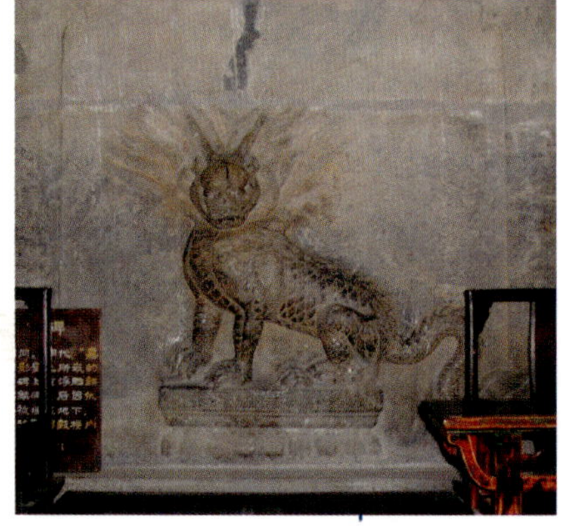

now displayed in the main hall of the Drum-Tower Cultural Relics Protection Bureau.

Fuxue Hutong and Wen Tianxiang

Northeast of the former Kuan Jie (Wide Street), there is an old lane called Fuxue Hutong. Still in the lane is the Shuntianfuxue (Following-the-Mandate-of-Heaven School) set up in the Ming Dynasty, which gave the lane its name. During the Yuan Dynasty, the northwestern part of the lane was home to the prison run by the capital's ordnance department. Wen Tianxiang, a famous patriotic minister of the Southern Song Dynasty (1127-1279), was imprisoned here after being captured. For more than three years, he was kept in a very damp dungeon, where he wrote the celebrated *Zhengqige* ("Song of Righteousness"). Kublai Khan (the fifth emperor of the Yuan Dynasty) once went to

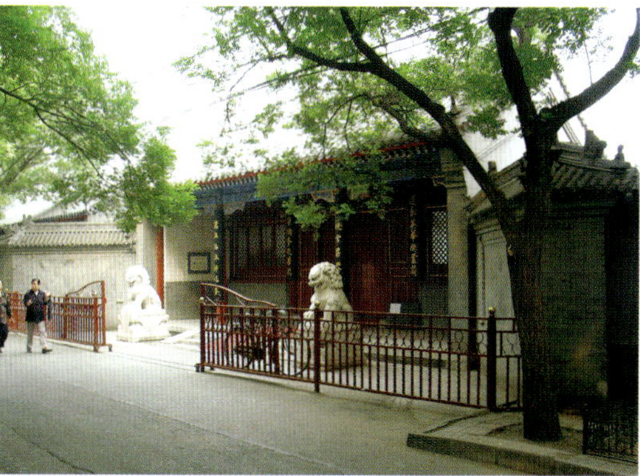

The paifang (memorial arch) in front of the Ming Dynasty school Shuntianfuxue (Following-the-Mandate-of-Heaven School)

Today's Fuxue Primary School

the prison to induce Wen Tianxiang to capitulate. Wen Tianxiang replied: "I would rather die for my country." He was later executed at Chaishi (today's Jiaodaokou in Dongcheng District). Later generations had a temple built at the prison site in memory of Wen Tianxiang. According to folklore, the old jujube tree in front of Xiangdian (Palace of Enjoyment) in the temple, with its trunk leaning south, was planted by Wen Tianxiang, showing that "Prime Minister Wen's heart is like a compass needle that always points south." Today, the Prime Minister Wen Memorial Temple is on Beijing Municipality's list

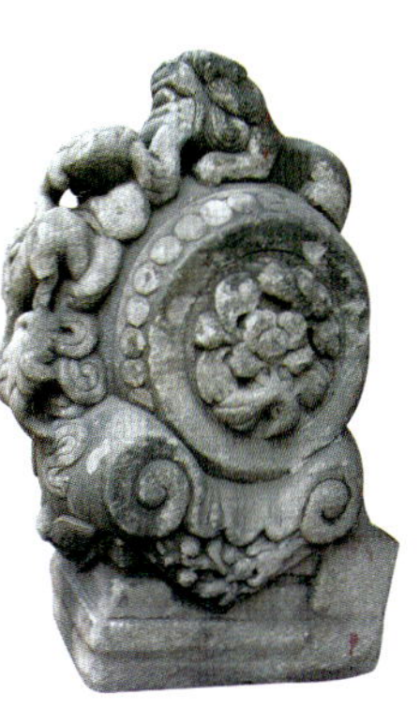

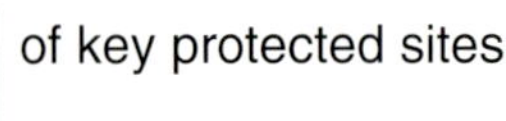

of key protected sites.

Legend of Tieyingbi Hutong (Iron Screen Lane)

Inside Deshengmen (Moral Victory Gate) is Tieyingbi Hutong (Iron Screen Lane). How did it get its name? It came from the screen in front of Huguo Desheng An (Defending-the-Nation Moral-Victory Nunnery). In the volcanic rock, craftsmen used their superb skills to vividly carve lions playing with silk balls on the front and kylins (Chinese unicorns) and green pine trees on the back. A folktale about the screen has been spread among the people to this day. When the city of Beijing was being built, there was a dragon couple in Youzhou Prefecture (today's northern Hebei Province) who had settled down in a quiet place. However, they complained that the northwest wind blew so wildly that it filled the entire sky. They were afraid that so much sand would accumulate that the newly built city would be covered in it sooner or later if the wind kept blowing. Where would it all end? The couple decided to go out to see what was happening. Reaching the northwestern corner of the city, they found an old woman in rags holding a yellow bag in her hand. Nearby stood a little boy holding a white bag in his hand and chatting with the old woman. The little boy

Two young *hutong* residents

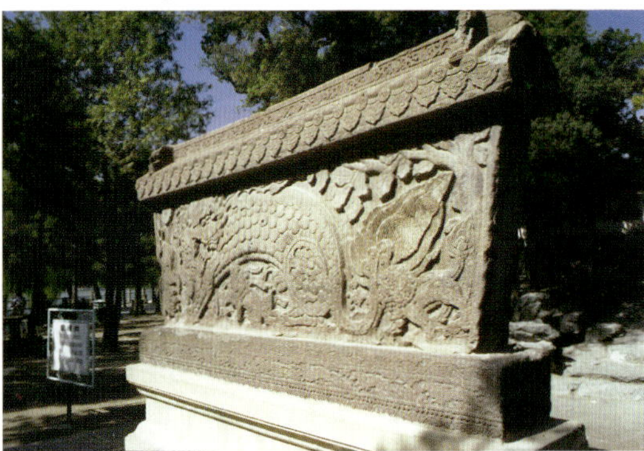

The iron screen in Beihai Park

shouted loudly: "Whoever gets in my way will be buried!" At the same time, he grabbed a handful of sand from his bag and threw it up into the sky. The old woman did likewise and shook out some sand. At once there was a rolling sea of sand. The dragon couple realized that the woman was the Wind Goddess and the boy was the Cloud God, who used magic arts to cause such wild winds. Then the dragon couple turned into two giant dragons and spurted spring water from their mouths to wash away the sand. The Wind Goddess and Cloud God were so frightened that they turned tail and ran. The sky then calmed down, and less and less sand fell on the city. People carved the screen to commemorate the dragon couple's contribution. Because the screen is the color of iron, people call it Tieyingbi (Iron Screen). During the Yuan Dynasty, it was placed at the opening of the city wall outside Deshengmen. Later it was moved in front of the nunnery, where it remained during the Ming and Qing dynasties. The lane was named Iron Screen Lane. Today, the Iron Screen stands in Beihai Park.

A kindergarten in a *hutong*

Legend of Jiuxian Qiao (Wine God Bridge)

East of the highway to Beijing airport is an area with streets named after Jiuxianqiao (Wine God Bridge): Jiuxianqiao Beilu, Nanlu, Donglu and Zhonglu (North, South, East and Central Wine God Bridge Road) and Jiuxianqiao Yijiefang to Jiuxianqiao Shiwujiefang (First to Fifteenth Wine God Bridge Streets). There is a legend about Jiuxianqiao. There used to be a remote village situated on the east and west banks of the Dongba River. The people living on each side of the river hoped to get a conve-

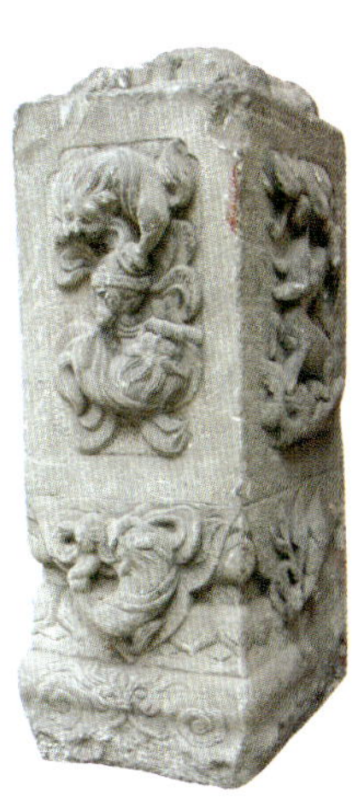

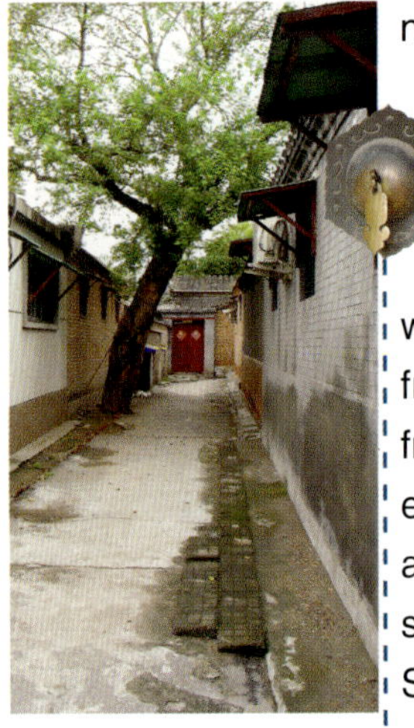

A peaceful lane

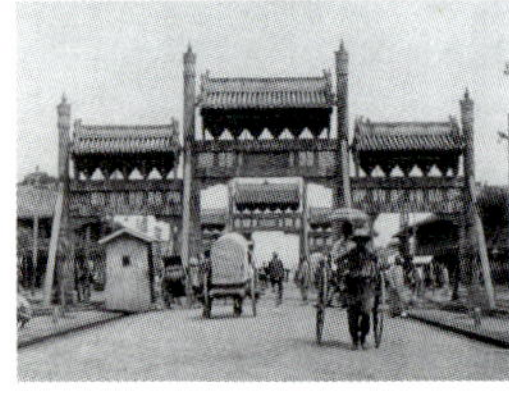

The Xisi (West Four) Pailou (decorated ceremonial archway) at the time of the Republic of China

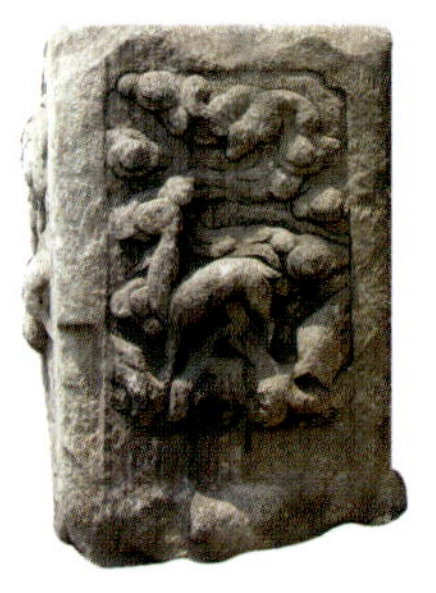

nient bridge built but they could not afford it. One day, a flagstone bridge suddenly appeared across the river. Everyone became curious and dared not be the first to cross the bridge. When the sun was setting in the west, an old man with a grey beard approached from a distance, energetically pushing a cart, from both sides of which hung two big containers with more than 400 *jin* (200 kilograms) of alcohol in total. The old man moved quickly and soon reached the middle of the bridge. Suddenly, his cart rolled to the east and the two containers of alcohol on that side fell in the river. The villagers hurried to the bridge to help the old man, only to find that he had disappeared together with his cart. Puzzled, they smelled the odor of alcohol from the river. They ladled out some water to taste it and found that it had the flavor of alcohol. They thought that the old man must have been the Alcohol God and that he had helped them build the bridge. So the flagstone bridge was named Jiuxianqiao (Alcohol God Bridge), and a little temple called Jiuxian Miao (Alcohol God Temple) was set up at the end of the bridge. Today, the bridge has gone and so has the temple. According to the elderly people in this area, there really was a little flagstone bridge with granite balusters and a few granite foundation stones.

***Pailou* (decorated archways):**

The *pailou* or decorated archway is a unique architectural feature of Chinese buildings. It has three functions: as a decoration that adds vigor to the main building; as a memorial to honor or commemorate someone or something; and as a dividing line between lanes, similar to a door. As the capital of the Yuan, Ming and Qing dynasties, Beijing had many palaces, temples and royal gardens, and there were also many events and people to honor and commemorate. Moreover, archways worked as boundaries between lanes in neat formations. All these factors meant Beijing had more archways than other cities. At the end of the Qing

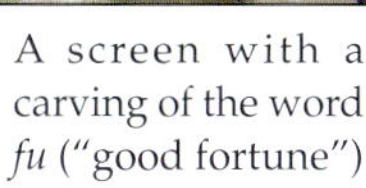

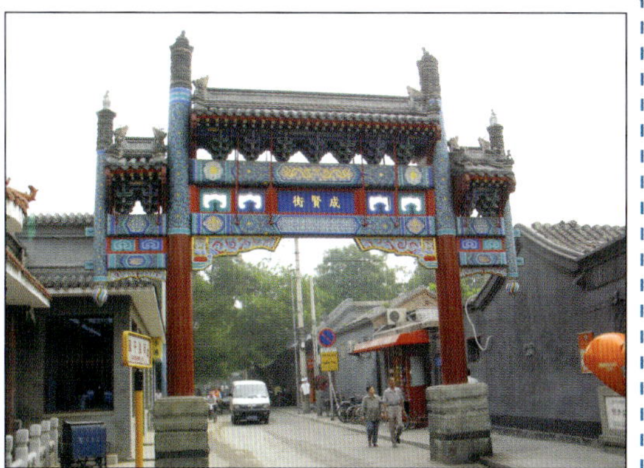

A screen with a carving of the word *fu* ("good fortune")

Dynasty, there were 57 archways of different sizes.

The biggest archway is the first structure at the southern end of the Ming Tombs and is made of white marble.

Dismounting Stones in Lanes

A dismounting stone set up during the Qing Dynasty to help people dismount their horses can still be seen today at the Guozijian (Imperial College) and Donghuamen (Eastern Flower Gate). On the stone in the Chinese and Manchu languages are the words "Civil and military officials dismount horses here." Officials had to dismount their horses at the stone to show their respect for the emperor.

Ancient Pagoda Trees

A pagoda tree (Chinese scholar tree) was planted on each side of the archway in front of a large quadrangle house. The trees were

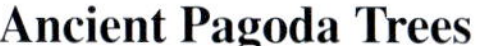
Rubbings of Confucius are quite popular.

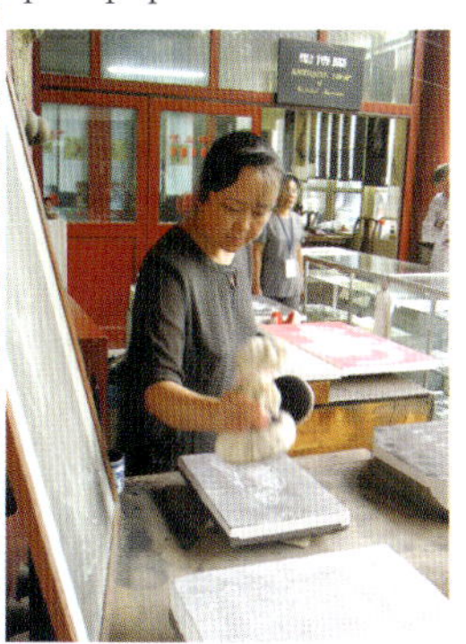

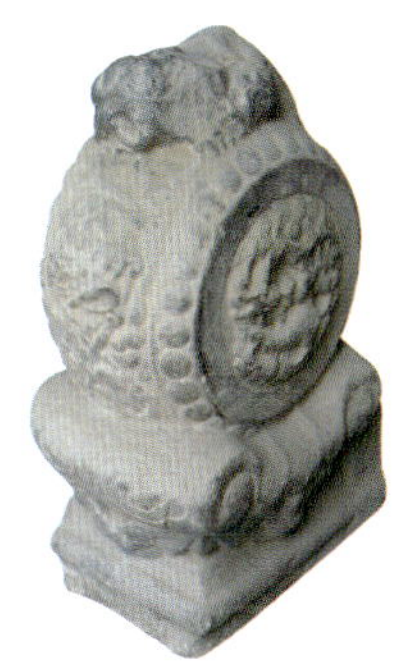

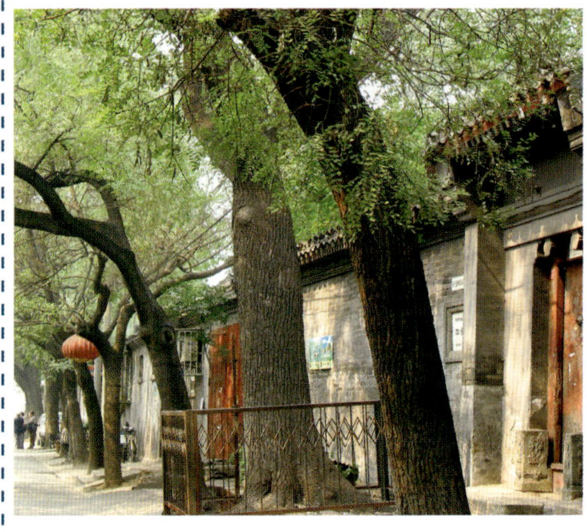

planted at the same time as the quadrangle house was being built. A proverb that spread among the people said: "Whether or not a house is old depends on whether or not the pagoda tree is big." This means that the year in which a quadrangle house was built can be confirmed by the age of the pagoda trees in front of it.

A lane in winter

Mount Tai Stones

In the early 1960s, people could still find big and small carved stones built into the wall of a quadrangle house courtyard or in the wall of the southern *daozuo* room (opposite the principal rooms and usually facing north). On those stones were carved the words "Taishan Shi Gandang" (either "Shi Gandang of Mount Tai", in reference to a heroic martial arts master called Shi Gandang, or "Mount Tai dares to resist"). The inscribed words implied overwhelming power because Mount Tai has been regarded since ancient times as the greatest of China's five sacred mountains. The "Mount Tai" stones were believed capable of guarding the house. Today, such carved stones are very rarely seen in the old lanes.

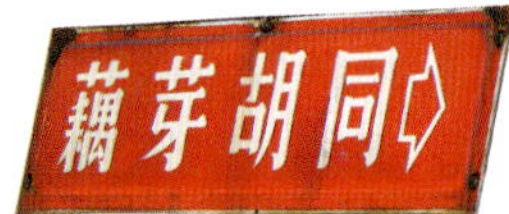

The Mount Tai Stone in Ouya Hutong (Lotus Root Sprout Lane)

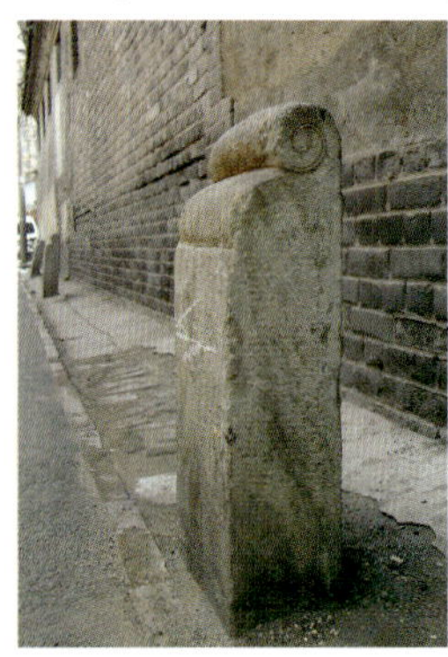

Mounting and Dismounting Stones and Tethering Posts

Nowadays, in front of the archways of big quadrangle houses, you can still see pairs of rectangular blue stones. The front of them usually measures 90 by 70 centimeters or 70 by 60 centimeters. At their bases are steps of the same width. These pairs of giant stones are for mounting and dismounting a horse. They differed according to the rank of each house owner of the Qing Dynasty. On the wall of the quadrangle house's southern *daozuo* room (opposite the principal rooms and usually facing north), there were usually three or four stone holes with iron rings inserted in them. The stone holes, at a height of 1.5 meters above the ground, were used to tether horses.

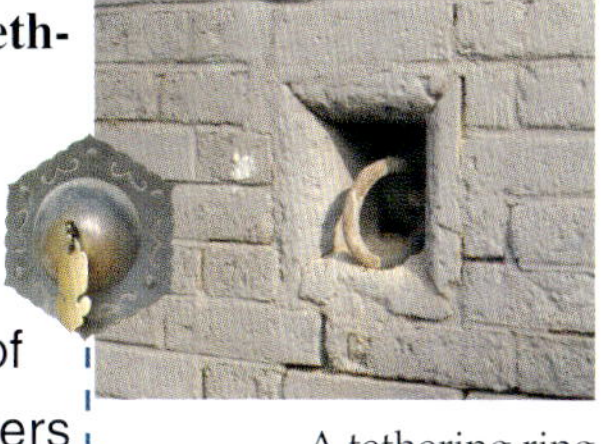

A tethering ring in a stone wall

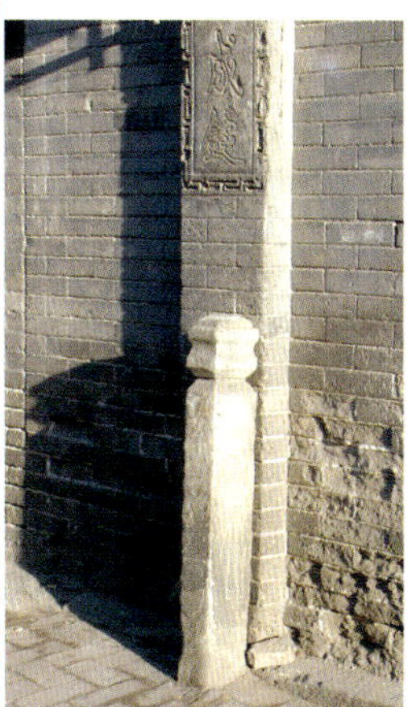

A tethering post

A stone for mounting and dismounting

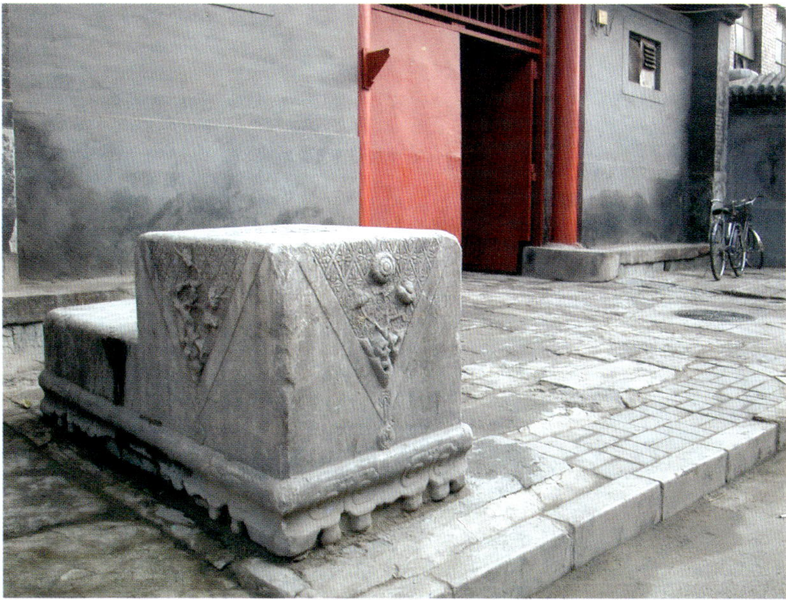

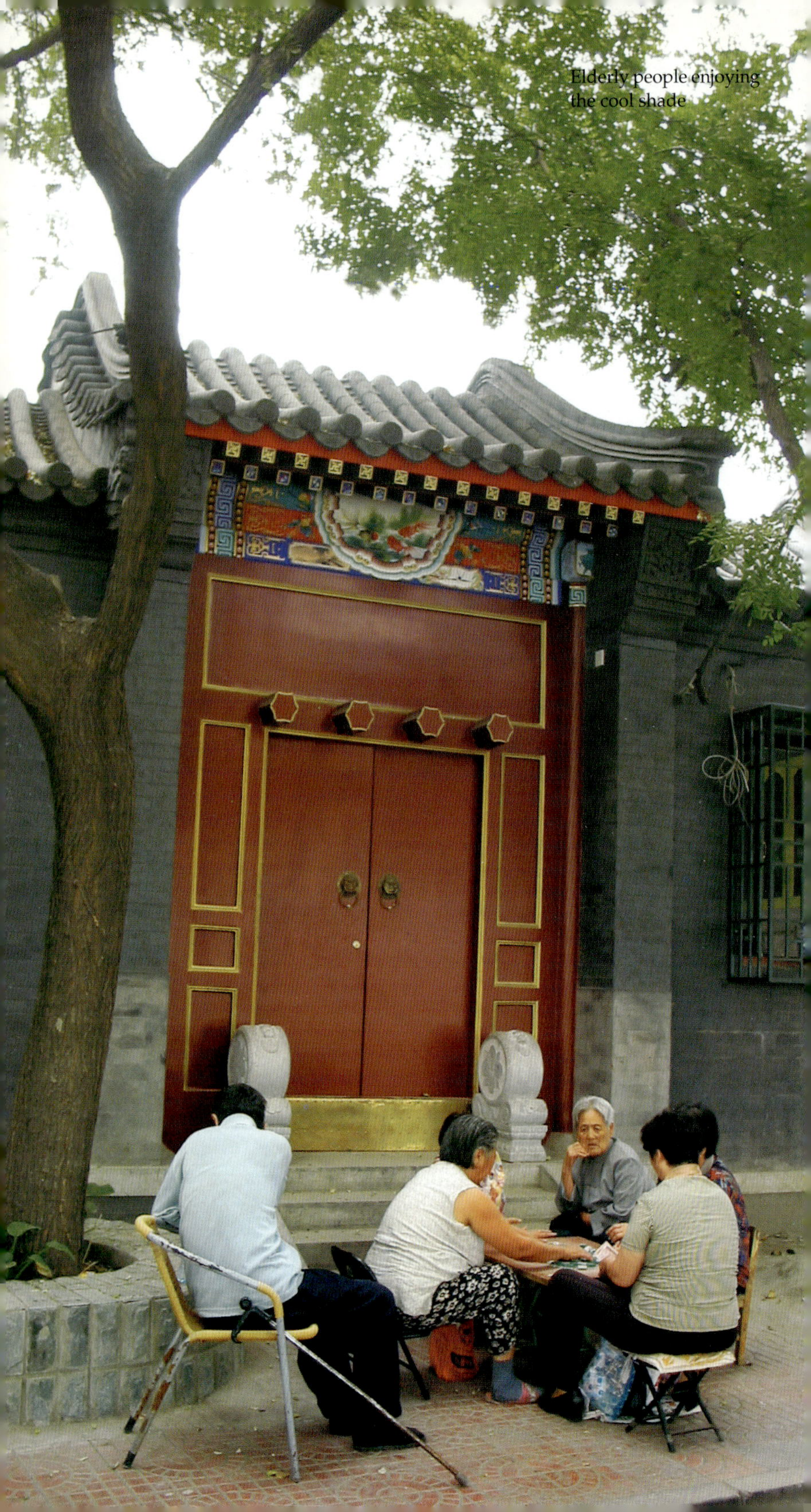

Elderly people enjoying
the cool shade

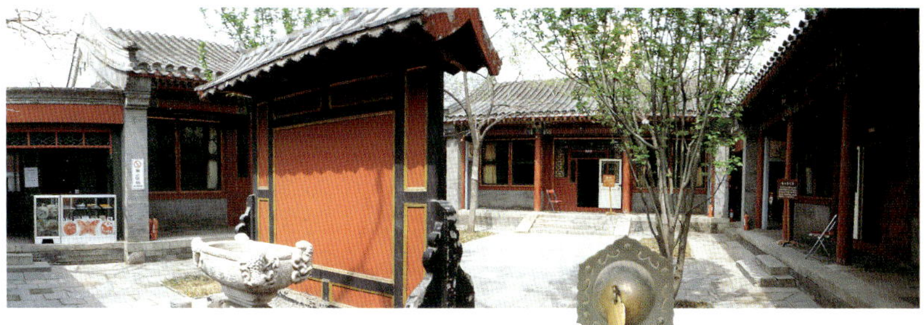

II. Quadrangle Houses

The quadrangle house that was Mei Lanfang's former home

The quadrangle house or *siheyuan*, a typical architectural style for residences in Beijing, appeared at the same time as *hutong* during the Yuan Dynasty, constituting an important part of the *hutong* system. In 1276, Dadu, the Grand Capital of the Yuan Dynasty, was built but was lacking in residents. Therefore, Kublai Khan ordered the former residents in the Zhongdu, the Middle Capital of the Jin Dynasty (in present-day southwestern Beijing), to move to the new capital. People then started building quadrangle houses.

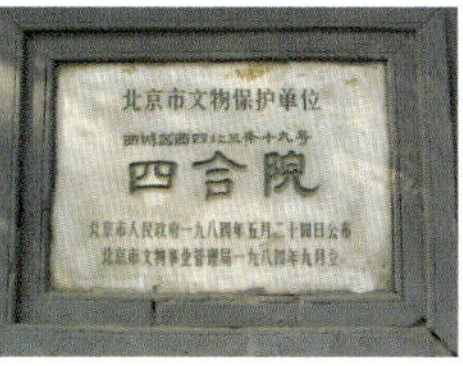

The sign of a protected quadrangle house

A quadrangle house is a unit with buildings on all four sides around an inner open courtyard. It was confined to one family, having only one external door and a screen inside, which would hide the interior even when the door was open.

The architectural design was influenced by Chinese traditional culture, in which set patterns should be followed. Top-class houses usually face south, with the room in the north considered the main room, and the gate is located in the southeast corner. According to the Eight

A bird's-eye view of quadrangle houses in Beijing

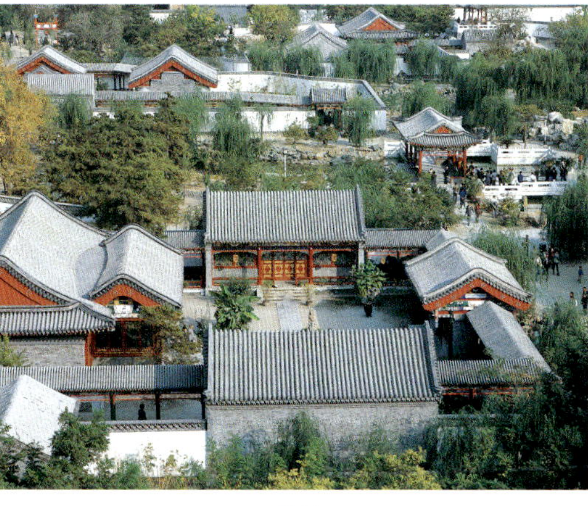

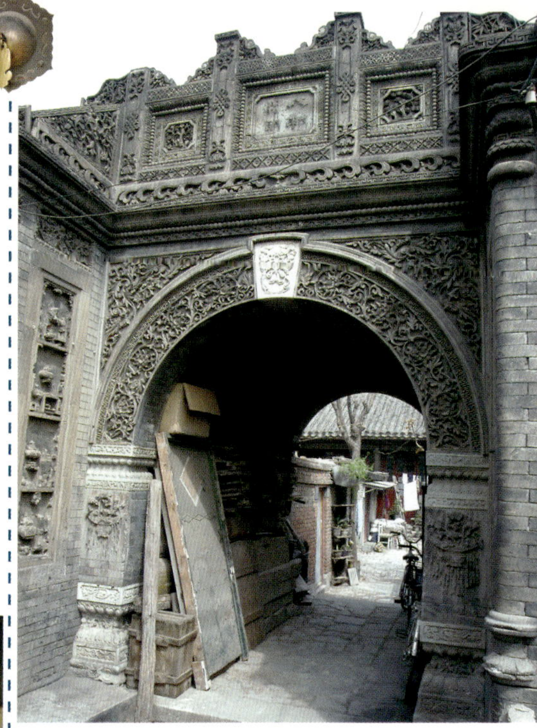

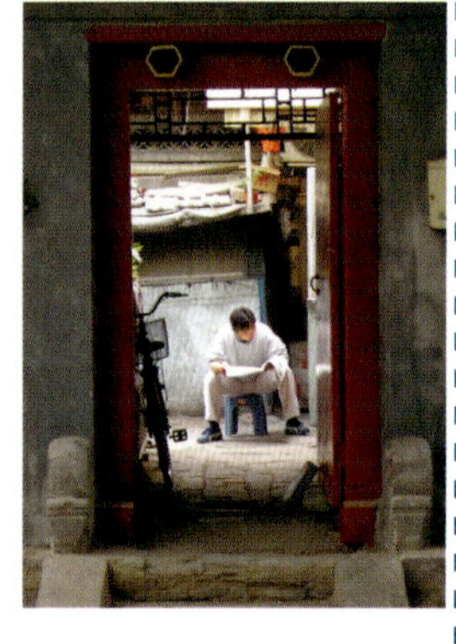

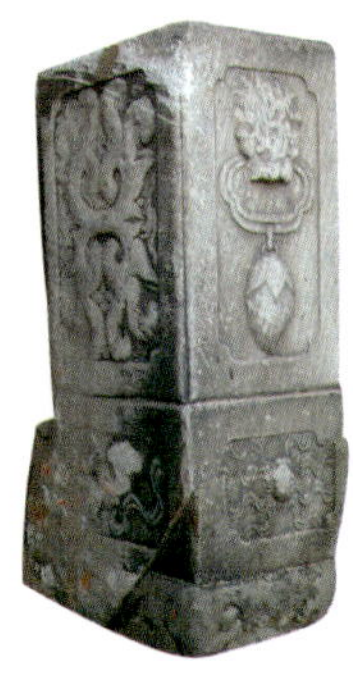

Trigrams in *The Book of Changes* (*Zhou Yi* or *Yi Jing*), the southeast is considered to be *feng* (wind), the north is considered to be *shui* (water), and *fengshui* (geomancy) represents propitiousness. (Only nobles' houses could have the doors set up on the central axis.) If the house was located on the south side of a lane, it was considered propitious to have the gate in the northwest.

Quadrangle houses of different sizes followed the same guideline whereby the buildings on all four sides would face the center, but they varied a great deal in terms of the walls, door decorations, steps and so on according to the rank of the owners. A small quadrangle house had one courtyard. A medium-sized quadrangle house consisted of an inner courtyard and an outer courtyard separated by a wall and linked by a gate in the partition wall along the central axis on the southern side. A large quadrangle house included a spacious main room (that is, the north room), a row of rooms or a storied building behind that, and long corridors on both sides of the gate. Some mansions of nobles and high-ranking officials even included seven or nine courtyards, with side courtyards and gardens. These mansions with spacious halls and extensive gardens were called *shenzhai dayuan* (literally "deep residence, big courtyard").

A screen wall outside the entrance to a house

Influenced by the feudal code of ethics, extended families living in quadrangle houses favored a strict order of seniority. The south-facing rooms were reserved for the elders. In the middle of these rooms was the central room for hosting gatherings, entertaining relatives and worshiping ancestors. The younger members of the family lived in the wing rooms or side courtyards. The rooms opposite the main room facing north were the living room or study and living quarters for servants. This order was strictly maintained.

A screen wall seen from inside an entrance

The quadrangle house, as a style of architecture, has lasted for several hundred years. Today, amid row upon row of high buildings and large mansions, old Beijingers still remain sentimentally attached to quadrangle houses.

Gates are the most characteristic building feature of quadrangle houses. There are two

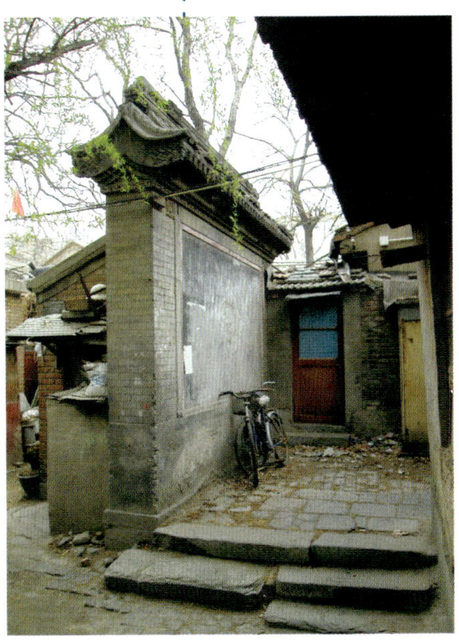

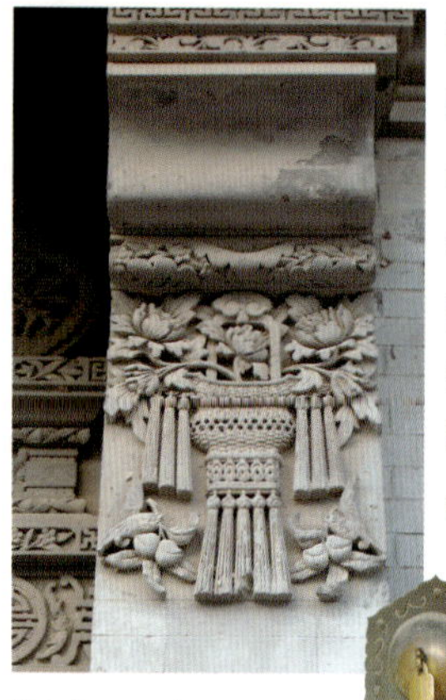
Brick carvings on a gate

types of quadrangle house gate. One type is built into an entrance of one bay or several bays, reserved for the middle and upper class. The other type is a gate joining two ends of the courtyard walls, for the lower classes. In the rigidly stratified feudal society, mansion gates with five bays and three doors or three bays and one door were of the highest category and reserved for princes. Located on the axis, they are truly spectacular, with specifically prescribed numbers of bays and steps, and decorations. Though diverse, the small wall-type corner gates used by the common people were built of bricks and were usually simple.

Some components of gates have both decorative and practical functions. Such door decorations include door clasps, door cymbals, and stone drums.

Door clasps, used to support gate posts, are so called because they worked like ancient Chinese hair clasps. For decoration, they are often carved with the words *jixiang* ("good luck"), *ping'an* ("safety") and *ruyi* (an S-shaped orna-

Elegant decorations on a floral-pendant gate

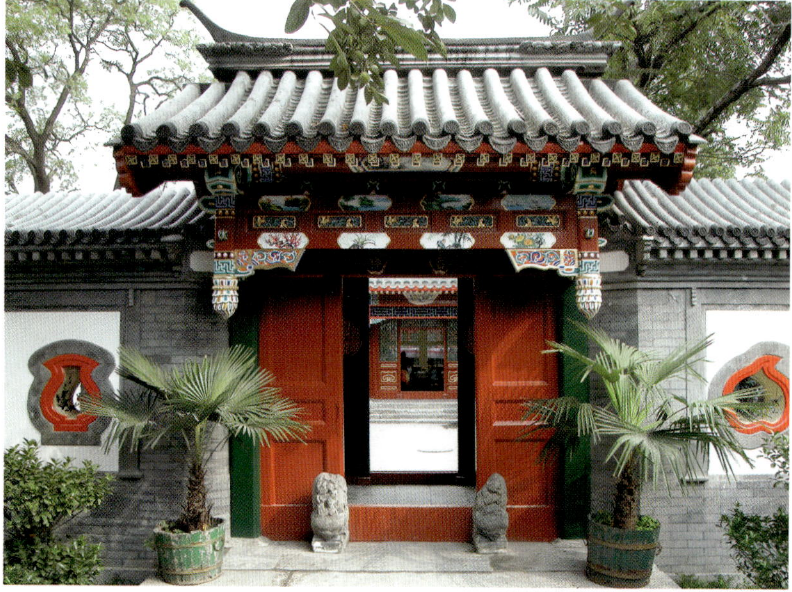

mental object, formerly a symbol of good fortune). Wide gates usually have four door clasps while small ones have only two.

The metal door cymbals or menbo function as doorbells. They look like the *bo* cymbal, a Chinese traditional percussion instrument, hence the name. Door cymbals are made of copper or iron, in the shape of a hexagon, with a protruding central part, into which was embedded a ring or *ruyi*. They are also used as doorknobs. A door cymbal in a prince's mansion is much more likely to be in the shape of an animal such as a dragon or lion with a big ring in its mouth. For this reason, it was also called a *menhuan* or door ring. Because the gate of a prince's mansion is massive, an animal shape is convenient for pulling it and for adding a more stately air.

Stone drums were important decorations on the gates of the relatively well-to-do. A stone drum consists of two parts: the *menzhenshi* or "gate pillow stone" and *baogushi* or drum-shaped stone block. The pillow stone inside the gate is square, with a hole in which the lower part of the door axle stands. The upper part of the axle is fixed into the lintel. In this way, the gate can turn to open and close without a hinge and can be inserted and removed easily. The drum-shaped stone block outside the gate is connected to the pillow stone. It is round at the top and square at the bottom, giving it a drum shape, hence the name. A variety of patterns for good luck are engraved all over the stone

Door clasps engraved with the word xi ("happiness")

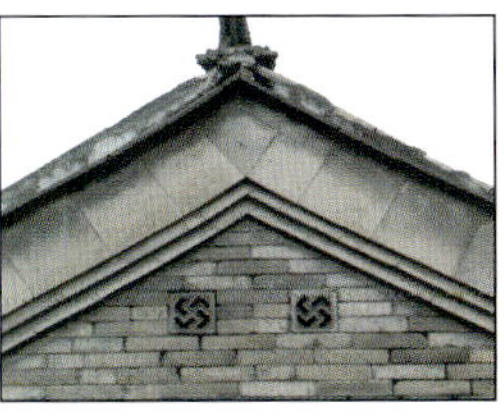

Air vents in a gable

Brick carvings on a screen wall at the entrance to a house

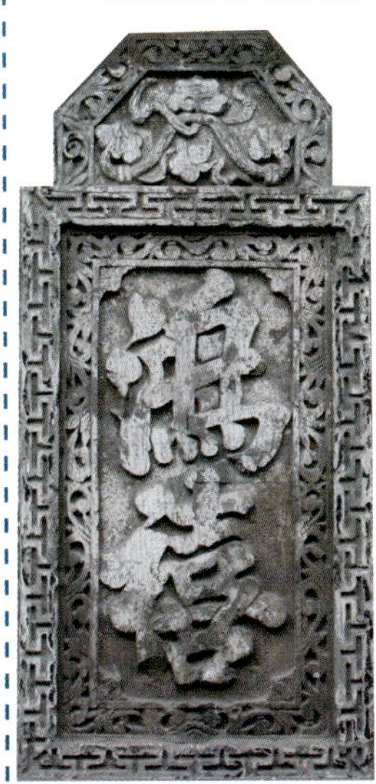

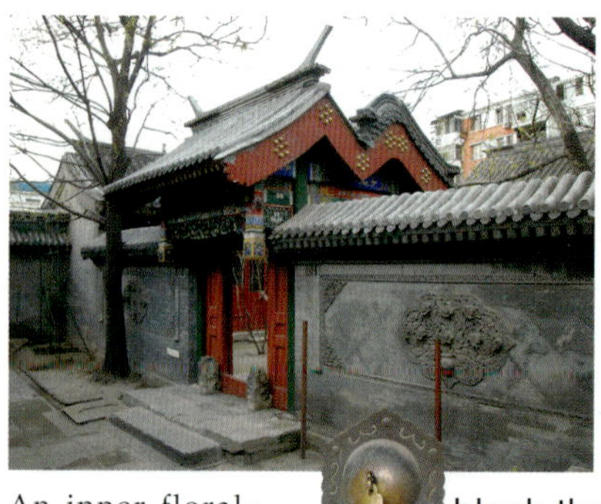

An inner floral-pendant gate with wall decorations on either side

drums.

Screen walls are another important part of quadrangle houses. According to the location, screen walls can be divided into two categories: screen walls at the entrance and those outside the entrance. The former were built to block the view of passersby and to decorate a courtyard while the latter were to keep the untidy eaves, walls or corners opposite the gate out of view. Divided by shape, there are *yizi* or single-line screen walls, mountain screen walls and wild-goose wing screen walls.

Single-line screens, whether inside or outside the gate, stand alone by the wing-room gable, outside the partition or in the opposite side of the lane.

So-called mountain screen walls are located mostly inside the entrance. As the courtyard is limited in space, a narrow roof is built on the wing room's gable to make it into a decorative screen wall. The screen wall and the gable

A corridor leading to a gate

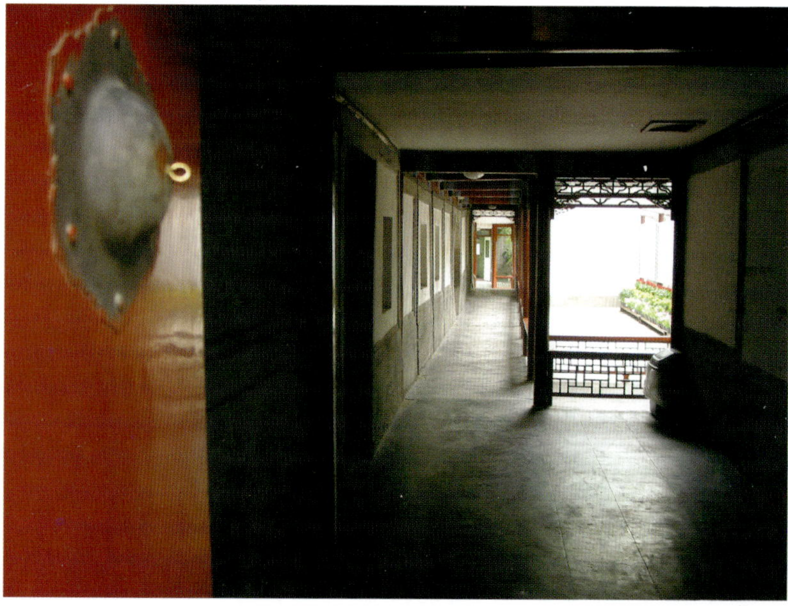

(which is called *shanqiang* or "mountain wall" in Chinese) share the same wall, hence the name "mountain screen wall."

Wild-goose wing screen walls, located opposite to the gate across the lane, stand alone or are attached to the wall facing the gate. The central part of them is shaped like a single-line screen wall but the two ends bend forward like the wings of a wild goose.

Most screen walls are built of brick and consist of a base, a central core and copestones on top. Generally, the central part of the screen wall inside the entrance is in the shape of a plaque, with the words *fu lu* ("happiness and high rank") or *hongxi* ("great happiness") carved on it.

Brick carvings were widely adopted in quadrangle houses in Beijing. Not only the prominent positions but also the windows, doors, walls, partition latticework, porticos and gutters are decorated with a variety of meticulous brick carvings. The artistry of these carvings reflects Beijing's customs and culture in concentrated form.

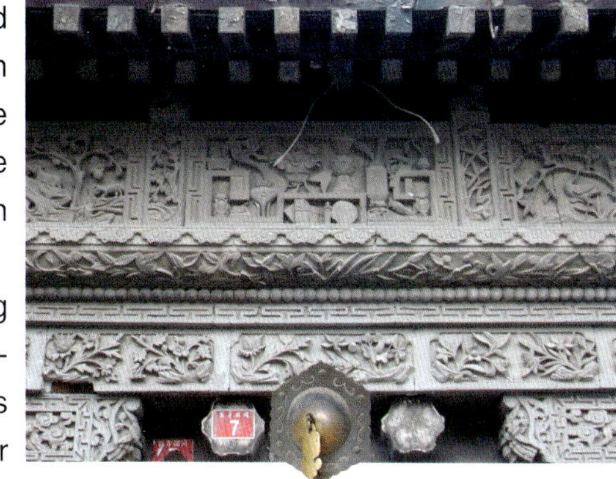

Traditional brick carvings on a gate's eave

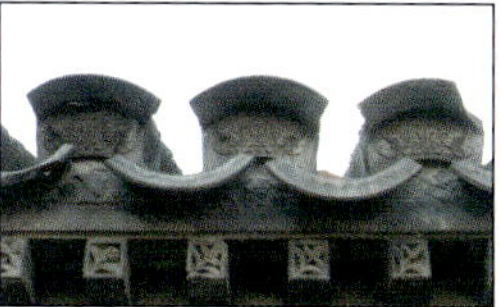

A metal decoration on a gate

Eave tiles

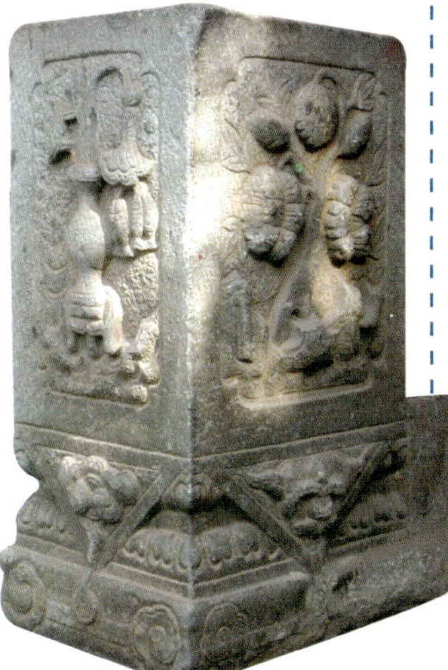

Very popular patterns on stone blocks are those of twin lotus flowers on one stalk, symbolizing conjugal affection; a vase, symbolizing constant safety; and a fish, symbolizing a surplus year after year.

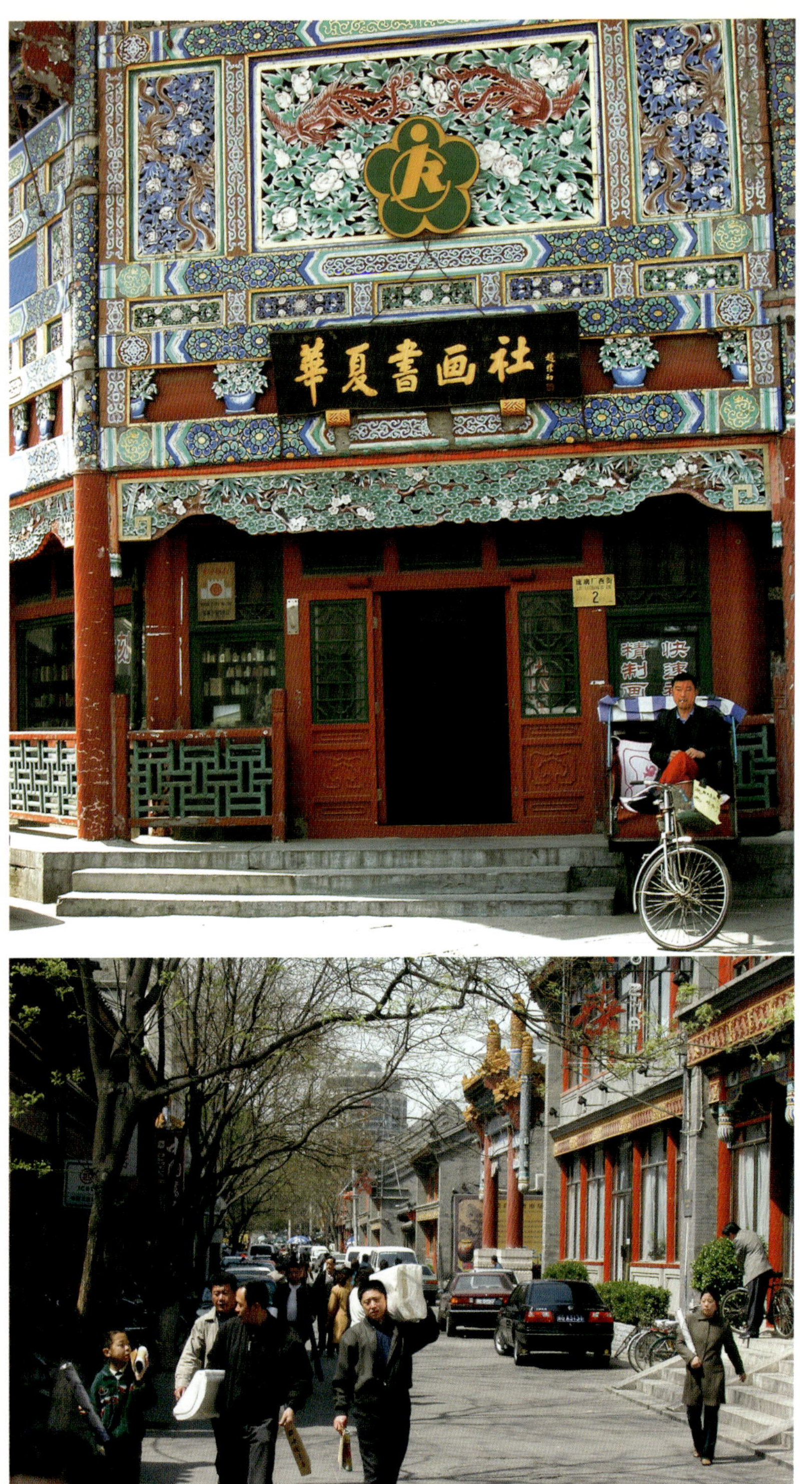

The cultural street Liulichang

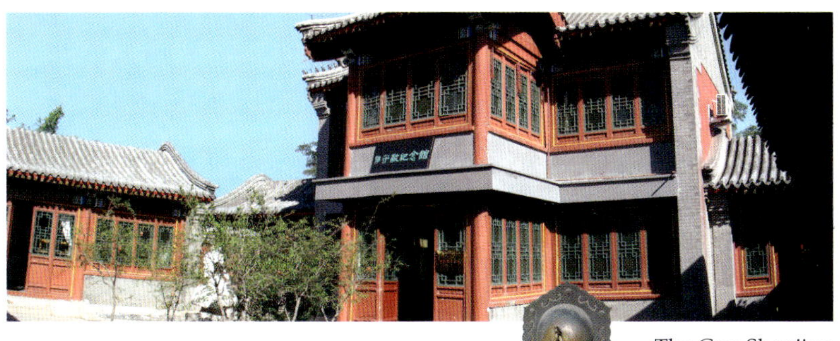

The Guo Shoujing Memorial

III. Former Homes of Historical Figures

As a famous historical and cultural city, Beijing has been home to many famous people. It is hard to say whether these famous residents brought fame to the quiet lanes or whether the history and culture of the lanes inspired the celebrity residents. But it is certain that, as an important part of Beijing, the residences of famous people have added new cultural significance to the city.

Guo Moruo's Former Home

Open 9 a.m. to 4 p.m., Tuesday to Sunday

Located at 18 Qianhai Xijie (West Qianhai Street) in Xicheng District, this was originally the garden of Prince Gong's Residence. Guo Moruo lived here for 15 years until his death. It has already been transformed into the Guo Moruo Memorial, a cultural relic under state

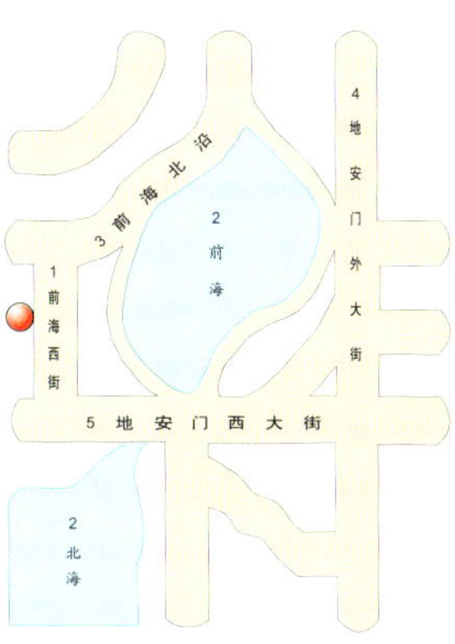

1. Qianhai Xijie (West Qianhai Street)
2. Qianhai (Front Lake), Beihai (North Lake)
3. Qianhai Beiyan (the north bank of Front Lake)
4. Di'anmenwai Dajie (Gate of Earthly Peace Outer Street)
5. Di'anmen Xidajie (Gate of Earthly Peace West Street)

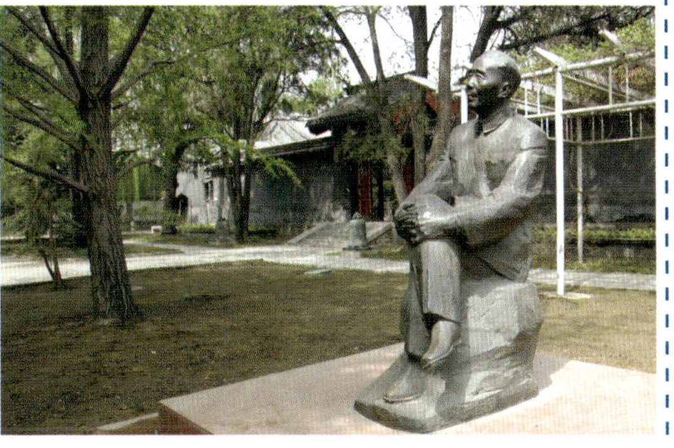

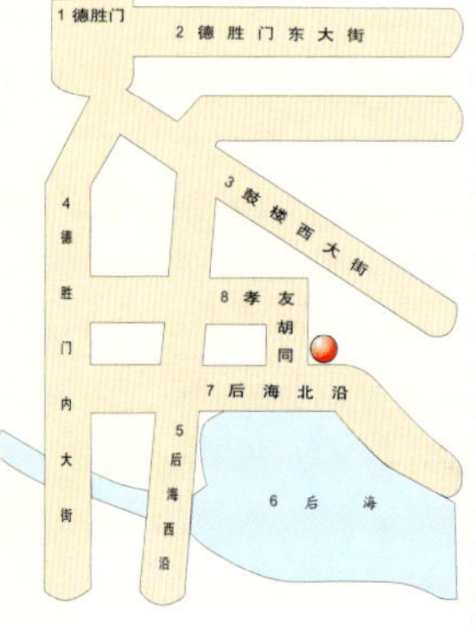
A ticket for Soong Ch'ing-ling's former home

1. Deshengmen (Moral Victory Gate)
2. Deshengmen Dongdajie (Moral Victory Gate East Street)
3. Gulou Xidajie (West Drum Tower Street)
4. Deshengmennei Dajie (Moral Victory Gate Inner Street)
5. Houhai Xiyan (the west bank of Rear Lake)
6. Houhai (Rear Lake)
7. Houhai Beiyan (on the north bank of Rear Lake)
8. Xiaoyou Hutong (Filial Friend Lane)

protection.

Guo Moruo (1892-1978) was born in Leshan, Sichuan Province. He was an outstanding writer, poet, archaeologist and social campaigner.

He had many books published, including the historical plays *Wang Zhaojun*, *Qu Yuan* and *Cai Wenji*, and the poetry collection *The Goddesses*. There is an edition of his collected works.

Soong Ch'ing-ling's Former Home

Open 9 a.m. to 4 p.m. daily

Located at 46 Houhai Beiyan (the north bank of Lake Houhai) in Xicheng District, this was originally the garden of Price Chun's Palace. Soong Ch'ing-ling (Song Qingling) lived here from 1963 until her death. The two halls of the

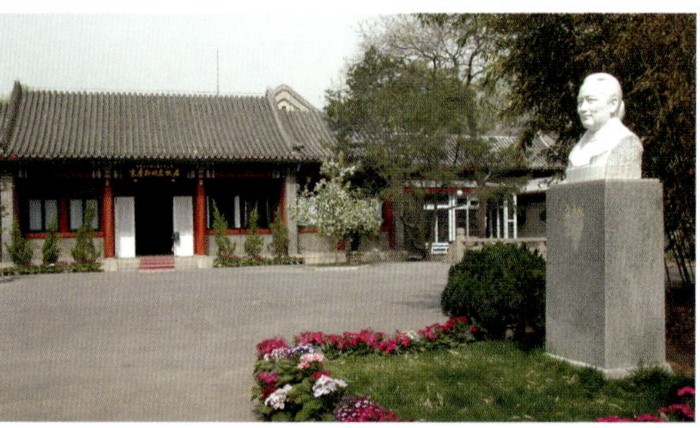

residence have since been turned into showrooms, with Soong Ch'ing-ling's pictures, letters and other memorabilia displaying her outstanding life. The residence is a cultural relic under state protection.

Soong Ch'ing-ling (1893-1981) was born in Shanghai but her family roots were in Wenchang in Hainan Province. In 1915, she married Sun Yat-sen in Japan. After his death in 1925, Soong adhered to Sun Yat-sen's three cardinal principles (alliance with Soviet Russia, co-operation with the Communist Party of

China, and assistance to the peasants and workers). After the founding of the People's Republic of China, Soong was given the largely honorary position of vice-chairperson and then chairperson of the republic.

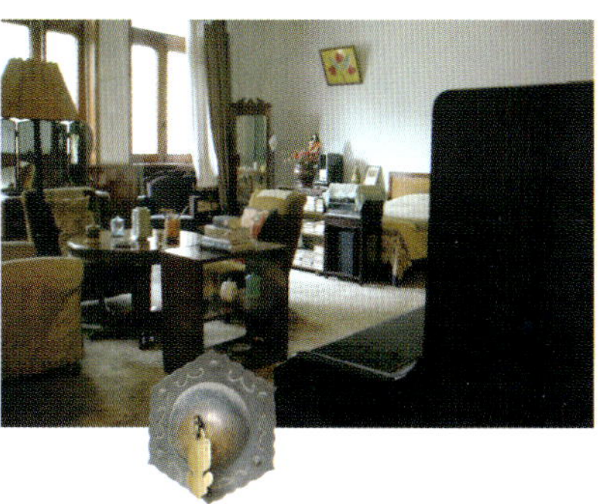

Kang Youwei's Former Home (Nanhai Guild Hall)

This is located at 43 Mishi Hutong (Rice Market Lane) in Xuanwu District. Kang Youwei lived here from 1882 to 1898.

Kang Youwei, a native of Nanhai (now the city of Foshan) in Guangdong Province, was the leader of the reform movement at the end of the Qing Dynasty. After the defeat of the political reform movement on September 21, 1898, he fled abroad. Today, the guild hall is public housing and is on Beijing's list of protected sites.

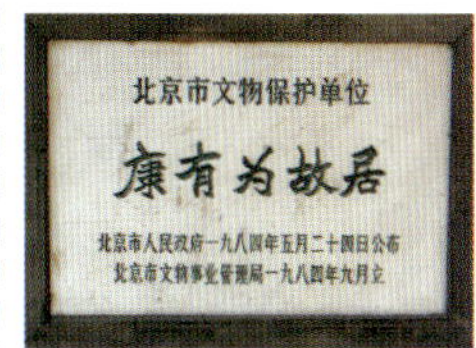

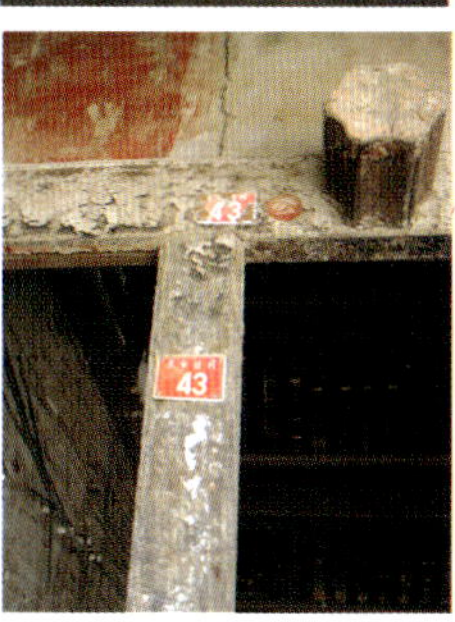

This gate still standing is probably very historic.

1. Luomashi Dajie (Mule & Horse Market Street)
2. Caishikou Dajie (Vegetable Market Entrance Street)
3. Mishi Hutong (Rice Market Lane)
4. Jiajia Hutong (Jia Family Lane)
5. Nanheng Dongjie (South Horizontal East Street)
6. Guozi Xiang (Fruit Alley)

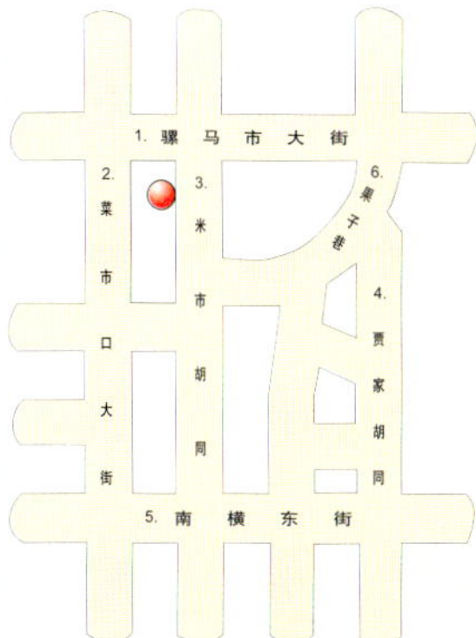

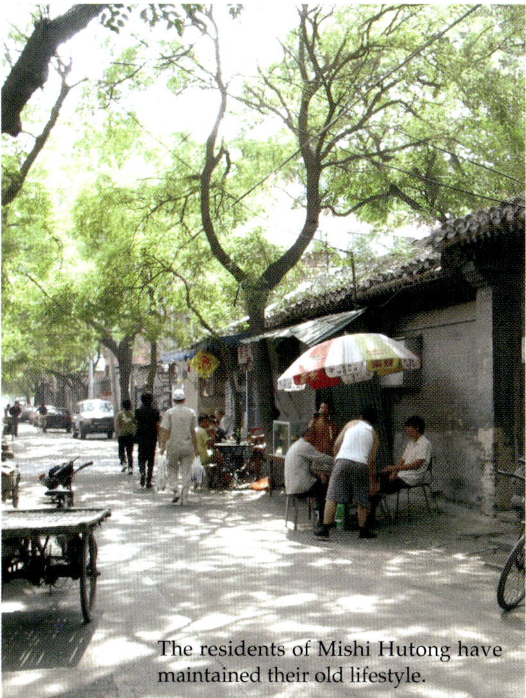

The residents of Mishi Hutong have maintained their old lifestyle.

Sun Yat-sen's Beijing Residences

The well-preserved residence at 23 Zhangzizhong Lu in Dongcheng District was Sun Yat-sen's last residence. It was originally the home of the noted diplomat Gu Weijun in the early period of the Republic of China.

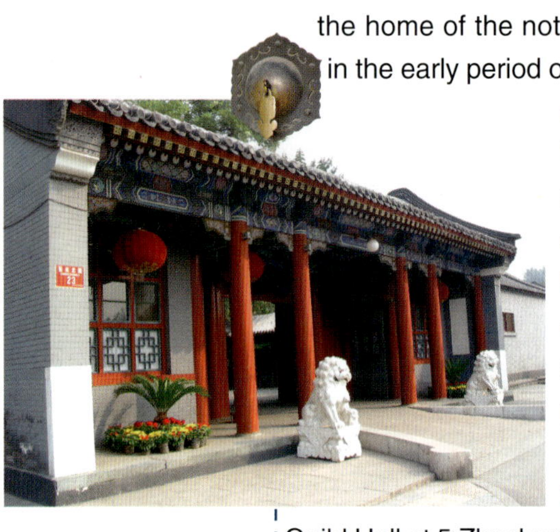

At the end of 1924, Sun Yat-sen came to Beijing and lived in this residence until his death on March 12, 1925. It is an official guesthouse now and on Beijing's list of protected sites.

In 1912, Sun Yat-sen lived in the Zhongshan Guild Hall at 5 Zhuchao Jie (Pearl Court Street) in Xuanwu District. After his death, his coffin was kept in Biyun Si (Azure Cloud Temple) in the Fragrant Hills in Beijing's western suburbs from April 1925 to May 1929.

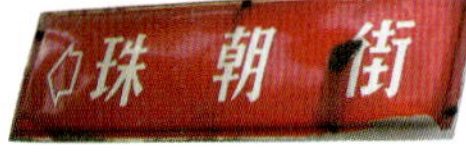

The sign for Zhuchao Jie (Pearl Court Street)

Wooden carvings at Zhongshan Guild Hall at 5 Zhuchao Jie (Pearl Court Street)

1. Meishuguan Houjie (Art Gallery Back Street)
2. Zhangzizhong Lu (Zhang Zizhong Road)
3. Dongsi Beidajie (East Four North Street)
4. Dafosi Dongjie (Big Buddha Temple East Street)

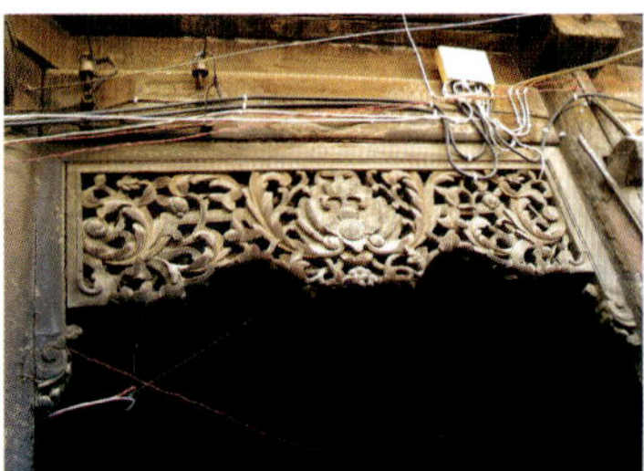

Sun Yat-sen (1866-1925) was originally called Sun Wen. He was a native of Xiangshan County (now Zhongshan) in Guangdong Province. To overthrow the Qing Dynasty, he founded the Xing Zhong Hui (Society for the Revival of China) and Tong Meng Hui (Chinese Revolutionary League), with the aim of "driving away foreign invaders to restore the sovereign integrity of China, establishing the Republic and equalizing land ownership." He developed the Three People's Principles (nationalism, democracy, and the

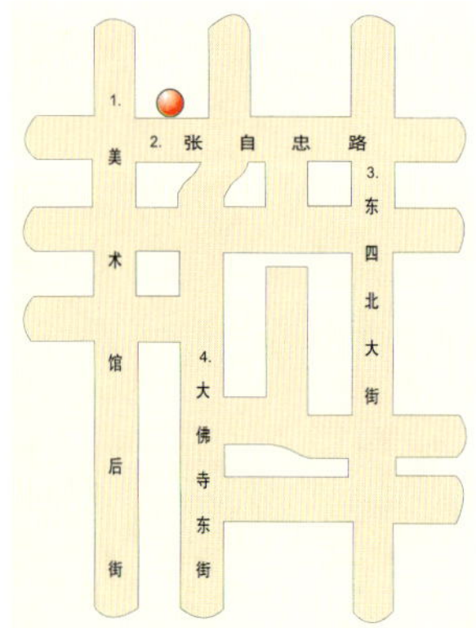

44

people's livelihood) and organized many armed uprisings. After the 1911 Revolution succeeded, Sun was elected provisional president of the Republic of China.

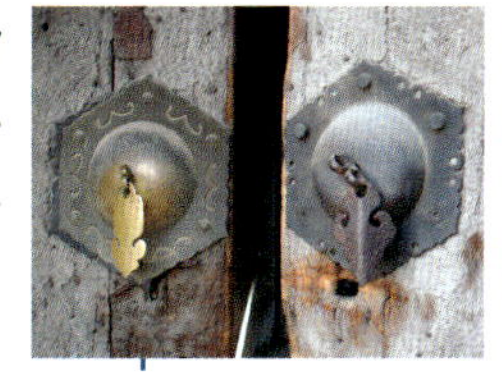
The old gate of Li Dazhao's former home

Li Dazhao's Former Home

Located at 24 Wenhua Hutong (Literary Glory Lane) in Xicheng District, this was the Beijing residence where Li Dazhao spent the most time. Li lived here from 1920 to 1922. It is now public housing on Beijing's list of protected sites.

Li Dazhao (1889-1927) was a native of Leting County in Hebei Province. He led the May 4th Movement in 1919, established the Beijing Communist Group in 1920, helped Sun Yat-sen enact the three cardinal principles (alliance with the Soviet Union and the Chinese Communist Party and support for the workers and peasants). He was one of the founders of the Chinese Communist Party.

Lu Xun's Former Home

Open 9 a.m. to 4 p.m., Tuesday to Sunday

The house at 21 Xisantiao (Third West Lane), Gongmenkou (Palace Gate Entrance) near Fuchengmen in Xicheng District was the last home of Lu Xun and his mother in Beijing. They lived here from 1924 to 1926 and it is on

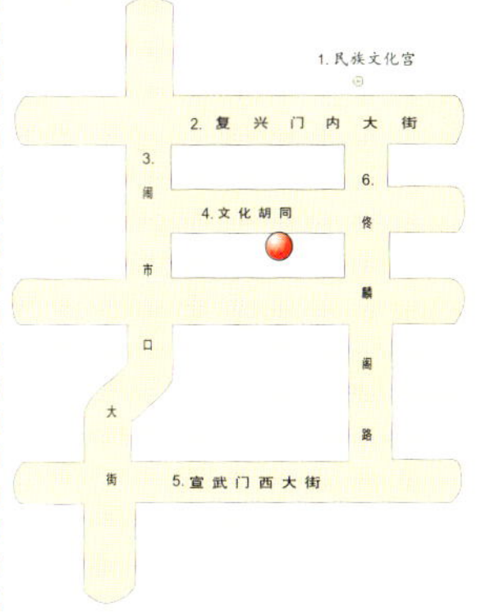

1. The National Cultural Palace
2. Fuxingmennei Dajie (Gate of Revival Inner Street)
3. Naoshikou Dajie (Busy Market Entrance Street)
4. Wenhua Hutong (Literary Glory Lane)
5. Xuanwumen Xidajie (Gate of Proclaimed Military Strength West Street)
6. Tonglinge Lu (Tong Linge Road)

1. Fuchengmen Beidajie (Fuchengmen North Street)
2. Qingta Hutong (Blue Tower Lane)
3. Gongmenkou Ertiao (Palace Gate Entrance Second Lane)
4. Fuchengmennei Beijie (Inner Fuchengmen North Street)
5. Fuchengmennei Dajie (Inner Fuchengmen Street)
6. Gongmenkou Toutiao (Palace Gate Entrance First Lane)
7. Gongmenkou Santiao (Palace Gate Entrance Third Lane)

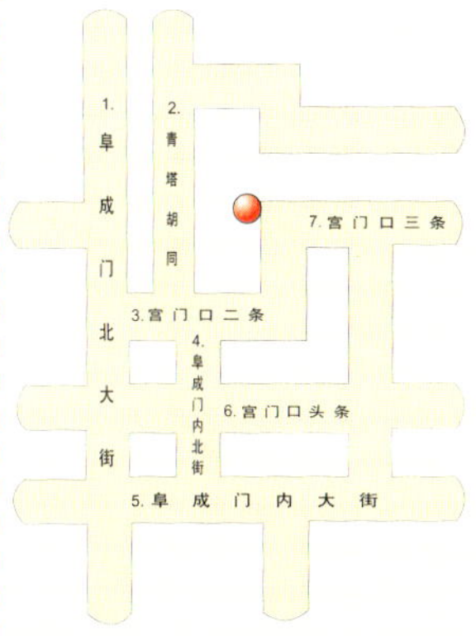

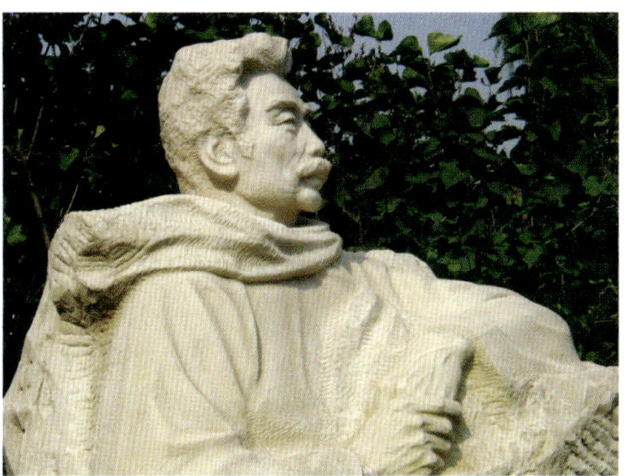

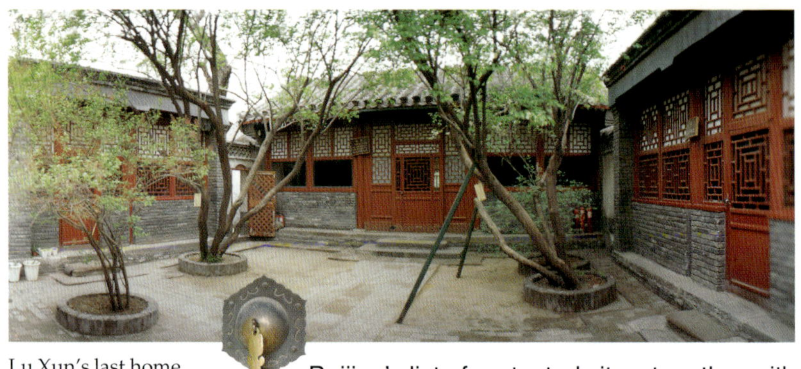
Lu Xun's last home in Beijing

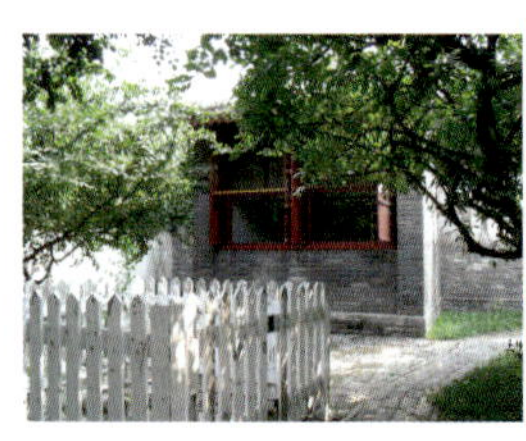
Lu Xun completed many of his works in this small house

Lu Xun's home at Banjie Hutong (Half Lane) outside Xuanwumen (Gate of Proclaimed Military Strength)

Beijing's list of protected sites, together with the Lu Xun Museum. Lu Xun previously lived in the Shaoxing Guild Hall in Nanban Jie (South Half Street) outside Xuanwumen (Gate of Proclaimed Military Strength) from May 1912 to November 1919. He stayed at 11 Badaowan (Eight Bends) in Xizhimen from November 1919 to July 1923 and moved to 61 Zhuanta Hutong (Brick Tower Lane) in the Xisi area in August 1923.

Lu Xun was the pen name of Zhou Shuren (1881-1936), a native of Shaoxing in Zhejiang Province and a well-known writer, thinker and revolutionary.

Many of Lu Xun's writings have been published, and there is an edition of his complete works. His greatest works include *A Madman's Diary*, *The True Story of Ah Q*, *The New-Year Sacrifice*, and *Wild Grass*.

The Lu Xun Museum opens from 9 a.m. to 4 p.m. and closes on Monday.

Lu Xun's home at Badaowan (Eight Bends) in Xizhimen (Straight West Gate)

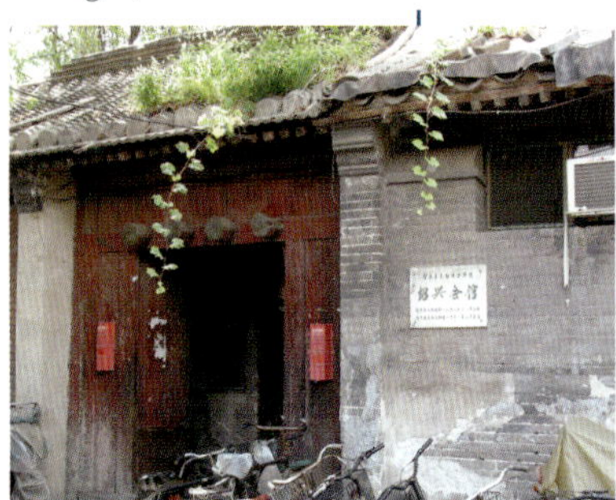

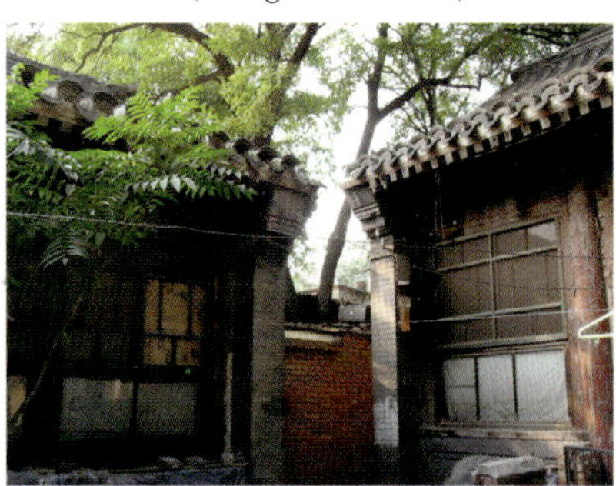

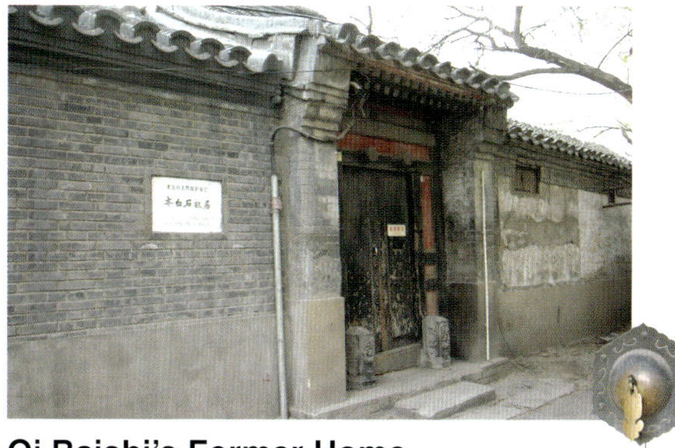

Qi Baishi's Former Home

This is located at 13 Kuache Hutong (Getting on a Cart Lane) inside Picai Hutong (Introducing Talent Lane) in Xicheng District. Qi Baishi moved here in 1926 and lived here until his death. Today, it is the home of his descendants and is on Beijing's list of protected sites.

Qi Baishi (1864-1957) was originally called Qi Chunzhi and was a carpenter in his early years. At the age of 27, he started to learn how to paint and write poems. In 1956, the World Peace Council awarded him its International Peace Award. In 1963, he was included on a list of "World Cultural Celebrities."

Mei Lanfang's Former Home

Open 9 a.m. to 4 p.m., Tuesday to Sunday

Located at 9 Huguosi Jie (Defending-the-Nation Street) in Xicheng District, this was the home of Mei Lanfang from 1950 until his death. It has since been turned into the Mei Lanfang Memorial and is on Beijing's list of protected sites.

Mei Lanfang (1894-1961) was born in Beijing but his family came from Taizhou in Jiangsu Province. He was a great master of Peking opera. He started to learn the art of opera when he was eight and made his debut at the age of 10. Regarded as the best of the four great

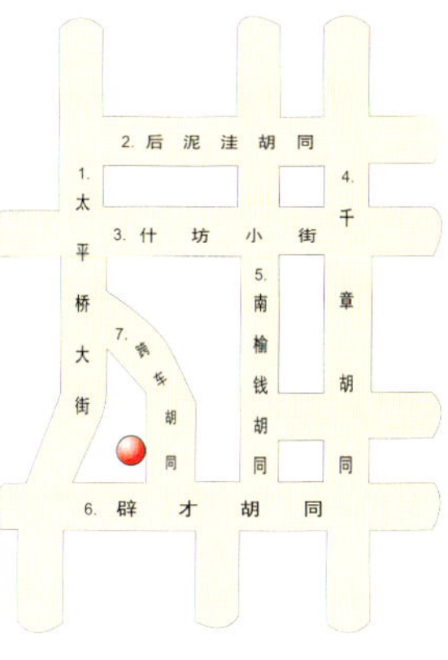

The area around Qi Baishi's former home is always changing.

1. Taipingqiao Dajie (Bridge of Peace and Tranquility Street)
2. Houniwa Hutong (Back Mud Pit Lane)
3. Shifang Xiaojie (Ten Lanes Small Street)
4. Qianzhang Hutong (Thousand Seals Lane)
5. Nanyuqian Hutong (South Elm Seeds Lane)
6. Picai Hutong (Introducing Talent Lane)
7. Kuache Hutong (Getting on a Cart Lane)

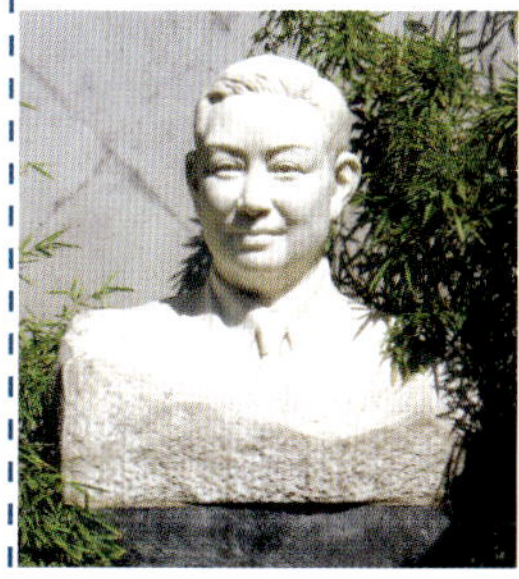

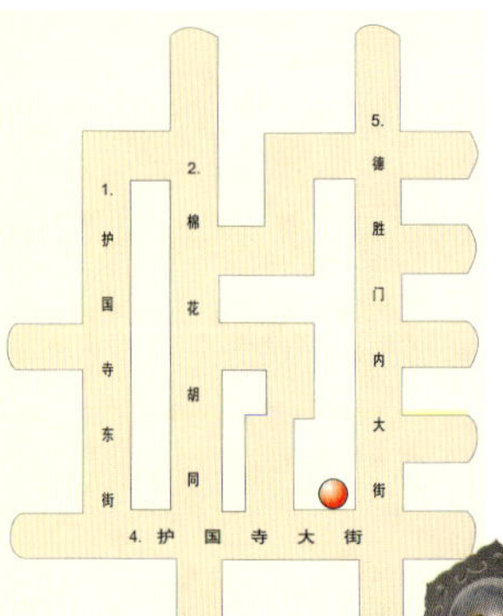

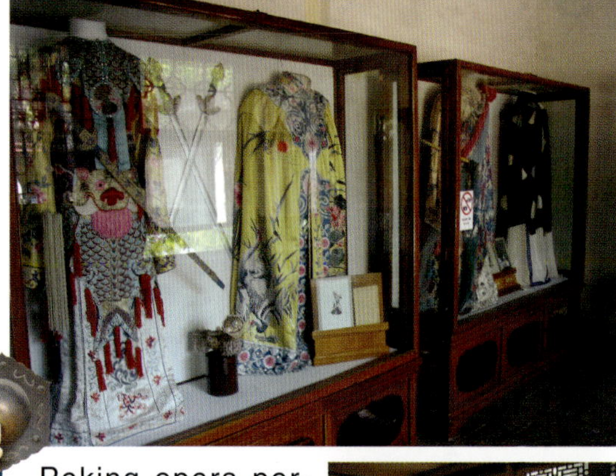

1. Huguosi Dongjie (Defending-the-Nation Temple East Street)
2. Mianhua Hutong (Cotton Lane)
3. Huguosi Jie (Defending-the-Nation Temple Street)
4. Deshengmennei Dajie (Moral Victory Gate Inner Street)

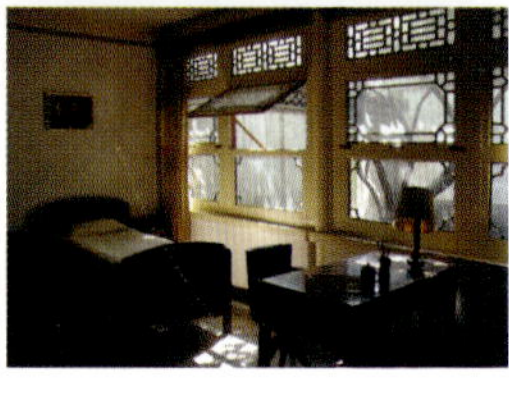

Peking opera performers of the female *dan* role (the three others being Cheng Yanqiu, Shang Xiaoyun and Xun Huisheng), he shaped his own style and gave birth to the Mei Lanfang school.

Lao She's Former Home

Open 9 a.m. to 5 p.m., Tuesday to Sunday

Lao She spent his childhood at 8 Xiaoyangjia Hutong (Little Sheep Pen Lane) in Xicheng District. As an adult, he moved to 19 Fengfu Hutong (Abundance Lane), north of Dengshikou Xijie (Lantern Market Entrance West Street) in Dongcheng District. The latter home is a traditional quadrangle house with two central courtyards. There are various flowers and trees, including two persimmon trees, which led to the courtyard being named Danshi Xiaoyuan (Red Persimmon Courtyard). It is on Beijing's list of protected sites.

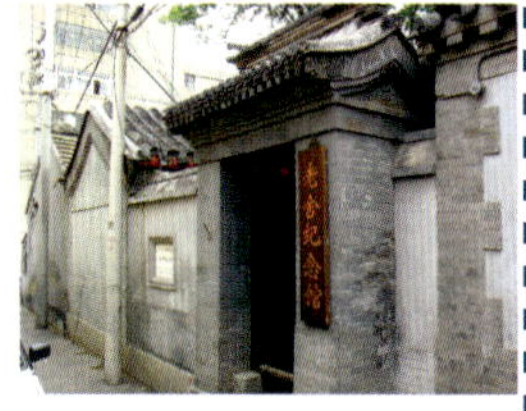

1. Beiheyan Dajie (North River Bank Street)
2. Donghuangchenggen Nanjie (East Imperial City Corner Wall South Street)
3. Fengfu Hutong (Abundance Lane)
4. Dong'anmen Dajie (Gate of Eastern Peace Street)
5. Wangfujing Dajie (Well in the Prince's Mansion Street)

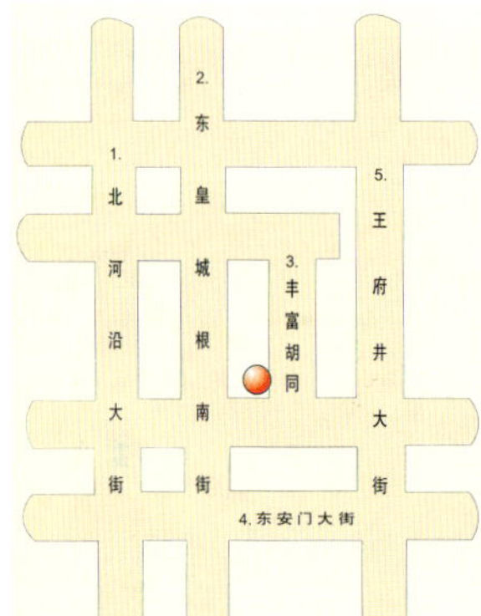

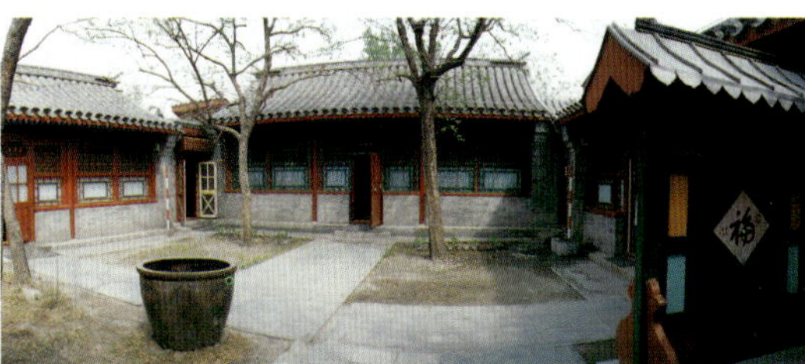

The well-known writer Lao She (1899-1966) was originally called Shu Qingchun and was born in Beijing. His works include the play *Teahouse* and the novels *Four Generations Under One Roof* (*The Yellow Storm*), *This Life of Mine*, *Beneath the Red Banner* and *Camel Xiangzi* (*Rickshaw Boy*). There is an edition of his collected works.

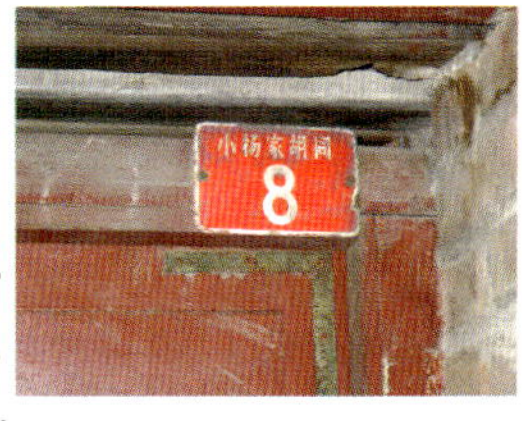

Lao She's childhood home

Mao Dun's Former Home

Open 9 a.m. to 4 p.m., Tuesday, Thursday and Saturday

Located at 13 Yuan'ensi Hutong (Round-Kindness Temple Lane) in Dongcheng District, this residence covers an area of 800 square meters. Mao Dun lived here from 1974 until his death. It is on Beijing's list of protected sites.

Mao Dun (1896-1981) was the pen name of Shen Dehong, a native of Tongxiang in Zhejiang Province. His works include the novel *Midnight* and the short stories *The Shop of the Lin Family* and *Spring Silkworms*. There is an edition of his complete works.

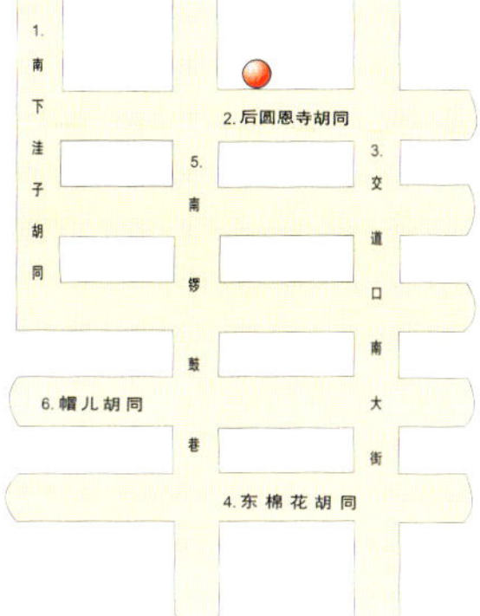

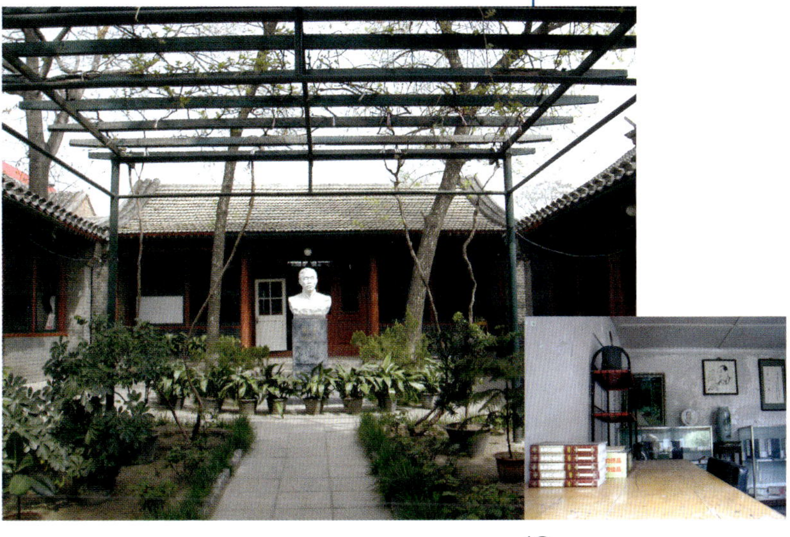

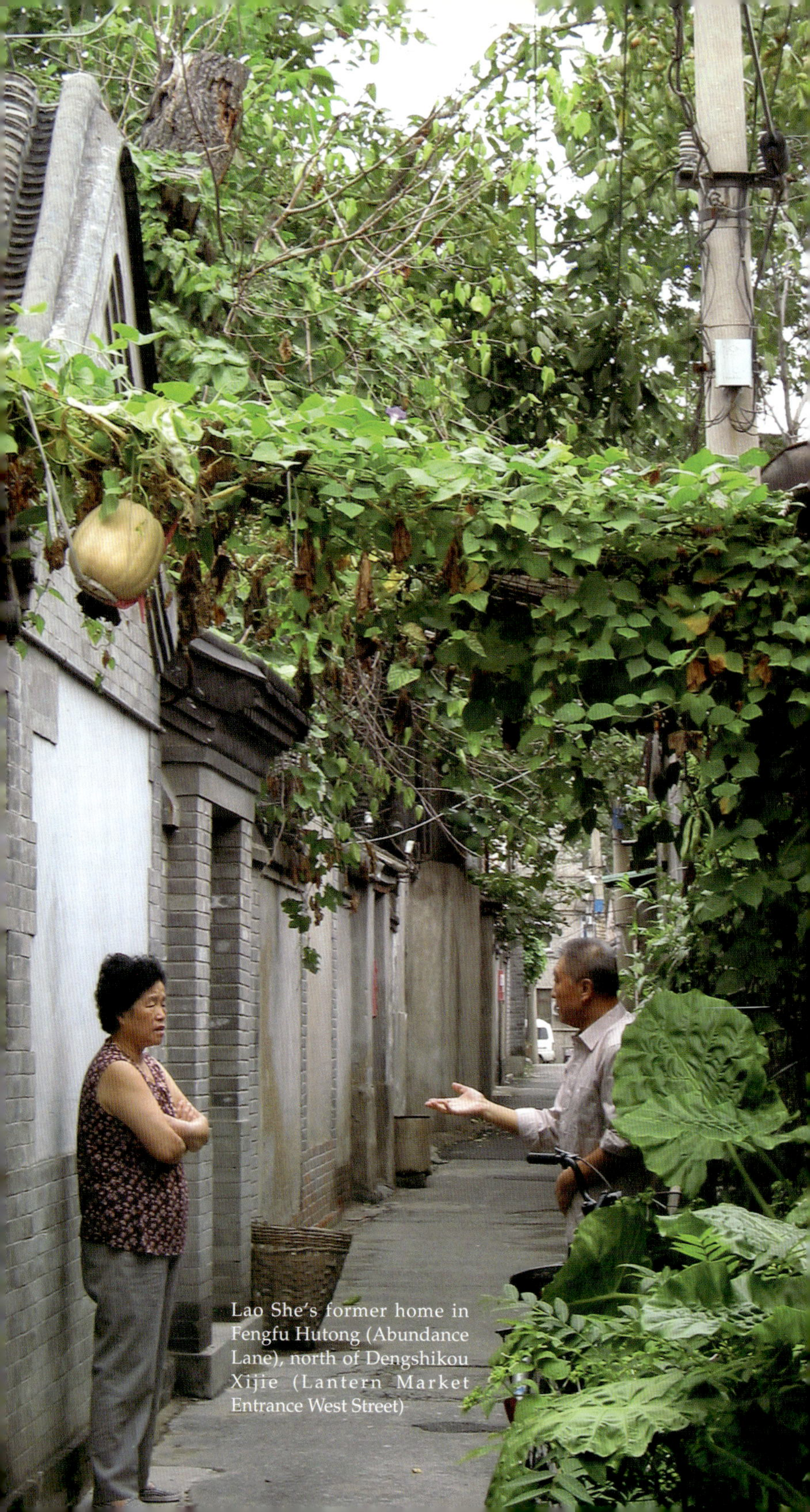
Lao She's former home in
Fengfu Hutong (Abundance
Lane), north of Dengshikou
Xijie (Lantern Market
Entrance West Street)

Cai E's Former Residence

This well-preserved residence with two courtyards is located at 66 Mianhua Hutong (Cotton Lane) in Xicheng District. This former home of Cai E is now public housing.

Cai E (1882-1916), originally called Gen Yin, was from Shaoyang in Hunan Province. He was a military strategist and active supporter of China's democratic revolution.

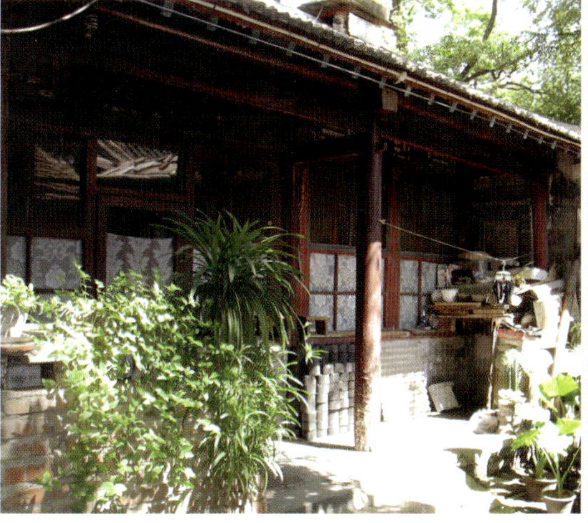

1. Huguosi Dongjie (Defending-the-Nation Temple East Street)
2. Mianhua Hutong (Cotton Lane)
3. Deshengmennei Dajie (Moral Victory Gate Inner Street)
4. Huguosi Jie (Defending-the-Nation Temple Street)

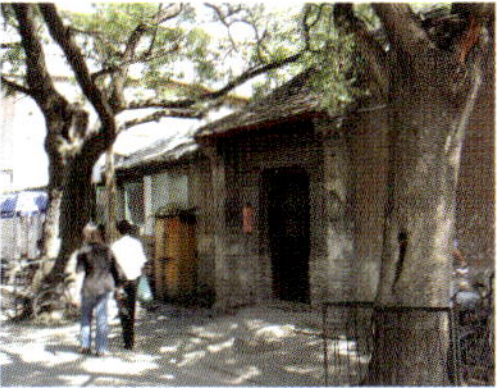

It is said that Cai E used to live in the old room in the left picture.

Cao Xueqin's Former Home

Open 8 a.m. to 5 p.m. daily

This is located at 39 Zhengbai Qi (Plain White Banner) at the foot of Xiangshan (Fragrant Hills) in Haidian District. In 1971, when

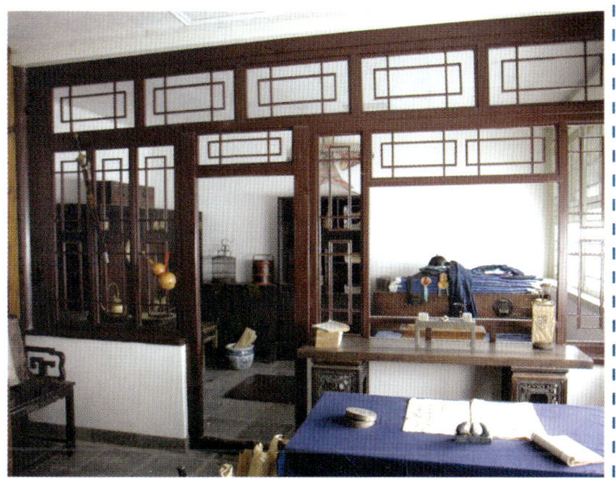

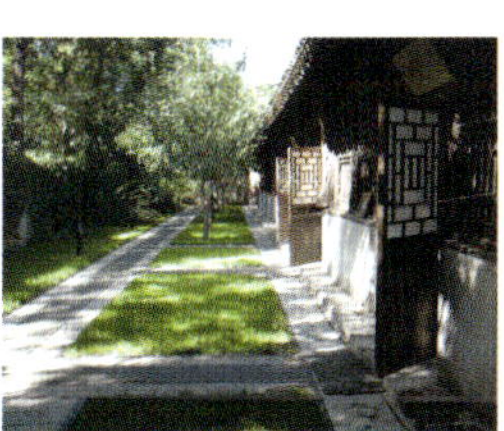

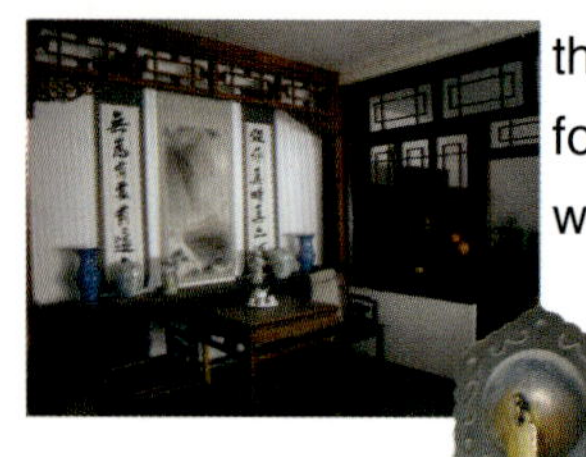

the house owner was renovating the house, he found some poems and couplets hung on the wall and later a few old boxes for books. Experts have identified the house as being where Cao Xueqin spent his later years. In April 1983, it was turned into the Cao Xueqin Museum .

Cao Xueqin (1715-64) was born in Nanjing to an eminent and wealthy family with roots in Fengrun in Hebei Province. When Cao Xueqin was 13 years old, his father was arrested and taken to Beijing due to a financial dispute. Cao Xueqin followed his father to Beijing. Living in poverty, he spent 10 years writing the renowned long novel *A Dream of Red Mansions*.

Dong Biwu's Former Home

Located at 24 Xiaoshiqiao Hutong (Small Stone Bridge Lane) in Jiugulou Dajie (Old Drum-Tower Street) in Xicheng District, this was origi-

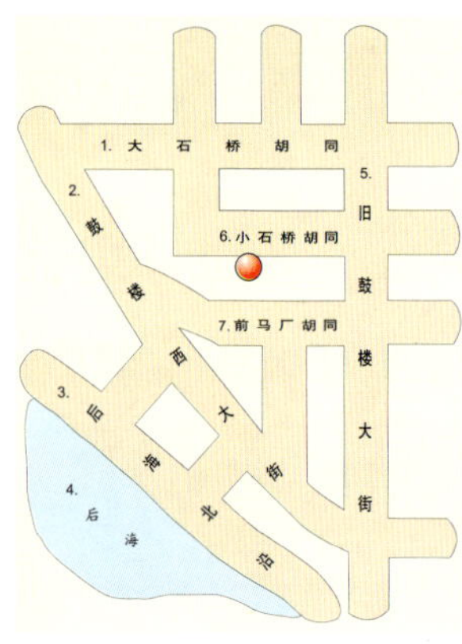

1. Dashiqiao Hutong (Big Stone Bridge Lane)
2. Gulou Xidajie (West Drum Tower Street)
3. Houhai Beiyan (the north bank of Rear Lake)
4. Houhai (Rear Lake)
5. Jiugulou Dajie (Old Drum Tower Street)
6. Xiaoshiqiao Hutong (Small Stone Bridge Lane)
7. Qianmachang Hutong (Former Horse Land Lane)

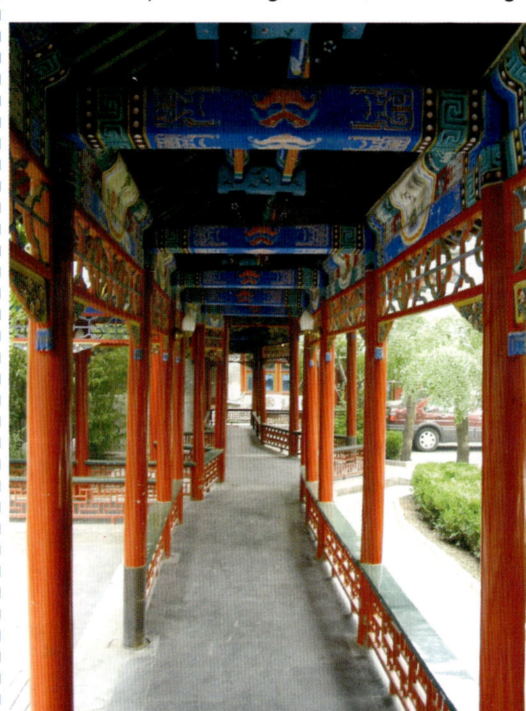

nally the house of Sheng Xuanhuai, minister of postal services during the Qing Dynasty. It thus got the name Shengyuan (Sheng Courtyard). Dong Biwu lived and received guests in the two-story building in the courtyard. Now it is the Zhuyuan (Bamboo Garden) Hotel and is a cultural relic under Xicheng District's protection.

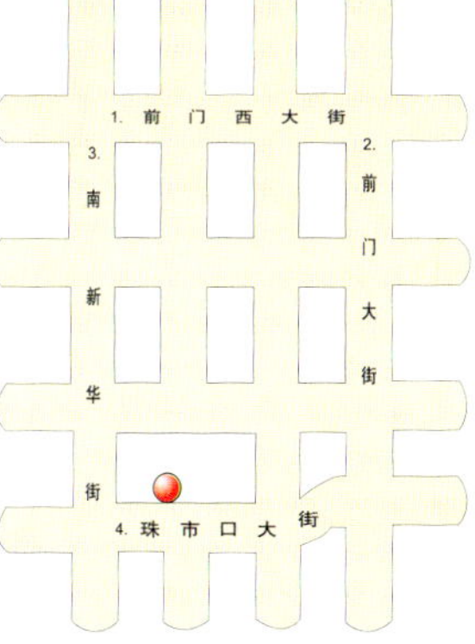

Dong Biwu (1886-1975) was a lawyer, scholar and educationist from Huang'an in Hubei Province. After liberation in 1949, he was elected vice president and served as acting president of the People's Republic of China.

Ji Xiaolan's Former Home

Open 9 a.m. to 4 p.m. Tuesday to Sunday

This is located on the north side of the street at 241 Zhushikou Xidajie (West Pearl Market Entrance Street) in Xuanwu District. With several courtyards, it is a cultural relic under Xuanwu District's protection.

Ji Xiaolan (1724-1805) was originally called Ji Yun. A native of Xian County in Hebei Province, he was a famous scholar during the Qing Dynasty. During his years as minister of rites and assistant grand secretary in the Grand

1. Qianmen Xidajie (Front Gate West Avenue)
2. Qianmen Dajie (Front Gate Avenue)
3. Nanxinhua Jie (South New China Street)
4. Zhushikou Dajie (Pearl Market Entrance Street)

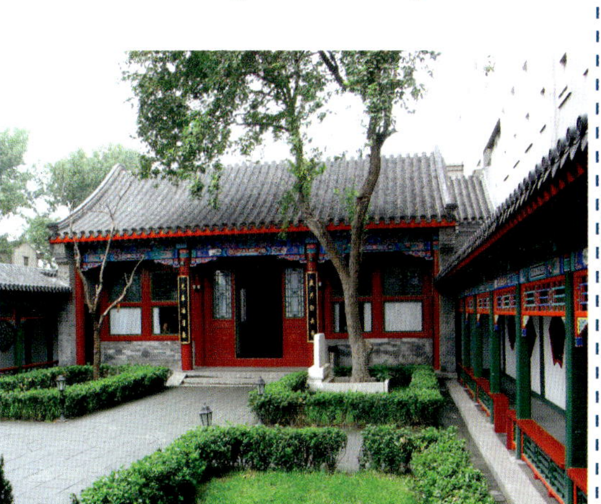

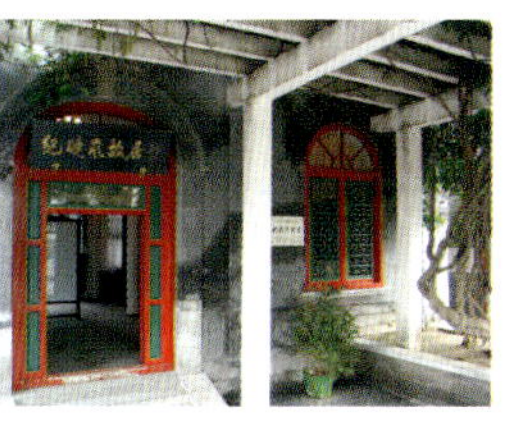

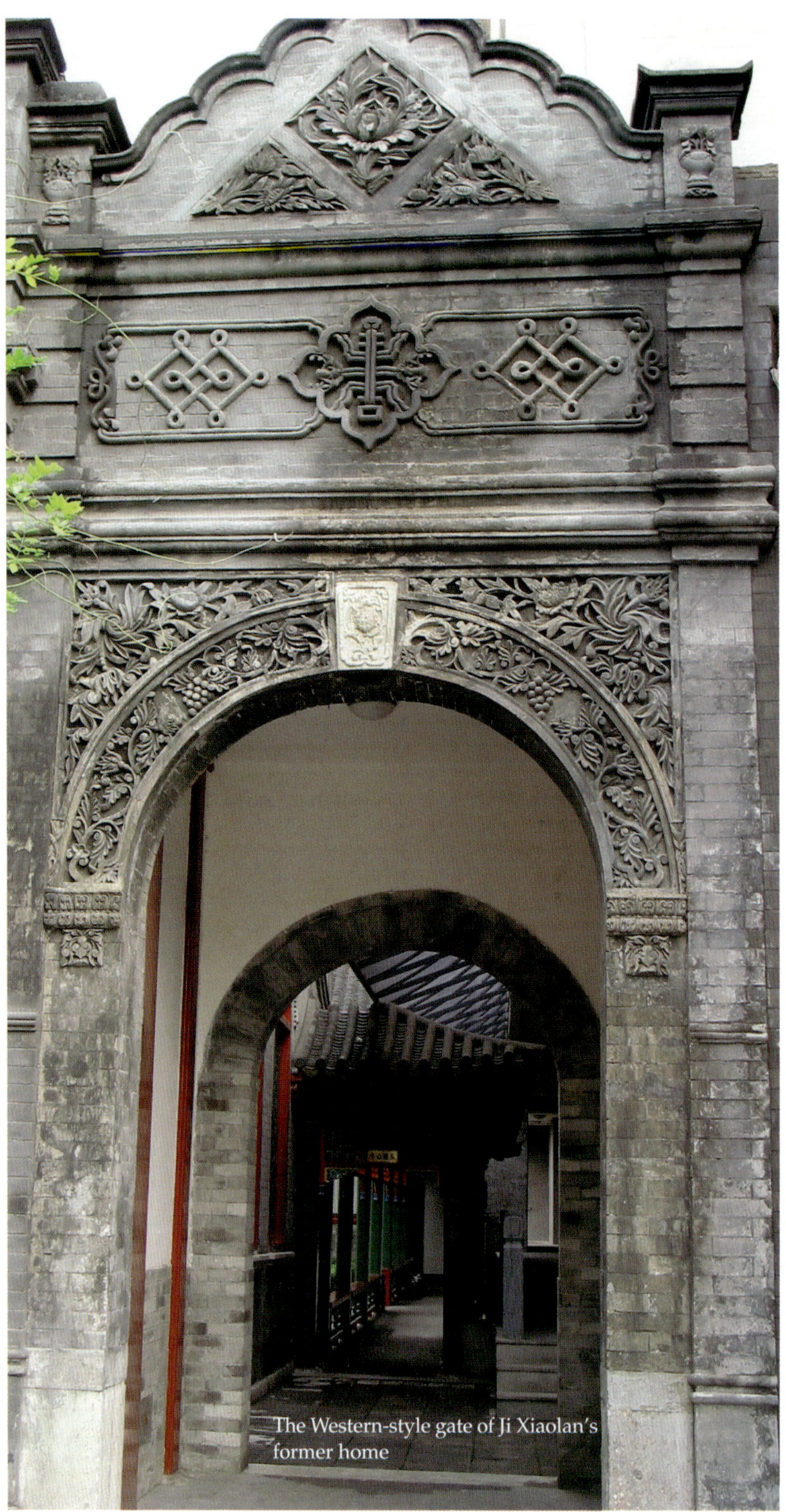

The Western-style gate of Ji Xiaolan's former home

Secretariat, he oversaw the compilation of the *Siku Quanshu* (*Complete Library of the Four Branches of Literature*) and wrote the 200-fascicle *Siku Quanshu Zongmu Tiyao* (*Siku Quanshu General Catalogue*) and *Yuewei Caotang Biji* (*Jottings from the Thatched Abode of Close Observations*).

1. Qianhai Beiyan (the north bank of Front Lake)
2. Di'anmenwai Dajie (Gate of Earthly Peace Outer Street)
3. Baimi Xie Jie (Polished Rice Oblique Street)
4. Qianhai (Front Lake)
5. Beihai (North Lake)
6. Di'anmen Xidajie (Gate of Earthly Peace West Street)
7. Qianhai Xijie (Front Lake West Street)

Zhang Zhidong's Former Home

This is located at 11 Baimi Xie Jie (Polished Rice Oblique Street) in Xicheng District. Its backyard is near the beautiful lake Qianhai in the Shichahai (Ten-Temple Lake) area, and the house has been turned into public housing.

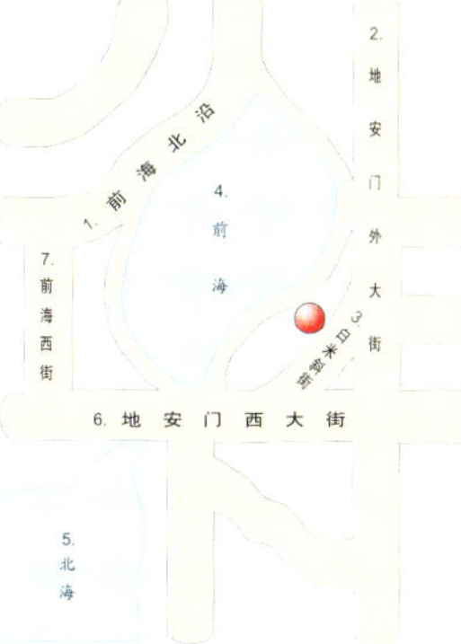

Zhang Zhidong (1837-1909) had his roots in Nanpi in Zhili Province (today's Hebei Province). He was an important official in the late Qing Dynasty and head of the Yangwu ("Foreign Affairs") faction. He held the position of governor-general of Guangdong and Guangxi and later of Hubei and Hunan provinces and was a great academician and minister of state.

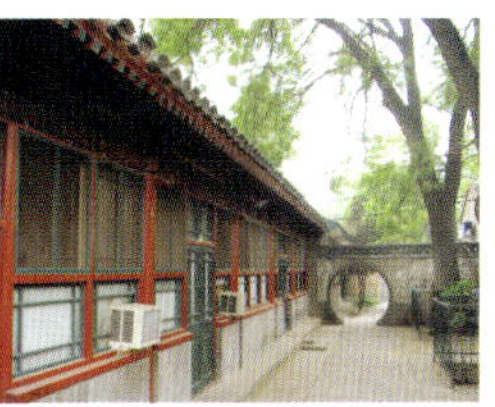

Upholding Western knowledge, he promoted heavy industry and the military industry, set up the State Mint Bureau, railroads and developed the postal service, searching for a way in which China could survive in the modern world by accommodating Western knowledge while preserving its traditional ways.

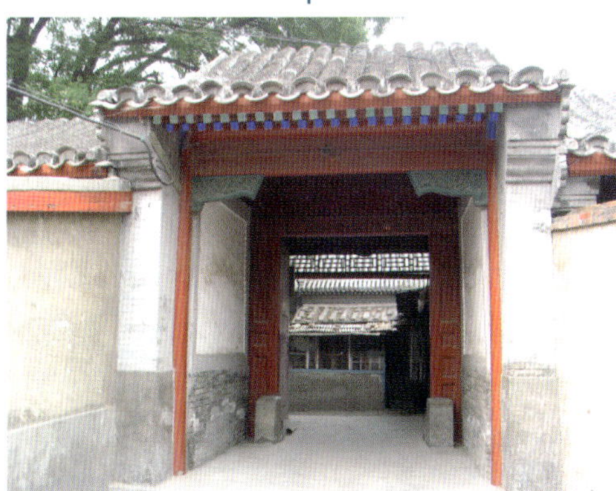

Shen Jiaben's Former Home

Located at 1 Jinjing Hutong (Golden Well Lane) in Xuanwu District, the house has been

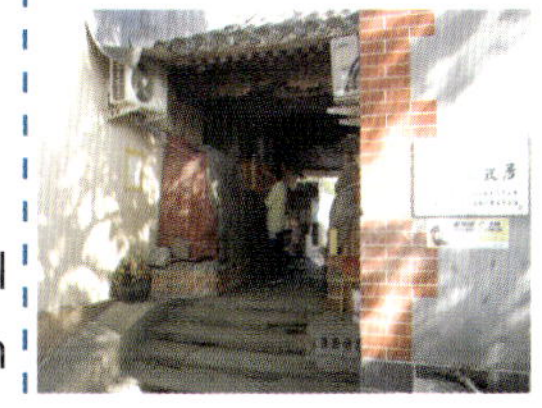

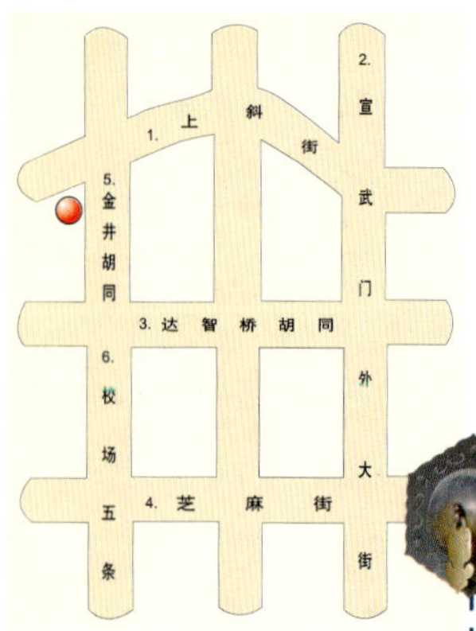

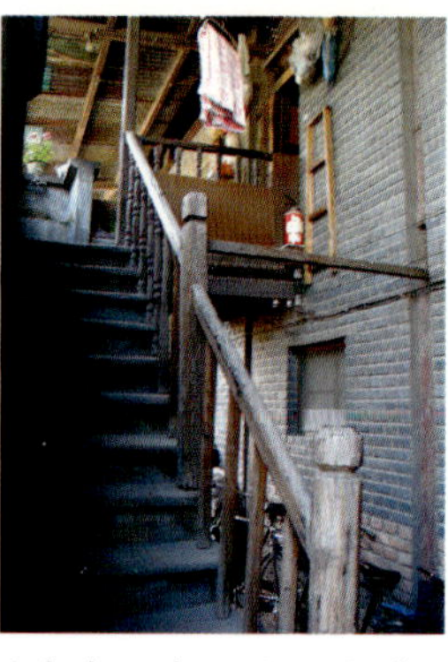

1. Shangxie Jie (Upper Oblique Street)
2. Xuanwumenwai Dajie (Gate of Proclaimed Military Strength Outer Street)
3. Dazhiqiao Hutong (Attaining Wisdom Bridge Lane)
4. Zhima Jie (Sesame Street)
5. Jinjing Hutong (Golden Well Lane)
6. Jiaochang Wutiao (Drill Ground Fifth Lane)

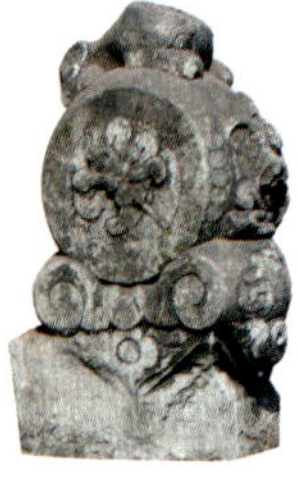

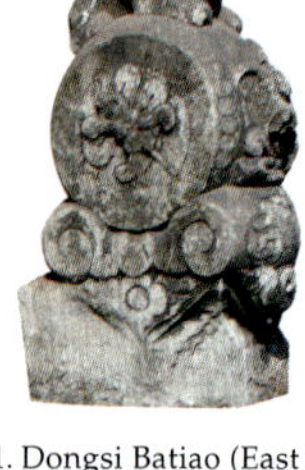

1. Dongsi Batiao (East Four Eighth Lane)
2. Dongsi Beidajie (East Four North Street)
3. Chaoyangmen Beixiaojie (Chaoyang Gate North Small Street)
4. Chaoyangmennei Dajie (Chaoyang Gate Inner Street)
5. Dongsi Liutiao (East Four Sixth Lane)

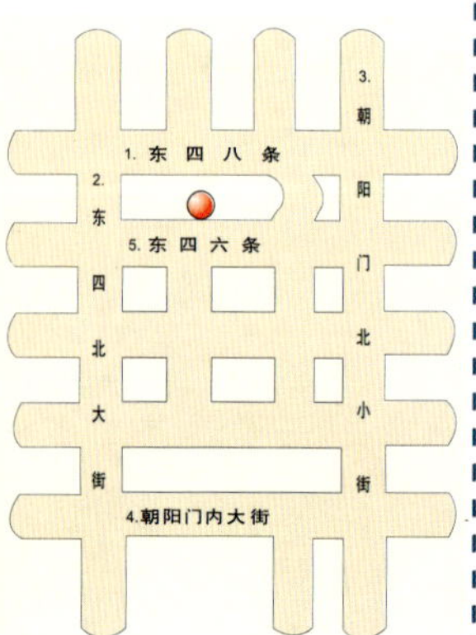

turned into public housing and is a cultural relic under Xuanwu District's protection.

The calligrapher Shen Jiaben (1840-1913) was from Gui'an in Zhejiang Province. He called for the late Qing Dynasty's legal system to be revolutionized and he initiated research into the modern Chinese legal system. In 1910, as vice president of China's congress, he presided over the editing of the first criminal code in modern Chinese history, the *New Criminal Law of the Qing Dynasty*.

Sha Qianli's Former Home

This is located at 55 Dongsi Liutiao (East Four Sixth Lane) in Dongcheng District. With three courtyards, it is a cultural relic under Dongcheng District's protection and is used as public housing.

The famous patriot Sha Qianli (1901-82) was one of the so-called "seven men of honor" of the 1930s. After liberation, he was elected vice president of the Chinese People's Political Con-

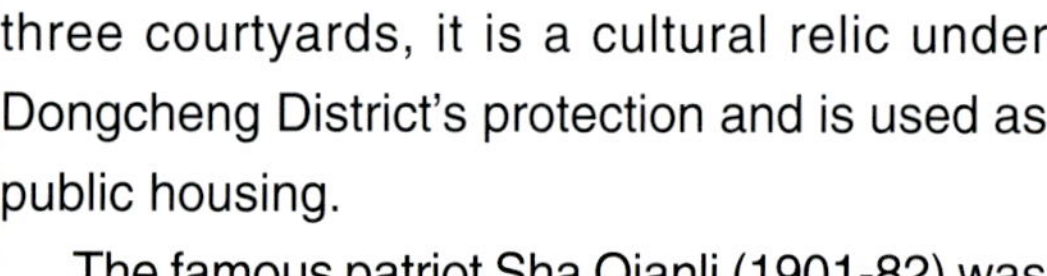

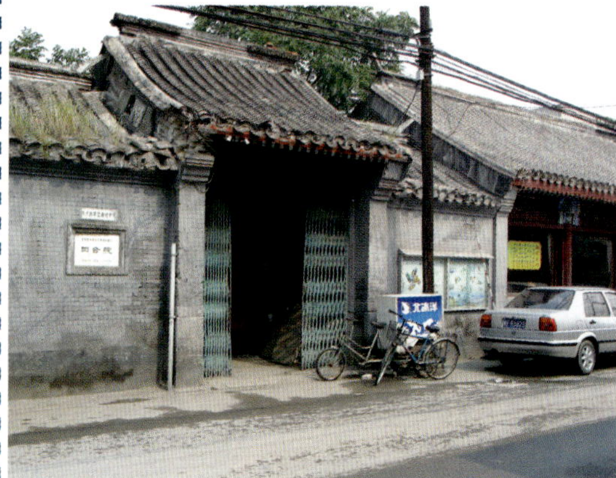

sultative Conference's Fifth Committee.

Song Jiaoren's Former Residence

Located in the northwest corner of Beijing Zoo in Xicheng District, this house is called Changguan Lou (Grand View Tower). The architecture is typically European and it is the only perfectly preserved Western-style holiday palace of Empress Dowager Cixi. In the early 1950s, the then Panchen Lama came to Beijing and lived here. Since 1980, it has been managed by Beijing Zoo.

Song Jiaoren (1882-1913) was from Taoyuan County in Hunan Province. He set up the Hua Xing Hui (China Rehabilitation Association) and later became the backbone of the Tong Meng Hui (Chinese Revolutionary League). After the Republic of China was founded, he enacted the Temporary Regulations of the Republic of China, which constituted China's first national fundamental law, equivalent to a constitution.

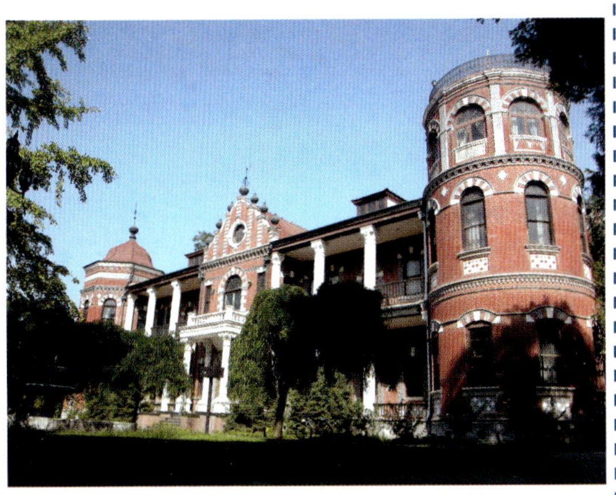

Lin Baishui's Former Home

Located at 1 Mianhua Toutiao (First Cotton Lane) to the north of Guozi Xiang (Fruit Lane) in Xuanwu District, this is where the renowned

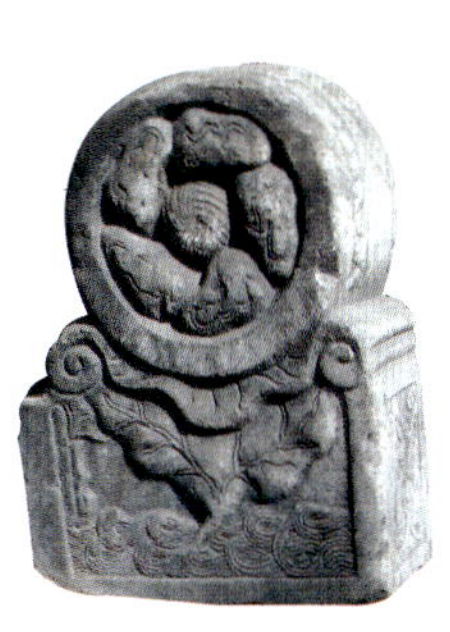

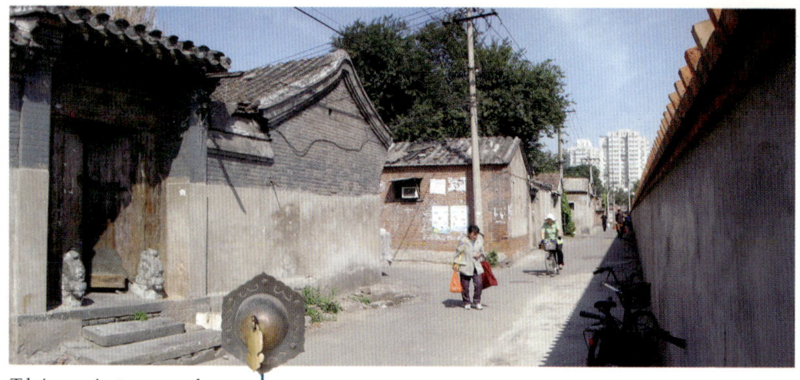

This picture shows Mianhua Ertiao (Second Cotton Lane). Buildings on the other side of the wall on the right of the picture, including Lin Baishui's former home, have been pulled down.

The protected former home of Ye Shengtao

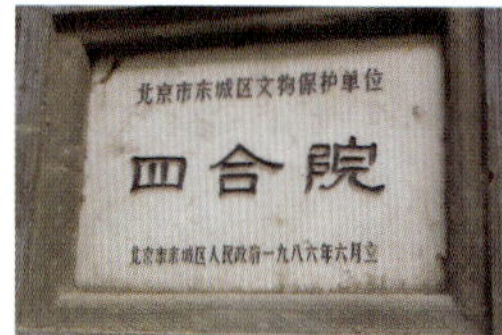

1. Dongsi Batiao (East Four Eighth Lane)
2. Chaoyangmen Beixiaojie (Chaoyang Gate North Small Street)
3. Dongsi Beidajie (East Four North Street)
4. Dongsi Liutiao (East Four Sixth Lane)
5. Chaoyangmennei Dajie (Chaoyang Gate Inner Street)
6. Dongsi Ertiao (East Four Second Lane)

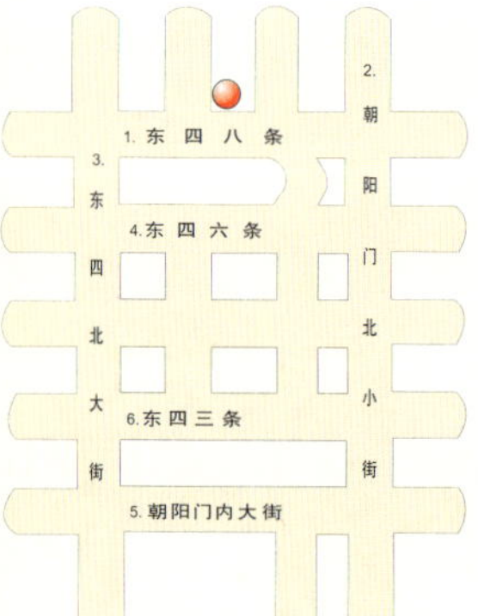

journalist Lin Baishui established *Shehui Ribao* (*Social Daily*). It was turned into public housing and has been demolished.

Lin Baishui (1874-1926) was originally called Lin Xie and also went by the alias Wan Li. He was from Fuzhou in Fujian Province and set up *Zhongguo Baihua Bao* (*China Vernacular Newspaper*), *Gongyan Bao* (*Public Speech Newspaper*) and other publications.

Ye Shengtao's Former Home

Located at 71 Dongsi Batiao (East Four Eighth Lane) in Dongcheng District, this house has three courtyards and a workplace now occupies this home.

Ye Shengtao (1894-1988) was originally called Ye Shaojun. From Suzhou in Jiangsu Province, he was a famous educationist, writer

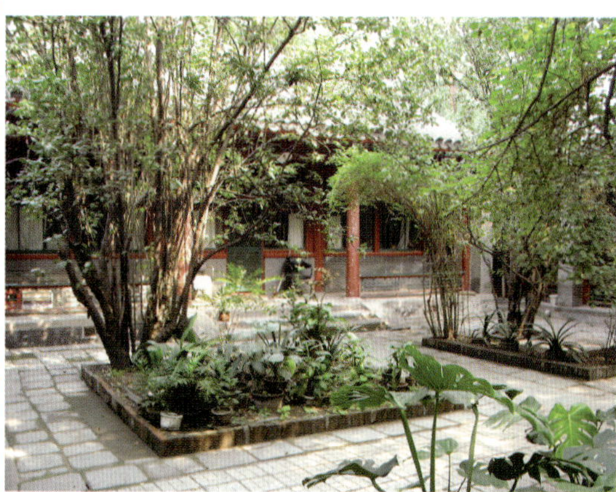

and editor. His works include the long novel *Schoolmaster Ni Huanzhi*, the short story *Estrangement* and the fairy tale *The Scarecrow*. After the People's Republic of China was founded, he was appointed vice president of the Chinese People's Political Consultative Conference and director of the Central Research Institute of Culture and History.

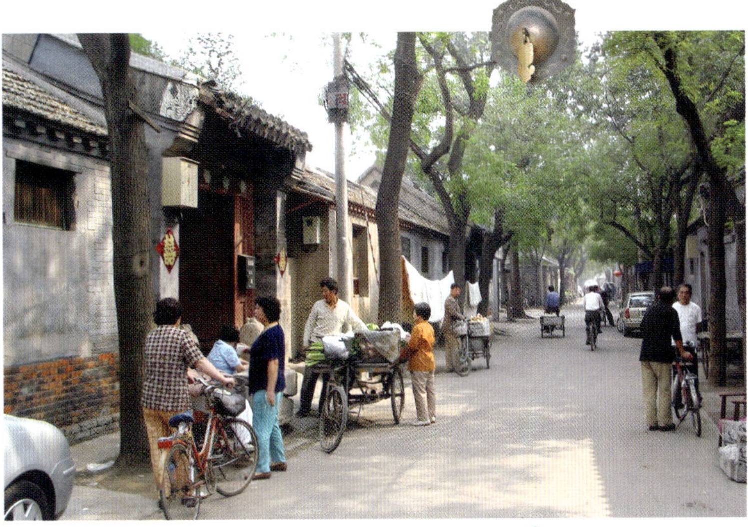

There are still many quadrangle houses on Dongsi Batiao (East Four Eighth Lane).

Zhang Henshui's Former Home

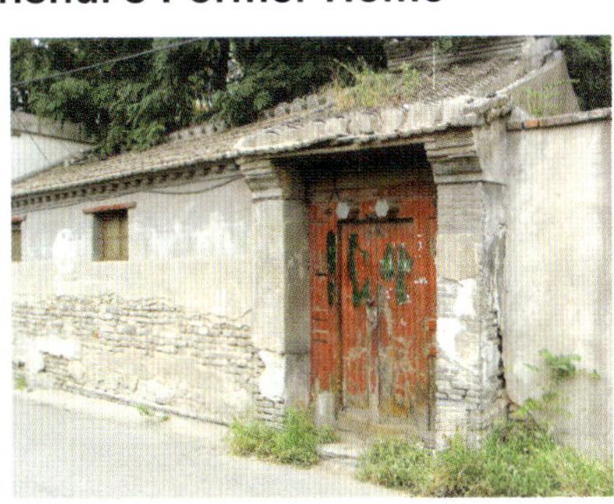

Located at 95 Zhuanta Hutong (Brick Tower Lane) in Xicheng District, this home was made into public housing and is listed for demolition.

Zhang Henshui (1895-1967) was originally called Zhang Xinyuan. A native of Guangxin in Jiangxi Province, he was one of China's best novelists. His novels include *Jinfen Shijia* (*The Story of a Noble Family* or *Golden Family*) and

1. Fuchengmennei Dajie (Inner Fuchengmen Street)
2. Xisi Nandajie (West Four South Street)
3. Taipingqiao Dajie (Bridge of Peace and Tranquility Street)
4. Zhuanta Hutong (Brick Tower Lane)
5. Bingmasi Hutong (Department of Military Forces Lane)

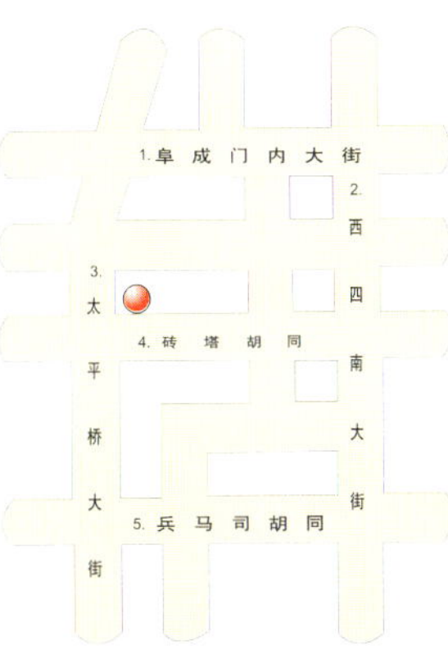

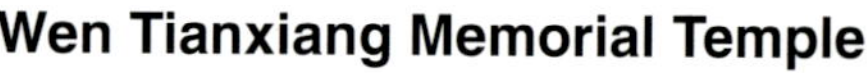

Tixiao Yinyuan (*Fate in Tears and Laughter*).

Wen Tianxiang Memorial Temple

Open 9 a.m. to 4 p.m. daily

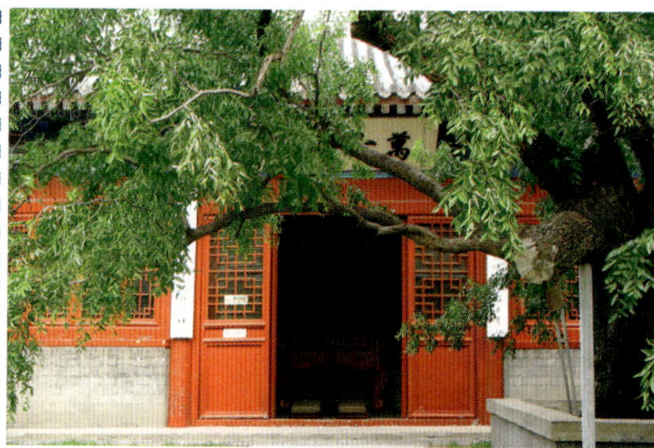

Wen Tianxiang Memorial Temple is located at 63 Fuxue Hutong (Prefectural School Lane) in Dongcheng District, to the east of Shuntian Fuxue (Following-the-Mandate-of-Heaven School), which is now Fuxue Primary School.

Wen Tianxiang (1236-83), a native of Luling in present-day Ji'an in Jiangxi Province, was a national hero and prime minister during the Southern Song Dynasty (1127-1279). He wrote the poem *Zhengqige* ("Song of Righteousness"), which ends with the two famous lines: "Since olden days, which man has lived and not died? / I'll leave a loyalist name in history!" The Prime Minister Wen Memorial is located on the site where Wen was imprisoned.

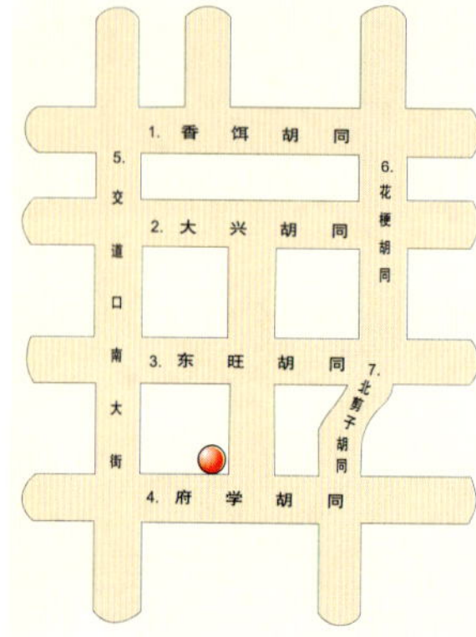

1. Xiangr Hutong (Savory Bait Lane)
2. Daxing Hutong (Great Prosperity Lane)
3. Dongwang Hutong (Eastern Flourish Lane)
4. Fuxue Hutong (Prefectural School Lane)
5. Jiaodaokou Nandajie (Cross-Lane Entrance South Street)
6. Huageng Hutong (Flower Stalk Lane)
7. Beijianzi Hutong (North Scissors Lane)

Yang Jiaoshan Memorial Temple

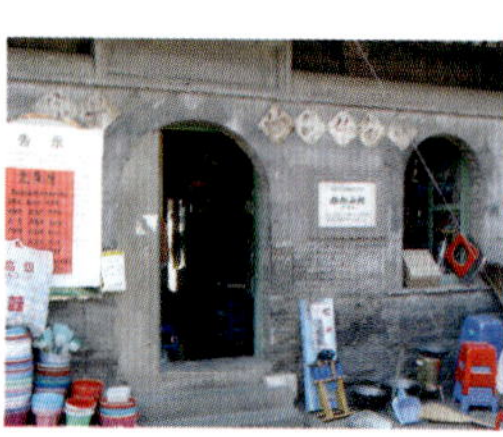

Yang Jiaoshan's former home is located at 12 Dazhiqiao Hutong (Attaining Wisdom Bridge

Lane) outside Xuanwumen (Gate of Proclaimed Military Strength) in Xuanwu District.

Yang Jiaoshan (1516-55) was originally called Yang Jisheng. A native of Rongcheng in Hebei Province, he was a successful candidate in the highest imperial examinations during the Ming Dynasty and was Vice Minister of War. Prime Minister Yan Song had Yang Jiaoshan imprisoned because Yang staunchly advocated fighting the nomadic invaders and accused the prime minister of corruption. Later Yang was executed at Xishi (now Xisi). During the reign of the Qing Emperor Qianlong, the main room of Yang's home was converted into a memorial temple, called Jingxian Tang (Revering Virtue Hall).

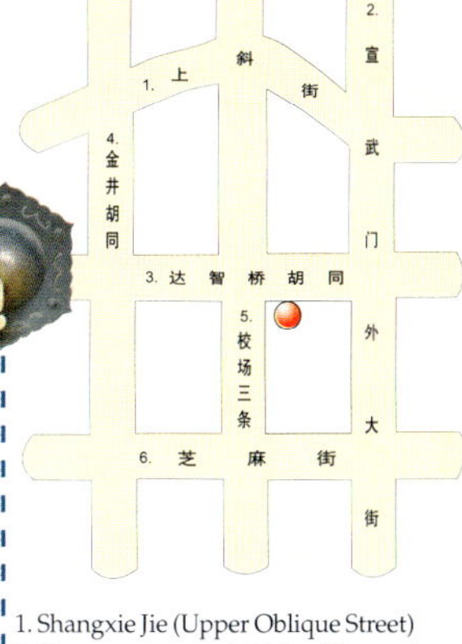

1. Shangxie Jie (Upper Oblique Street)
2. Xuanwumenwai Dajie (Gate of Proclaimed Military Strength Outer Street)
3. Dazhiqiao Hutong (Attaining Wisdom Bridge Lane)
4. Jinjing Hutong (Golden Well Lane)
5. Jiaochang Santiao (Drill Ground Third Lane)
6. Zhima Jie (Sesame Street)

This temple later became Songzhu An (Pine and Bamboo Hut) and is now public housing.

Guo Shoujing Memorial

Open 8 a.m. to 6 p.m. daily

Located by the northwest part of the Jishuitan (Reservoir Lake) in Xicheng District, this building was established during the Ming Dynasty and was originally called Zhenshui Guanyin An (Calm Water Guanyin Nunnery). It was renovated during Qing Emperor Qianlong's reign (1736-96) and was renamed Huitong Ci (Gathering and Connecting Temple). It was demolished during the 1960s when the subway was built but was rebuilt in 1986. The temple's courtyard is square and there is a two-story memorial building, which is now Guo Shoujing Memorial.

Guo Shoujing (1231-1316) was a native of Xingtai in Hebei Province. He was

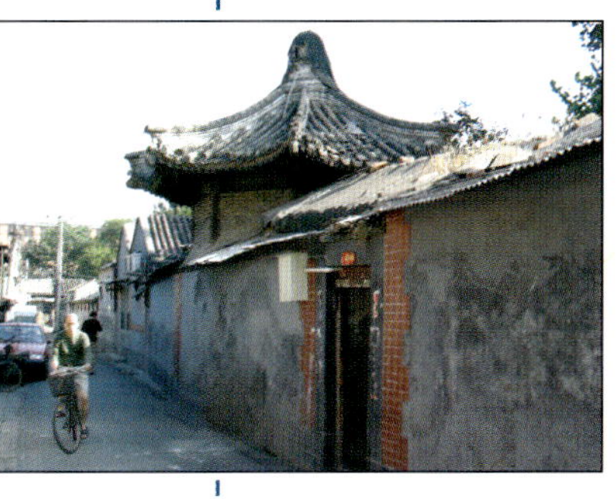

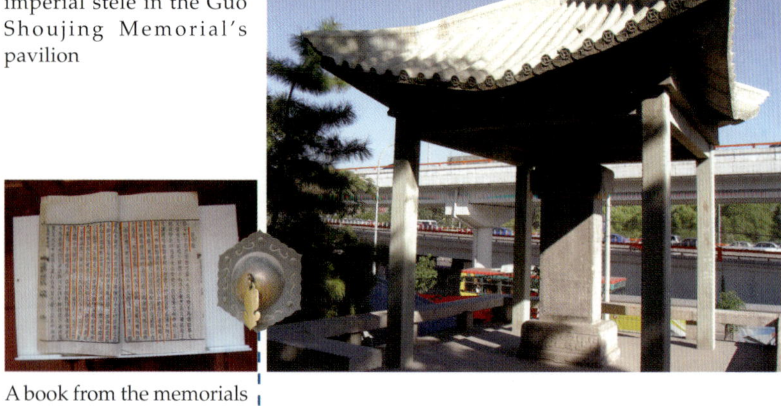

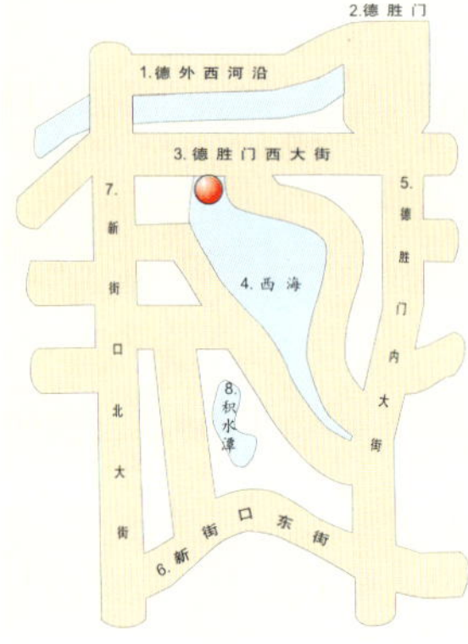

A book from the memorials collection

1. Dewai Xiheyan (the west bank outside Moral Victory Gate)
2. Deshengmen (Moral Victory Gate)
3. Deshengmen Xidajie (Moral Victory Gate West Street)
4. Xihai (West Lake)
5. Deshengmennei Dajie (Moral Victory Gate Inner Street)
6. Xinjiekou Dongdajie (New Street Entrance East Avenue)
7. Xinjiekou Beidajie (New Street Entrance North Avenue)
8. Jishuitan (Reservoir Lake)

a famous hydraulic engineer, astronomer and maker of scientific instruments in the Yuan Dynasty. He designed several water-conservation projects, including the diversion of the Yuquan (Jade Spring) and other water resources into the city and the connection of Beijing to the canal in southern China. These not only solved problems of insufficient water supplies but also gave southern merchants access to the capital Dadu, which greatly accelerated economic and cultural cooperation between the north and south of China. Guo's other notable achievement was the calendar he finished in 1280 while serving on the astrology commission. His calendar has 365.3425 days in a year, the accuracy of which is remarkable.

Zhu Yizun's Former Home

Located at 16 Haibai Hutong (Seaside Cypress Lane) outside Xuanwumen in Xuanwu District, this was once called the Shunde County Guild. It became an ordinary house and now has been pulled down.

Zhu Yizun (1629-1709), a native of Xiushui (now Jiaxing) in Zhejiang Province, was an influential writer and literary theorist in the early Qing Dynasty. The most influential of his works was *Rixia Jiuwen* (*Old Stories*), in which he wrote about Beijing's streets and lanes and folk customs and included allusions from classical works. As a record of the city's historical development and geographical environment and with everyday scenes, the book was regarded as an essential reference works for research into Beijing. He wrote *Old Stories* in Haibai Hutong.

Haibai Hutong (Seaside Cypres's Lane) still exists but its west side is being pulled down. Zhu Yiyun's former home has gone.

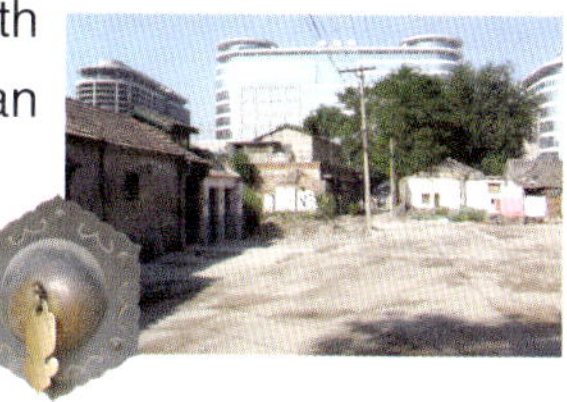

1. Meishuguan Houjie (Art Gallery Back Street)
2. Zhangzizhong Lu (Zhang Zizhong Road)
3. Dongsi Beidajie (East Four North Street)
4. Dafosi Dongjie (Big Buddha Temple East Street)
5. Yuqun Hutong (Group Raising Lane)
6. Wangzhima Hutong (Sesame Wang Lane)

Ouyang Yuqian's Former Home

Located at 5 Zhangzizhong Lu (Zhang Zizhong Road), this house is now used by the Central Academy of Drama as a dormitory building.

Ouyang Yuqian (1889-1962) was originally called Ouyang Liyuan. A native of Liuyang in Hunan Province, he was a renowned performer, playwright and theater director. After the People's Republic of China was founded, he was appointed vice president of the China Fed-

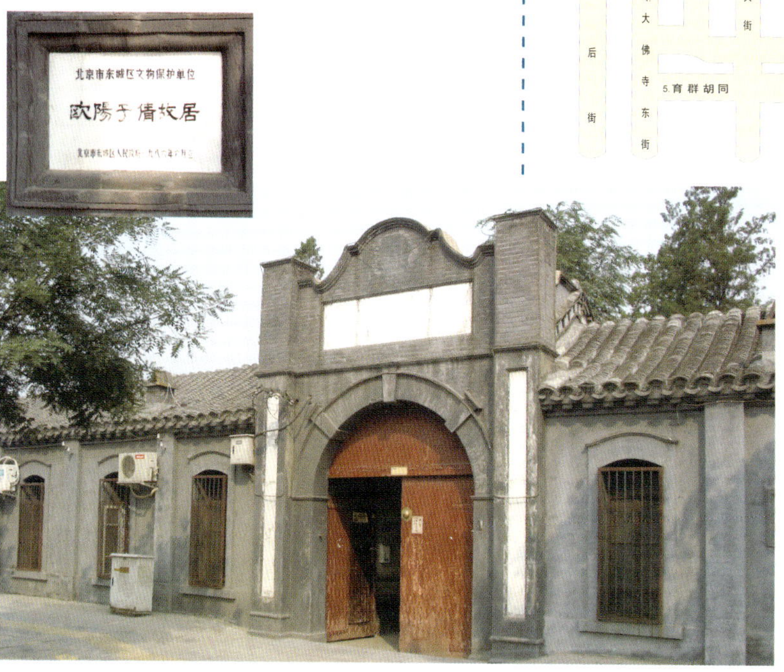

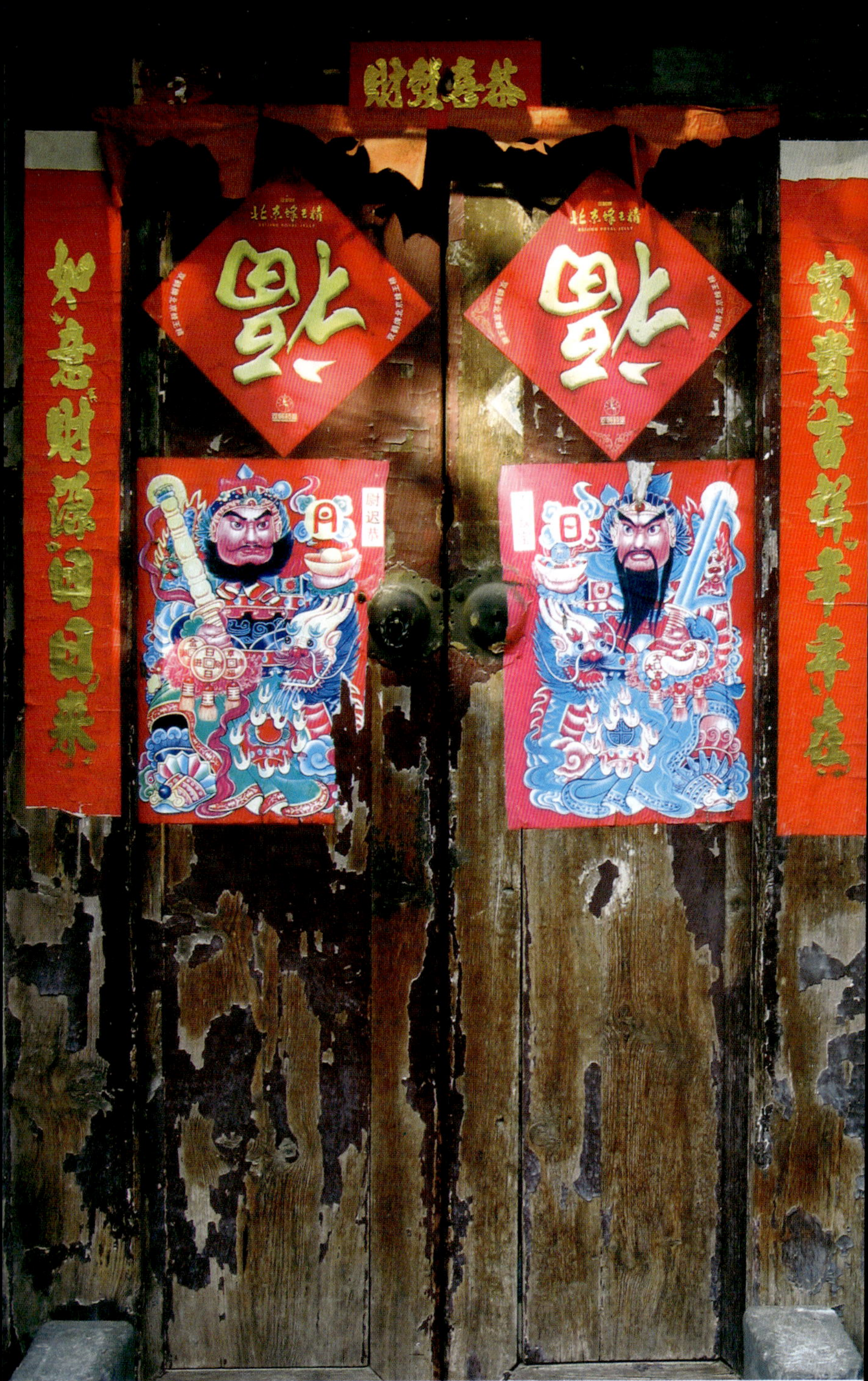

A gate at the entrance of Jiaochang
Sitiao (Drill Ground Fourth Lane)

eration of Literary and Art Circles and vice president of the China Dramatists Association.

Cheng Yanqiu's Former Home

This is located at 39 Xisi Beisantiao (West Four, Third North Lane) in Xicheng District, in a street originally named Baozi Hutong (Lopard Lane). The house has two south-facing courtyards and is now public housing and on Beijing's list of protected sites.

Cheng Yanqiu (1904-58), originally named Cheng Lin, was a famous Peking opera actor. Regarded as the second greatest of the four great Peking opera performers of the female *dan* role, he shaped his own style and gave birth to the Cheng School.

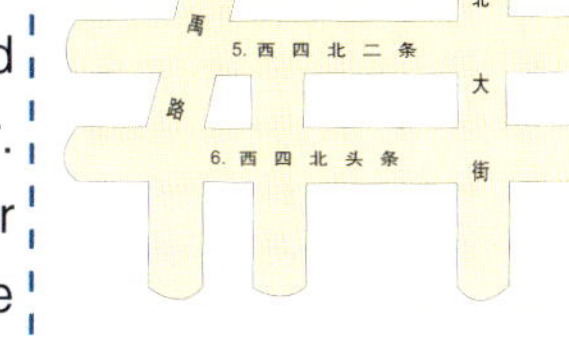

1. Xisi Beiqitiao (West Four Seventh North Lane)
2. Zhaodengyu Lu (Zhao Dengyu Road)
3. Xisi Beidajie (West Four North Street)
4. Xisi Beisantiao (West Four Third North Lane)
5. Xisi Bei'ertiao (West Four Second North Lane)
6. Xisi Beitoutiao (West Four First North Lane)

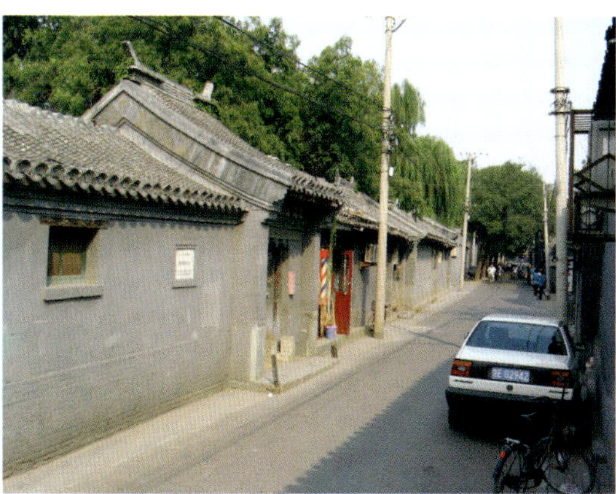

1. Xuanwumenwai Dajie (Gate of Proclaimed Military Strength Outer Street)
2. Xicaochang Jie (West Grazing Land Street)
3. Qiujia Jie (Qiu Family Street)
4. Tieyi Hutong (First Iron Lane)
5. Shanxi Jie (Shanxi Street)
6. Mianhua Xiaqitiao (Cotton Seventh Lower Lane)
7. Luomashi Dajie (Mule & Horse Market Street)

Xun Huisheng's Former Home

Located at 13A Shanxi Jie (Shanxi Street) outside Xuanwumen in Xuanwu District, this is a quadrangle house with a garden and is now public housing and is now public housing.

Xun Huisheng (1900-68), a native of Luoyang in Henan Province, was a famous

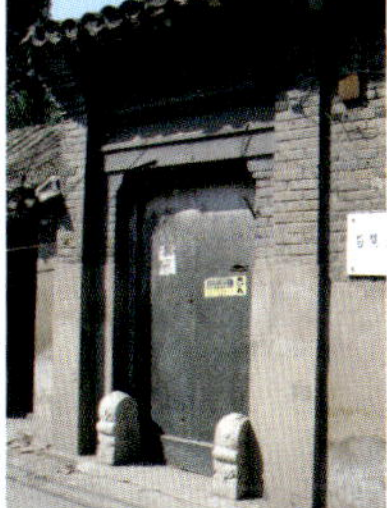

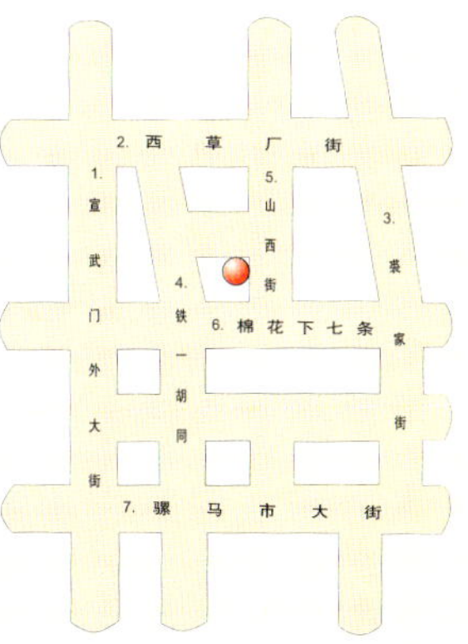

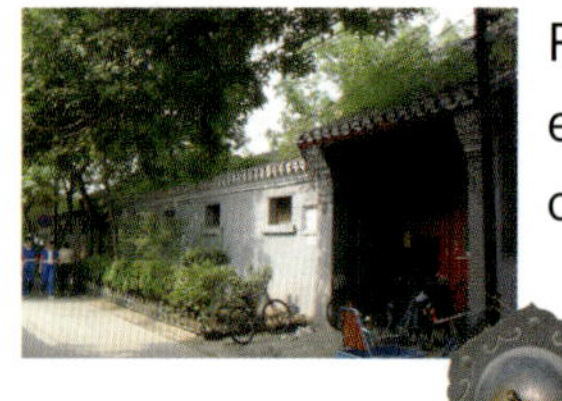

Peking opera actor. Regarded as the third greatest of the four great Peking opera performers of the female *dan* role, he shaped his own style and gave birth to the Xun School.

Tian Han's Former Home

Located at 9 Xiguan Hutong (Fine Tube Lane) in Dongsi Beidajie (East Four, North Street) in Dongcheng District, this has two courtyards and is now public housing on Beijing's list of protected sites. The Tian Han Foundation has an office there.

Tian Han (1898-1968), originally called Tian Shouchang, was a famous dramatist from Changsha in Hunan Province. He wrote the lyrics to the national anthem of the People's Republic of China and produced dramas such as *Chen Yuanyuan*, *Liren Xing* (*Beauties Stepping Out*) and *Princess Wencheng*. After the People's Republic of China was founded, he was appointed president of the China Federation of Literary and Art Circles.

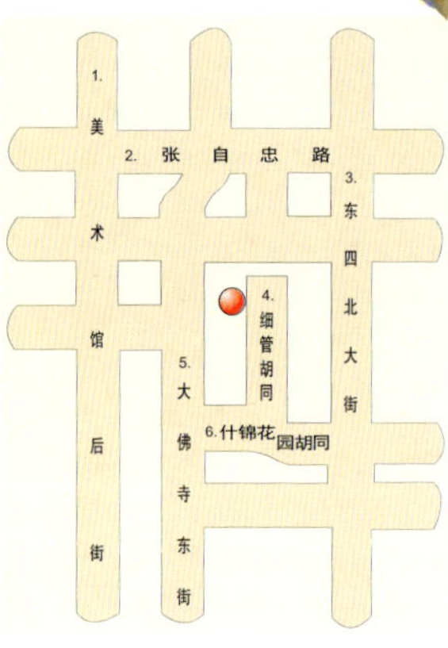

1. Meishuguan Houjie (Art Gallery Back Street)
2. Zhangzizhong Lu (Zhang Zizhong Road)
3. Dongsi Beidajie (East Four North Street)
4. Xiguan Hutong (Fine Tube Lane)
5. Dafosi Dongjie (Big Buddha Temple East Street)
6. Shijinhuayuan Hutong (Assorted Pattern Garden Lane)

1. Meishuguan Houjie (Art Gallery Back Street)
2. Zhangzizhong Lu (Zhang Zizhong Road)
3. Dongsi Beidajie (East Four North Street)
4. Shijinhuayuan Hutong (Assorted Pattern Garden Lane)
5. Yuqun Hutong (Group Raising Lane)

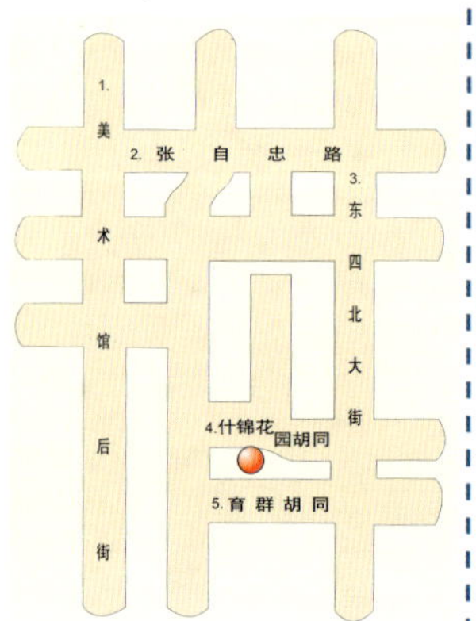

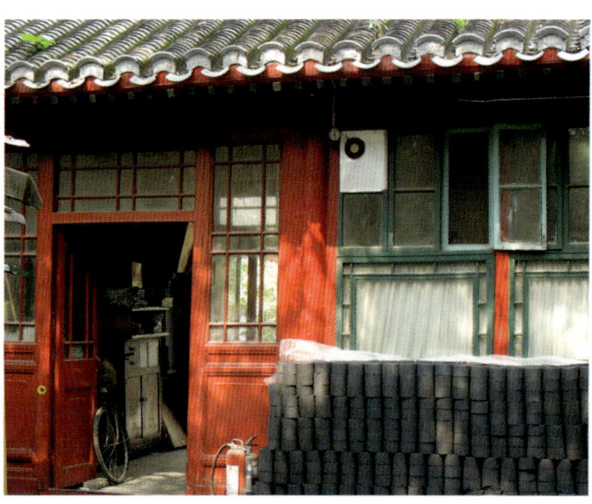

Wu Peifu's Former Home

Located at 19 Shijinhuayuan Hutong (Assorted Pattern Garden Lane) in Dongcheng

District, this example of late Qing Dynasty architecture is now occupied by a workplace.

Wu Peifu (1874-1939), a native of Penglai in Shandong Province, was an influential warlord during the Northern Warlords period of 1912 to 1927.

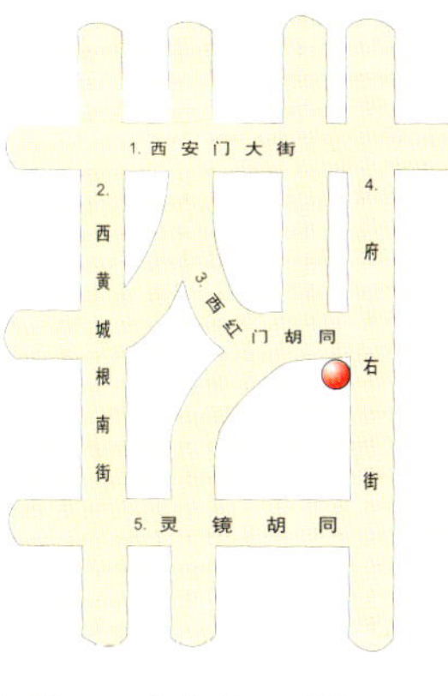

Zhang Zizhong's Former Home

Located in Fuyou Jie (Right Mansion Street) in Xicheng District, this building is now the Beijing Zizhong Primary School.

Zhang Zizhong (1891-1940), a native of Linqing in Shandong Province, was a famous patriotic general who fought the Japanese invaders during World War II. In 1947, Tieshizi Hutong (Iron Lion Lane) in Dongcheng District was renamed Zhangzizhong Lu (Zhang Zizhong Road) to commemorate General Zhang Zizhong.

1. Xi'anmen Dajie (Gate of Western Peace Street)
2. Xihuangchenggen Nanjie (West Imperial City Corner Wall South Street)
3. Xihongmen Hutong (West Red Gate Lane)
4. Fuyou Jie (Right Mansion Street)
5. Lingjing Hutong (Soul Mirror Lane)

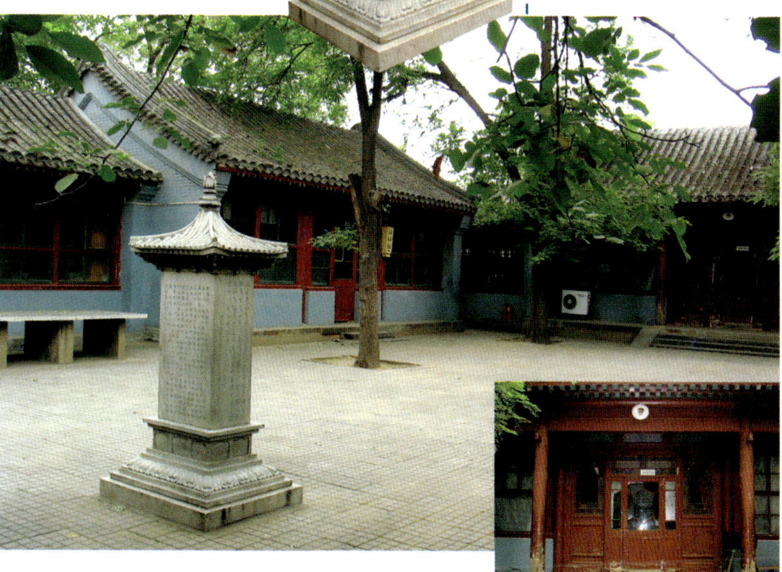

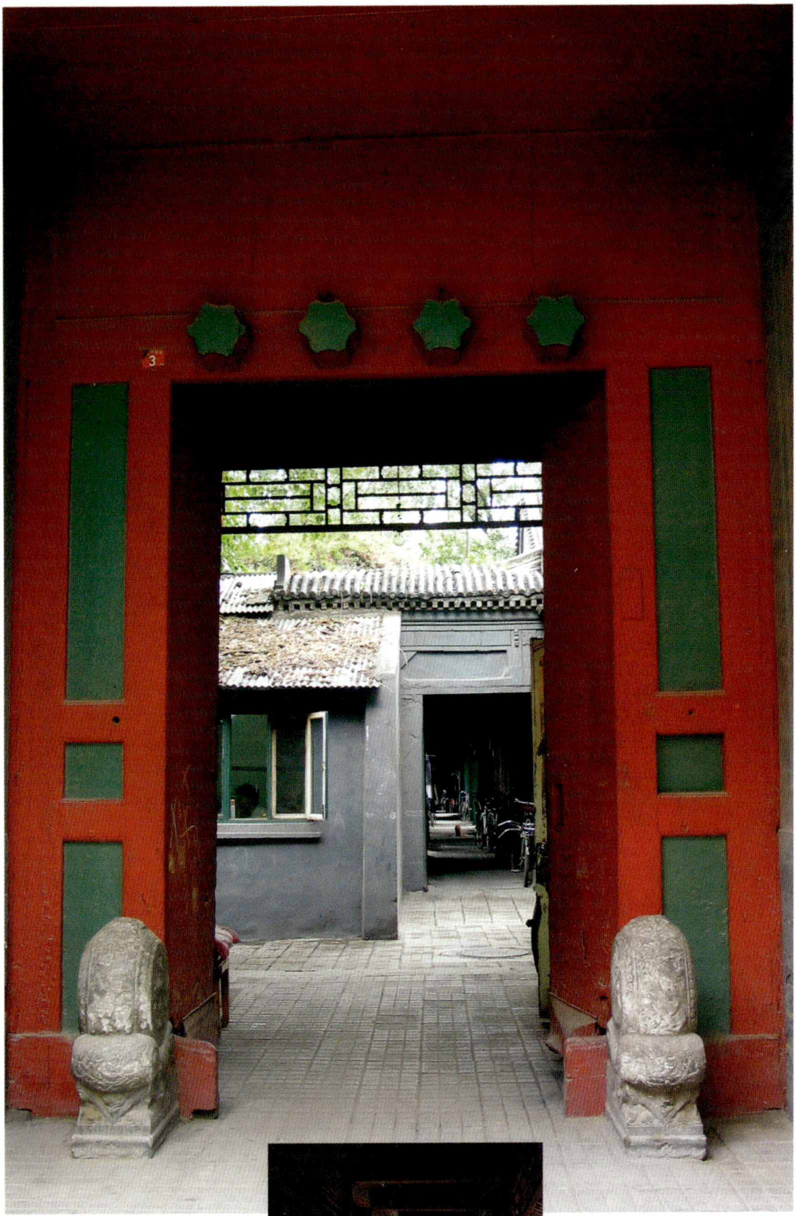

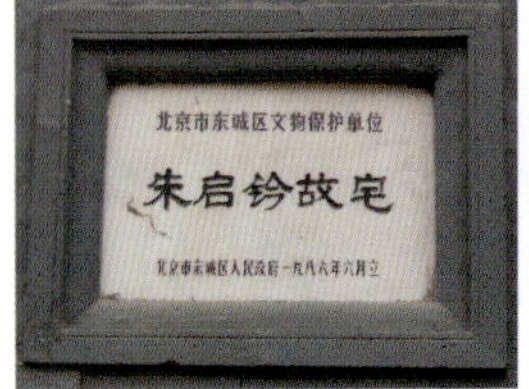

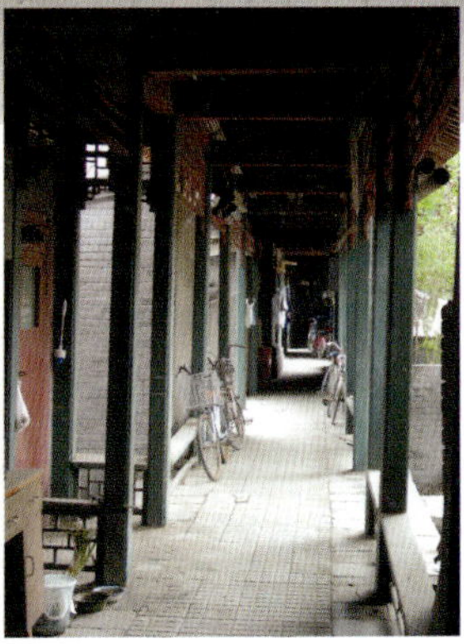

The building at 3 Zhaotangzi Hutong (Zhao's Hall Lane) has been kept in good condition. The picture above shows the gate, while the right-hand picture below shows the 50-meter-long corridor.

Zhu Qiqian's Former Home

Located at 3 Zhaotangzi Hutong (Zhao's Hall Lane) in Dongcheng District, this is a cultural relic under Dongcheng District's protection and is used for public housing now.

Zhu Qiqian (1871-1964) was from Kaiyang in Guizhou Province. Early in the Republic of China period, he was the cabinet minister responsible for transport, the cabinet minister in charge of internal affairs, and acting premier. His most significant contribution was the construction work done in Beijing in the early 20th century. After the People's Republic of China was founded, he was appointed to the Second and Third National Committees of the Chinese People's Political Consultative Conference.

Former Home of Zhang Shizhao and Qiao Guanhua

Located at 51 Shijia Hutong (Shi Family Lane) in Dongcheng District, this quadrangle house has three courtyards and is now public housing protected by Beijing Municipality.

The renowned scholar Zhang Shizhao (1881-1973) was from Changsha in Hunan Province. Early during the Republic of China period, he was president of Peking University

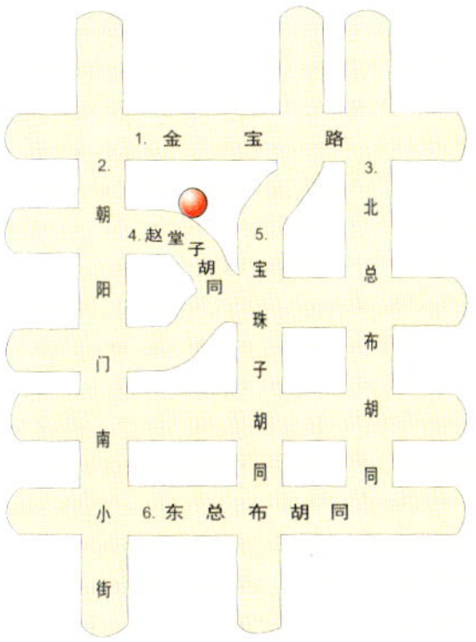

1. Jinbao Lu (Gold Valuables Road)
2. Chaoyangmen Nanxiaojie (Chaoyang Gate South Small Street)
3. Beizongbu Hutong (North Zongbu Lane)
4. Zhaotangzi Hutong (Zhao's Hall Lane)
5. Baozhuzi Hutong (Precious Pearl Lane)
6. Dongzongbu Hutong (East Zongbu Lane)

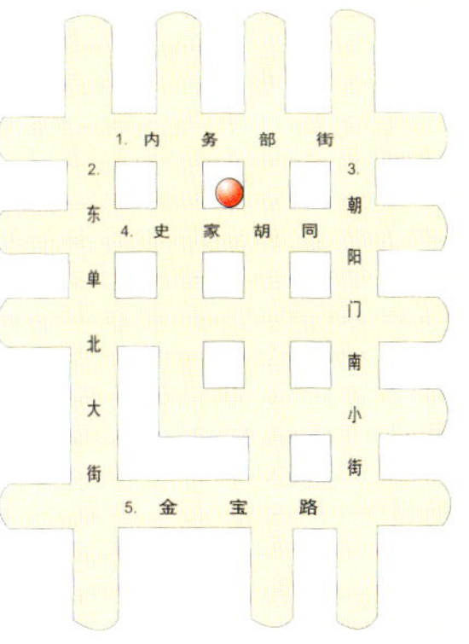

1. Neiwubu Jie (Ministry of Internal Affairs Street)
2. Dongdan Beidajie (East Single North Street)
3. Chaoyangmen Nanxiaojie (Chaoyang Gate South Small Street)
4. Shijia Hutong (Shi Family Lane)
5. Jinbao Lu (Gold Valuables Road)

There are many protected quadrangle houses along Shijia Hutong (Shi Family Lane).

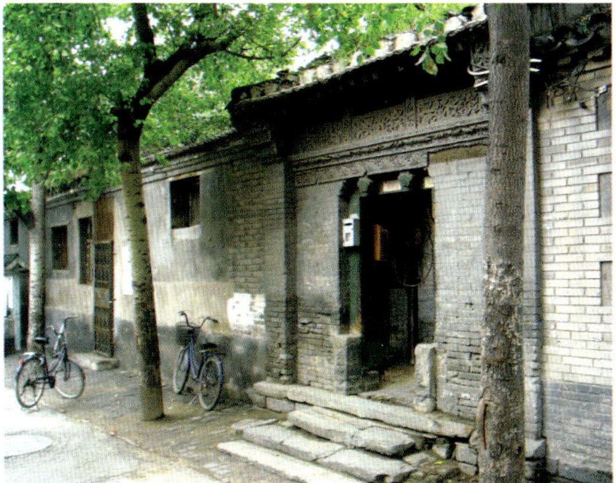

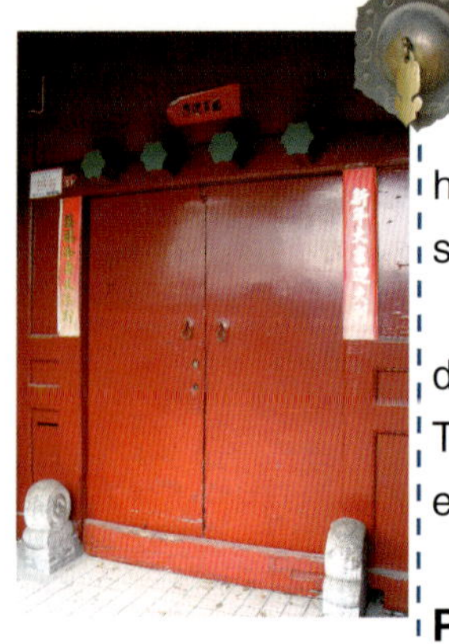

and China's attorney general. After the People's Republic of China was founded, he was appointed director of the Central Research Institute of Culture and History.

Qiao Guanhua (1913-83) was a well-known diplomat from Yancheng in Jiangsu Province. The son-in-law of Zhang Shizhao, he was foreign minister in the People's Republic of China.

President Yuan Shikai's Office

This is located at 3 Zhangzishong Lu (Zhang Zizhong Road) (originally Tieshizi Hutong or Iron Lion Lane) in Dongcheng District. It was the premier's office during the Beiyang government in 1919 and was the site of the Duan Qirui government. It has been included on Beijing's list of cultural sites under the title "The former location of the Duan Qirui government." A workplace now occupies Yuan Shikai's office.

Yuan Shikai (1859-1916) was from Xiangcheng County in Henan Province. He was a military commander, governor of Zhili (today's Hebei) Province and minister of Beiyang (today's Hebei, Liaoning and Shandong provinces) during the late Qing Dynasty and the first president of the Republic of China.

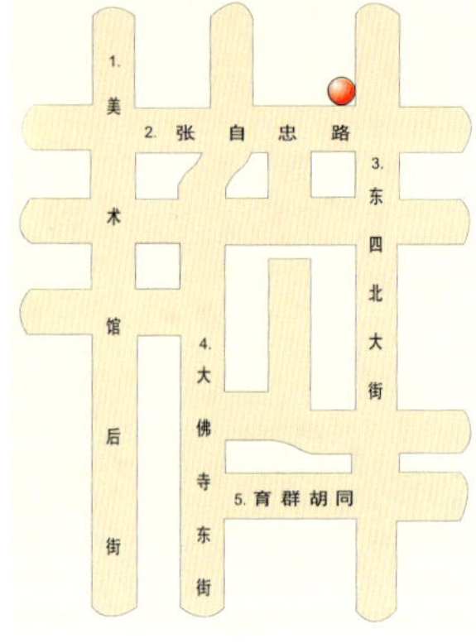

1. Meishuguan Houjie (Art Gallery Back Street)
2. Zhangzizhong Lu (Zhang Zizhong Road)
3. Dongsi Beidajie (East Four North Street)
4. Dafosi Dongjie (Big Buddha Temple East Street)
5. Yuqun Hutong (Group Raising Lane)

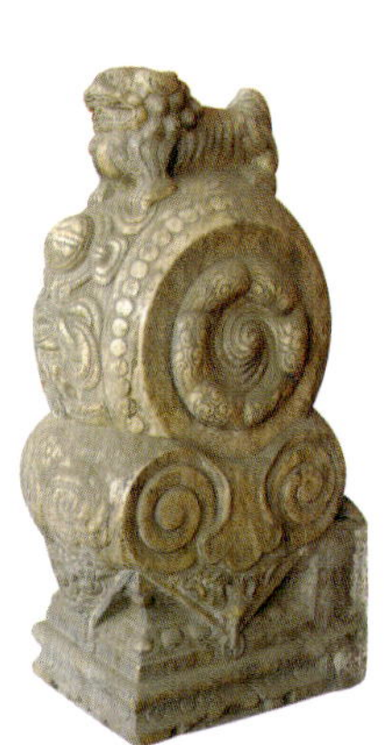

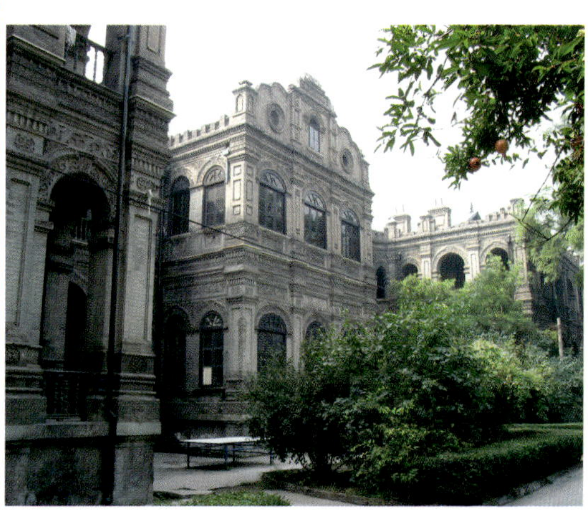

Yuan Chonghuan Memorial Temple

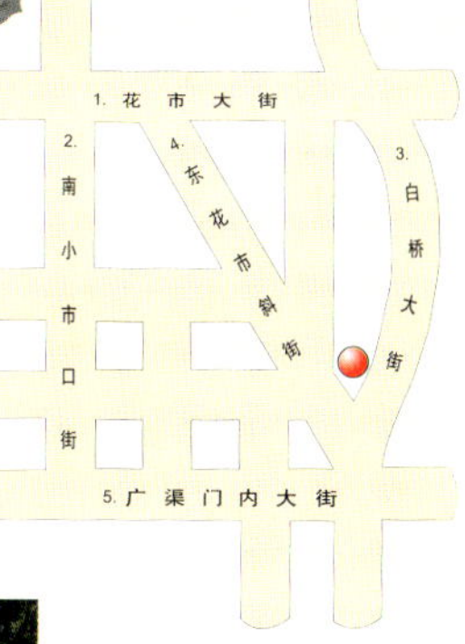

Located at Donghuashi Xie Jie (East Flower Market Oblique Street) inside Guangqumen (Wide Channel Gate) in Chongwen District, this is on Beijing's list of protected sites. It is now used as public housing.

Yuan Chonghuan (1584-1630), from Dongwan in Guangdong Province, was a well-known patriotic commander during the Ming Dynasty.

1. Huashi Dajie (Flower Market Street)
2. Nanxiaoshikou Jie (South Small Market Entrance Street)
3. Baiqiao Dajie (White Bridge Street)

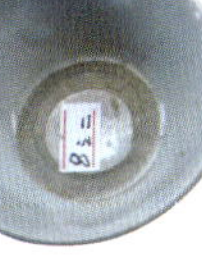
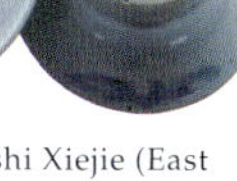

4. Donghuashi Xiejie (East Flower Market Oblique Street)
5. Guangqumennei Dajie (Wide Channel Gate Inner Street)

Liang Qichao's Former Home

Located at 23 Beigouyan Hutong (North Ditch Edge Lane), this residence has three courtyards facing east and is now used for public housing.

Liang Qichao (1873-1929), a native of Xinhui in Guangdong Province, was a famous politician, social campaigner, scholar and one of the main representatives of the 1898 Reform Movement.

1. Dongzhimennei Dajie (Straight East Gate Inner Street)
2. Xintaipingcang Hutong (New Peaceful Storehouse Lane)
3. Dongzhimen Nanxiaojie (Straight East Gate South Small Street)
4. Xiaoju Hutong (Small Chrysanthemum Lane)
5. Dongsi Shisitiao (East Four Fourteenth Lane)
6. Daju Hutong (Big Chrysanthemum Lane)

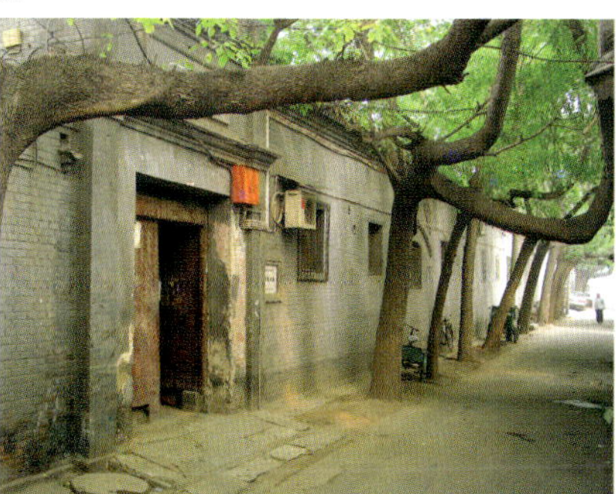

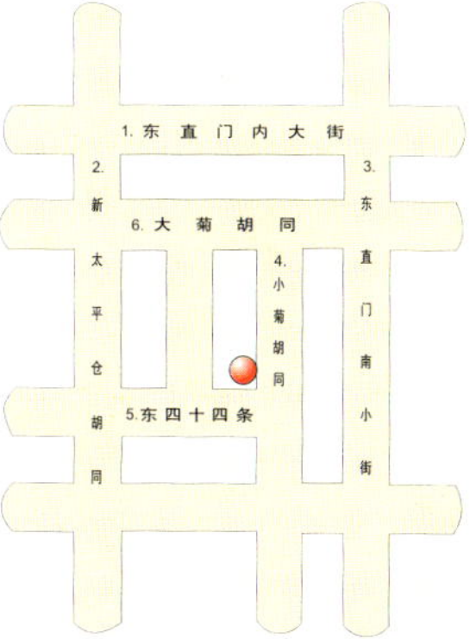

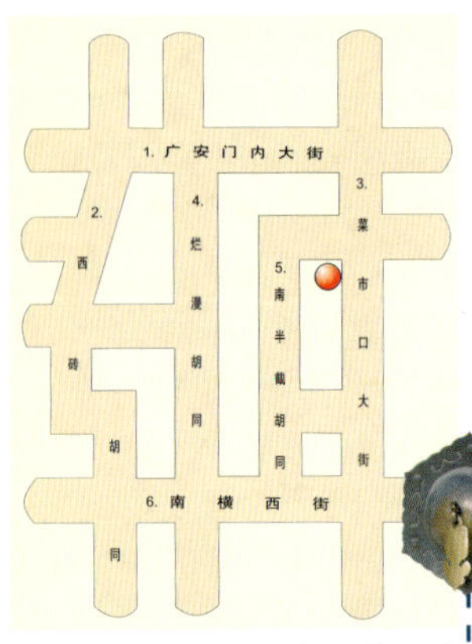

1. Guang'anmennei Dajie (Gate of Universal Peace Inner Street)
2. Xizhuan Hutong (West Brick Lane)
3. Caishikou Dajie (Vegetable Market Entrance Street)
4. Lanman Hutong or Lanmian Hutong (Mushy Noodle Lane)
5. Nanbanjie Hutong (South Half Lane)
6. Nanheng Xijie (South Horizontal West Street)

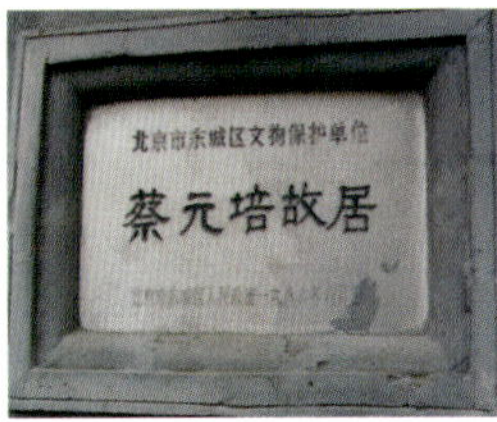

1. Nanxiawazi Hutong (South Depression Lane)
2. Houyuan'ensi Hutong (Round-Kindness Temple Back Lane)
3. Nanluogu Xiang (South Gong and Drum Alley)
4. Dongmianhua Hutong (East Cotton Lane)
5. Jiaodaokou Nandajie (Cross-Lane Entrance South Street)
6. Maor Hutong (Hat Lane)

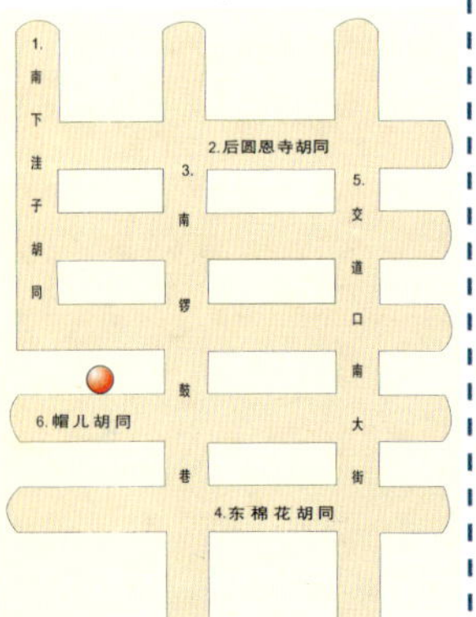

Tan Sitong's Former Home

Located at 41 Beibanjie Hutong (North Half Lane) in Xuanwu District, this is a cultural relic under Xuanwu District's protection. Today, it is used for public housing.

Tan Sitong (1865-98), from Liuyang in Hunan Province, was one of the main representatives of the 1898 Reform Movement and one of the movement's Six Men of Honor.

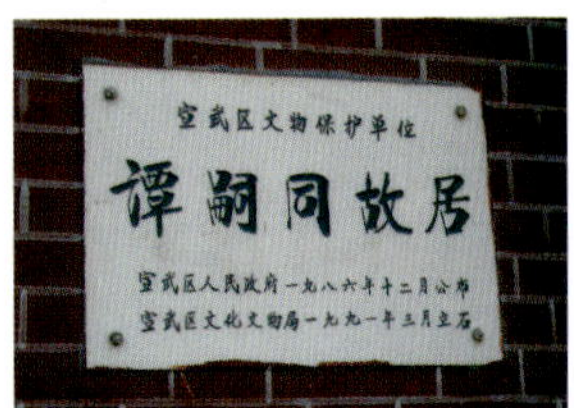

Cai Yuanpei's Former Home

Located at 75 Dongtangzi Hutong (Eastern Hall Lane) in Dongcheng District, this is a cultural relic under Dongcheng District's protection. This home continued to be used as public housing but the residents have been moved.

Cai Yuanpei (1868-1940), from Shaoxing in Zhejiang Province, was a celebrated educationist. During the May 4th Movement, he was president of Peking University.

Former Home of Empress Wanrong (wife of China's last emperor)

Located at 37 Maor Hutong (Hat Lane) in Dongcheng District, this residence has several

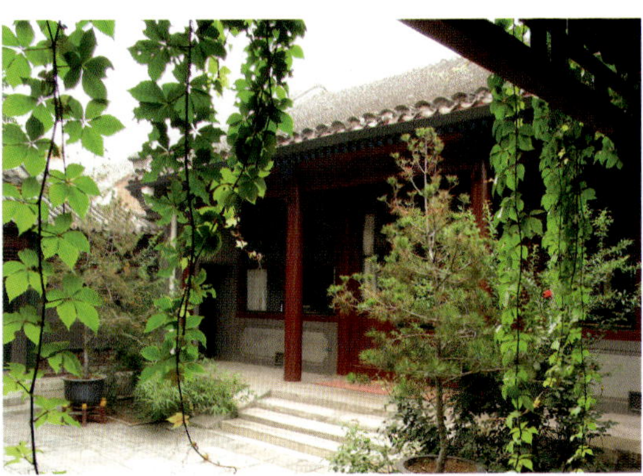

orderly courtyards and was the home of Empress Wanrong from 1906 to 1922. A workplace now occupies this home.

The Manchu Empress Wanrong (1906-46) married Pu Yi, China's last emperor, when she was 16, becoming the last empress.

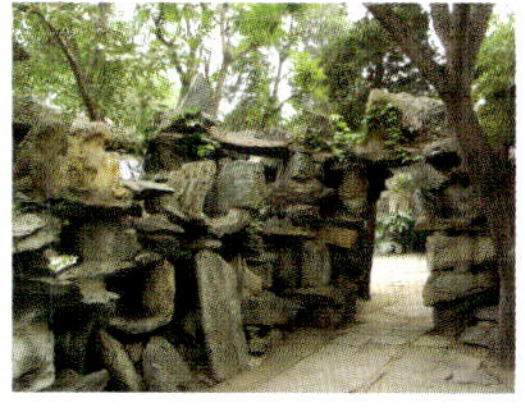

The rockery in Empress Wanrong's former home

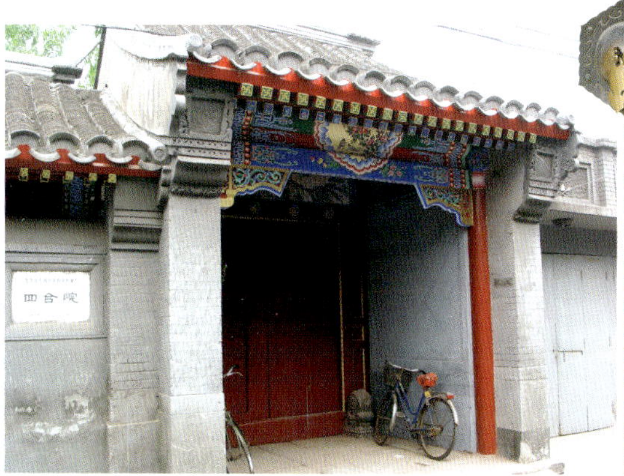

Feng Guozhang's former home at 11 Maor Hutong (Hat Lane)

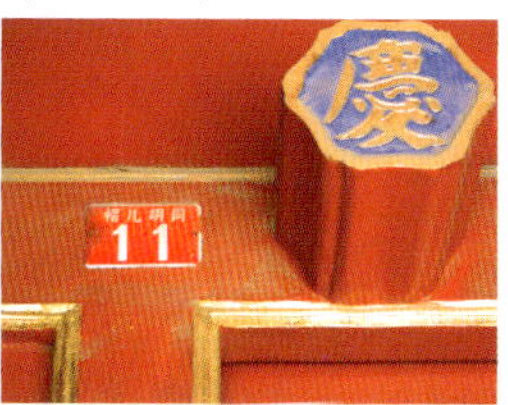

Many historical figures have lived in Maor Hutong (Hat Lane), at the entrance to which is a copper sign giving an introduction to the lane.

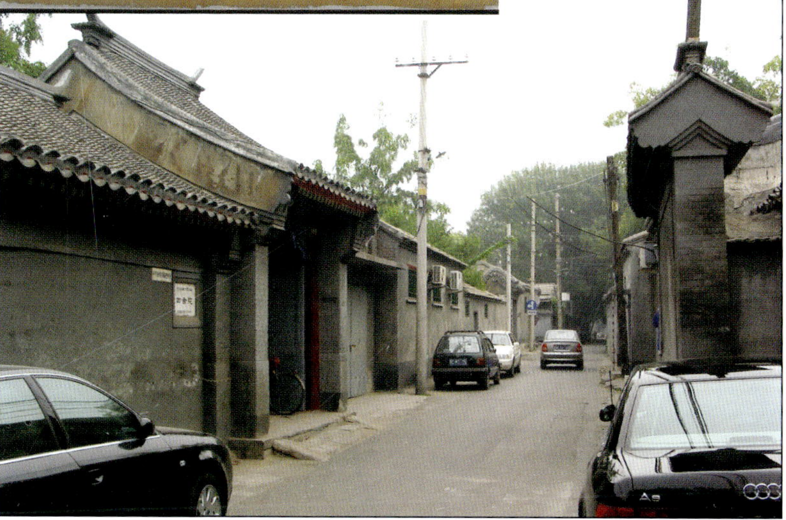

Reginald Johnston's Former Home

Located at 1 Youqizuo Hutong (Paint Workshop Lane) in the Di'anmen (Gate of Earthly Peace) area of Xicheng District, this residence has several courtyards and was the home of Reginald Johnston (whose Chinese name was Zhuang Shidun) from 1919 to 1931. Today, it is used for public housing.

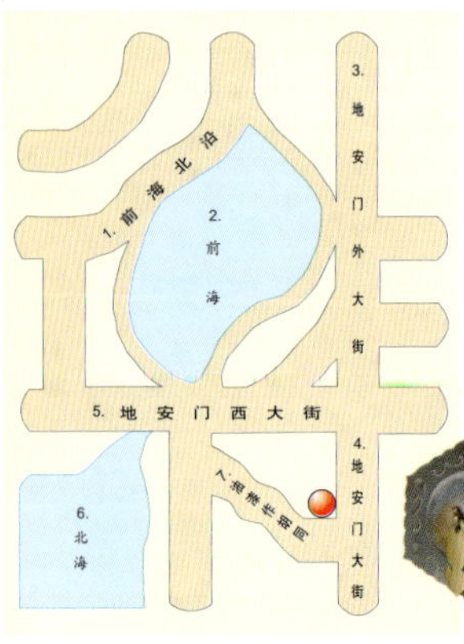

1. Qianhai Beiyan (the north bank of Front Lake)
2. Qianhai (Front Lake)
3. Di'anmenwai Dajie (Gate of Earthly Peace Outer Street)
4. Di'anmen Dajie (Gate of Earthly Peace Street)
5. Di'anmen Xidajie (Gate of Earthly Peace West Street)
6. Beihai (North Lake)
7. Youqizuo Hutong (Paint Workshop Lane)

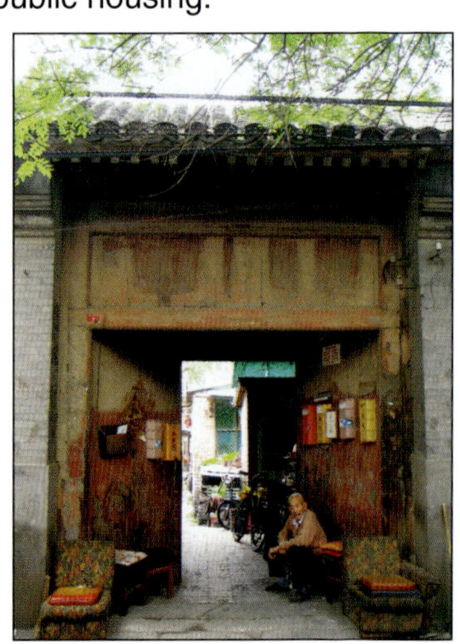

Reginald Johnston (1874-1938), a Scotsman, was the loyal English teacher of Emperor Pu Yi, China's last emperor, upon whom he had a significant influence.

Yu Qian Memorial Temple

Located at 23 Xibiaobei Hutong (West Mount Lane) in Dongcheng District, facing south, this quadrangle is used for public housing now.

Yu Qian (1398-1457), from Qiantang (now Hangzhou) in Zhejiang Province, was a celebrated politician and military strategist during the Ming Dynasty. He wrote the famous poem *Shihui Yin* (*Ode to Lime*).

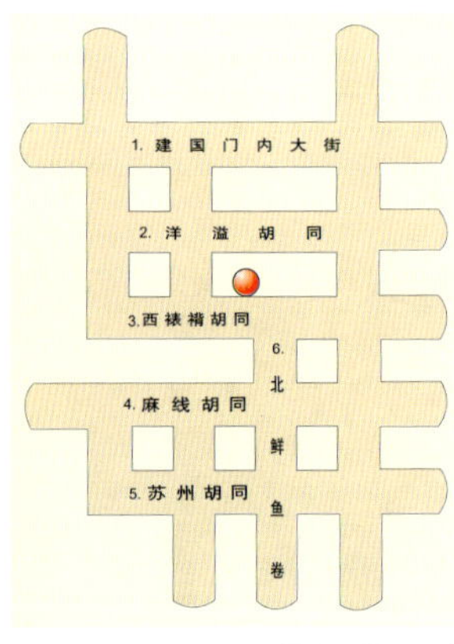

1. Jianguomennei Dajie (Gate of Constructing the Nation Inner Street)
2. Yangyi Hutong, or Yangrou Hutong (Mutton Lane)
3. Xibiaobei Hutong (West Mount Lane)
4. Maxian Hutong (Twine Lane)
5. Suzhou Hutong (Suzhou Lane)
6. Beixianyu Xiang (North Fresh Fish Alley)

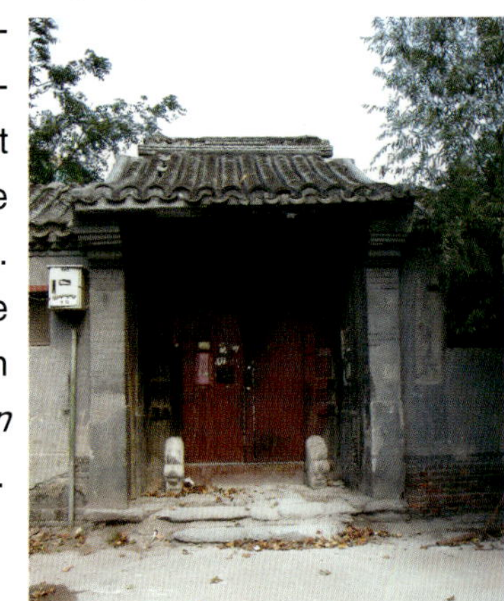

Mao Zedong's Former Home

Located at 15 Doufuchi Hutong (Bean Curd Pond Lane) behind the Drum Tower (Gulou) in Dongcheng District, this has two courtyards and is now used for public housing.

In 1918 and 1919, Mao Zedong lived at 8 Ji'ansuo Zuoxiang (Lucky Peaceful Place Left Lane), Sanyanjing (Three Wells), Jingshan Dongjie (East Coal Hill Street).

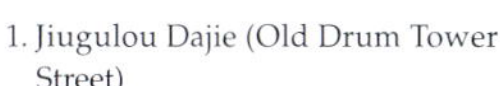

1. Jiugulou Dajie (Old Drum Tower Street)
2. Doufuchi Hutong (Bean Curd Pond Lane)
3. Caochang Beixiang (Grazing Land North Alley)
4. Bell Tower
5. Drum Tower
6. Gulou Dongdajie (East Drum Tower Street)

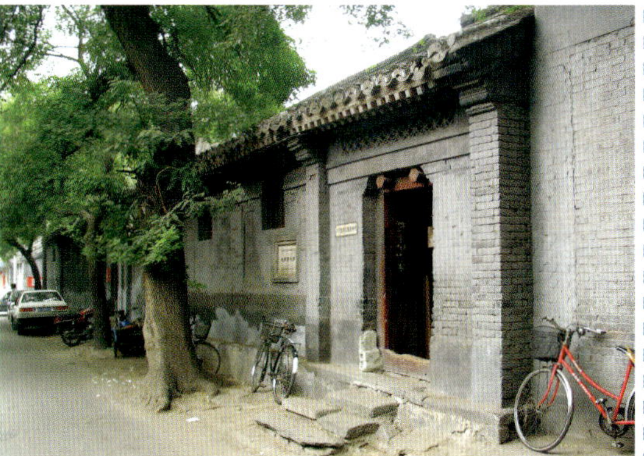

15 Doufuchi Hutong (Bean Curd Pond Lane)

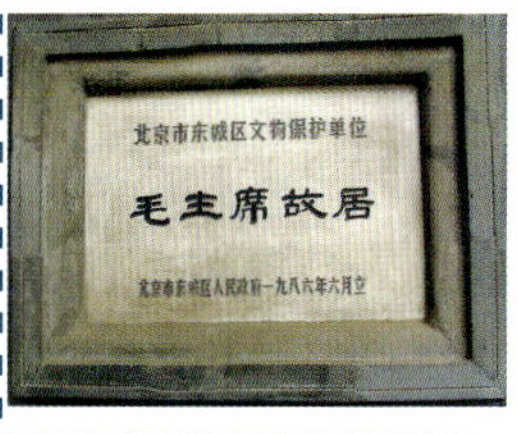

Mao Zedong (1893-1976), was from Shaoshan in Xiangtan, Hunan Province. Founder of the People's Republic of China, he was a great politician,

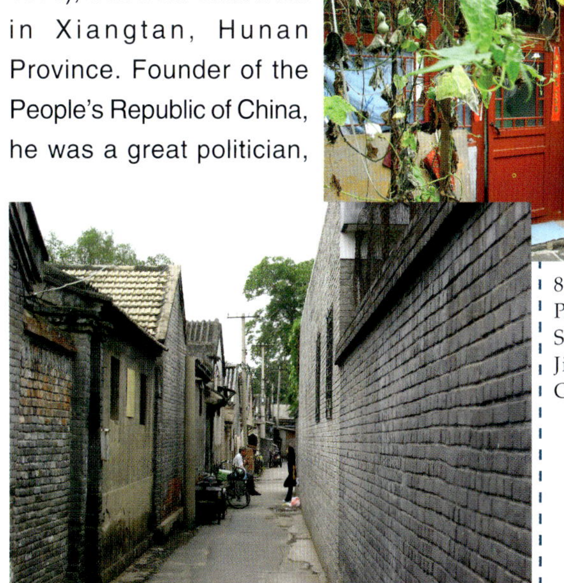

8 Ji'ansuo Zuoxiang (Lucky Peaceful Place Left Lane) in Sanyanjing (Three Wells), Jingshan Dongjie (East Coal Hill Street)

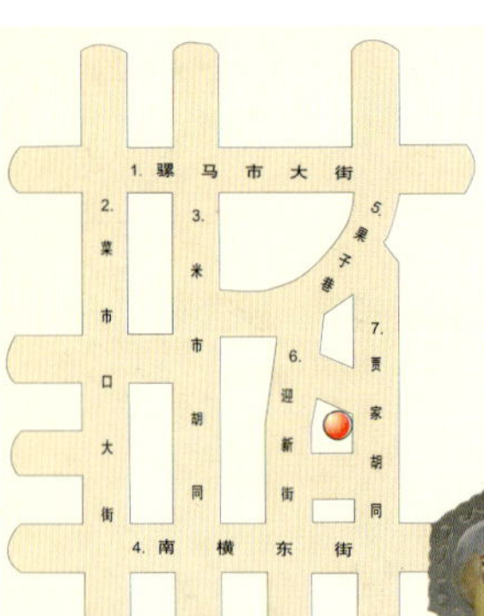

1. Luomashi Dajie (Mule & Horse Market Street)
2. Caishikou Dajie (Vegetable Market Entrance Street)
3. Mishi Hutong (Rice Market Lane)
4. Nanheng Dongjie (South Horizontal East Street)
5. Guozi Xiang (Fruit Alley)
6. Yingxin Jie (Welcoming New Arrivals Street)
7. Jiajia Hutong (Jia Family Lane)

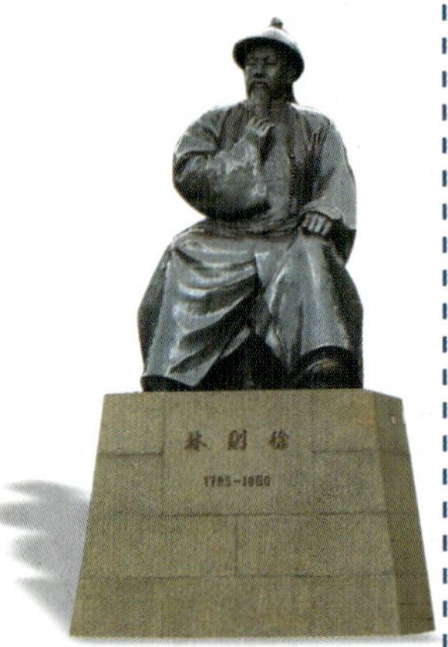
A statue of Lin Zexu

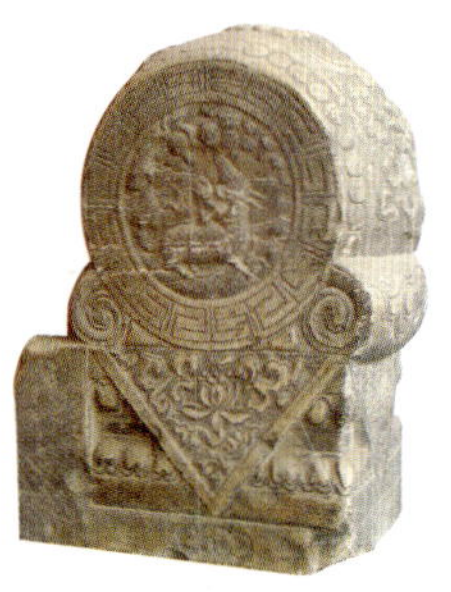

philosopher, strategist and poet.

Lin Zexu's Former Home

Located at 31 Jiajia Hutong (Jia Family Lane) in Xuanwu District, this is used for public housing now.

Lin Zexu (1785-1850), from Fuzhou in Fujian Province, was a celebrated patriot during the Qing Dynasty and was the leader of an anti-drug campaign. He launched the burning of opium at Humen, which was regarded as the jumping-off point of the Chinese people's anti-imperialist campaign and which sparked off the first well-known Opium War of 1840 to 1842.

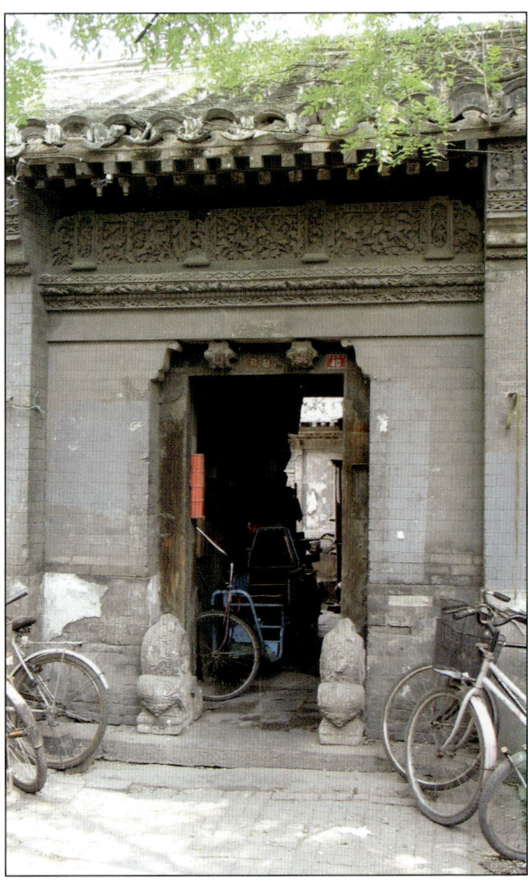

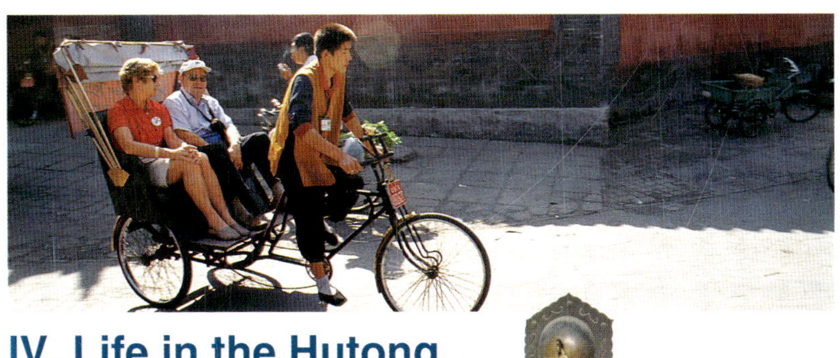

IV. Life in the Hutong

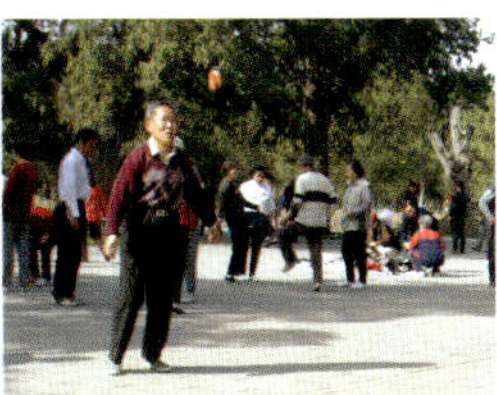

The dates of Chinese festivals are in accordance with the traditional Chinese calendar, which is the lunar calendar rather than the solar-based Gregorian calendar. There is a big or small festival in almost every month but the most celebrated ones are the Spring Festival on the first day of the first lunar month, the Dragon Boat Festival on the fifth day of the fifth lunar month, and the Mid-Autumn Festival on the 15th day of the eighth lunar month. The charm and inter-

Every morning, big parks and gardens by the streets of Beijing are crowded with people doing their morning exercises. Some jog, some walk with caged birds and others practice Taijiquan or sword. More and more people do morning exercises nowadays.

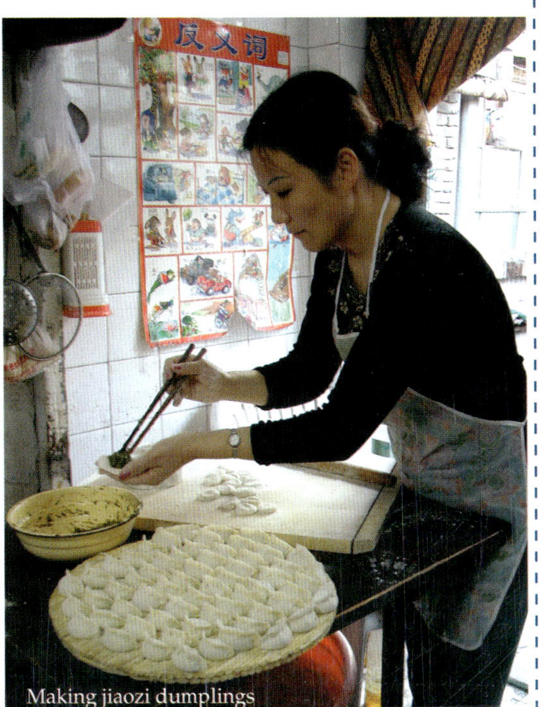

Making jiaozi dumplings

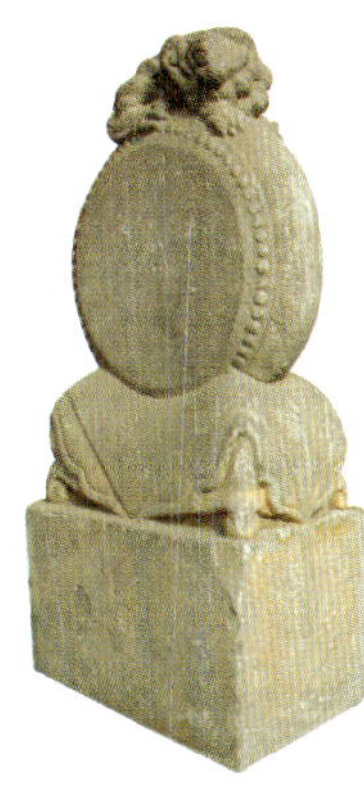

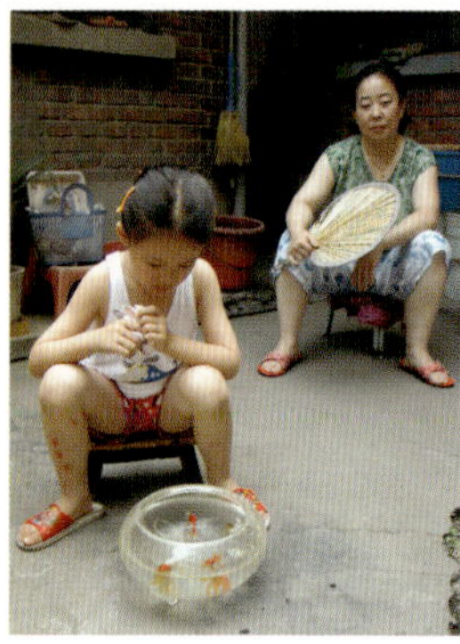
Feeding goldfish

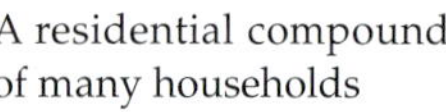
A residential compound
of many households

Making *zongzi*
(pyramid-shaped
glutinous rice
dumplings wrapped
in bamboo or reed
leaves)

esting life of the *hutong* can best be seen in the traditional celebrations of these festivals.

Laba Porridge and Laba Garlic

The twelfth month of the lunar year is called Layue. *Laba* literally refers to the eighth day of the 12th lunar month and it indicates that Spring Festival is approaching. On that day, the most important activity for every family is making laba porridge. This is made with a variety of ingredients, including different kinds of rice, dried fruit, and pulses such as kidney beans and peas. When people eat the porridge, they like to add some extra flavoring, such as sugar, rose petals, and sweet-scented osmanthus. Some people with particular tastes prefer to boil some less commonly eaten grains such as the seed of Job's tears, glutinous rice, water chestnuts, Gorgon fruit, and lotus seeds. In the boiled porridge, they also

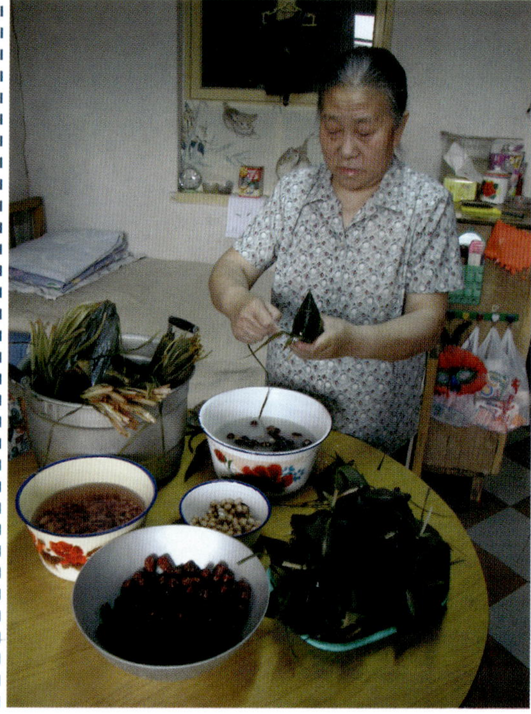

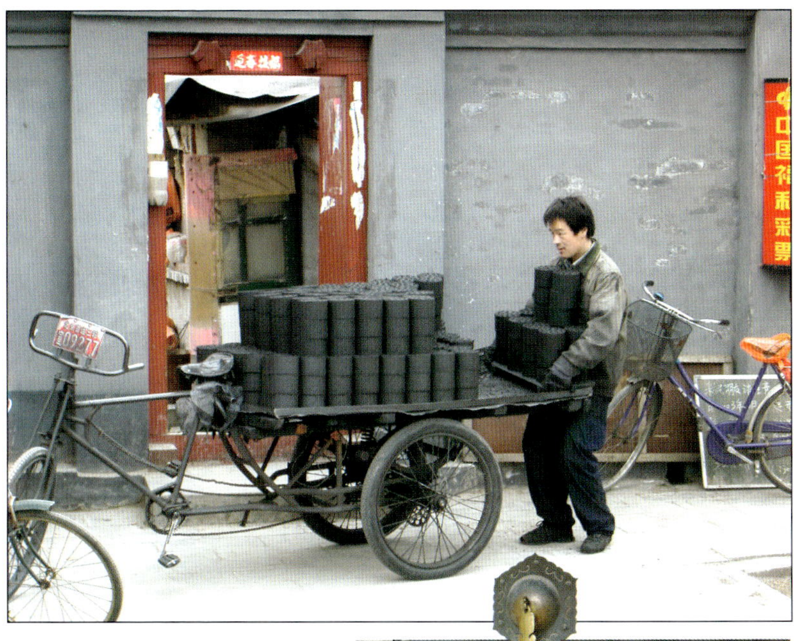

put some preserved fruit such as dried litchi and longan pulp, and shredded green and red plums, arranged in beautiful designs, to please both the eye and the taste buds.

In addition to *laba* porridge, Beijingers like to pickle *laba* garlic on *laba* day. They peel some cloves of garlic, put them in an earthenware jar, top it up with vinegar, seal it and keep it in a warm place until lunar New Year's Eve. The pickled garlic looks as green as jade and has a sour taste. It is eaten with *jiaozi* dumplings.

Coal stoves are widely used in Beijing's lanes for cooking and heating. A man delivers coal briquets in the top picture, and women make their own coal balls in the lower picture.

Spring Cleaning and Offering Sacrifices to the Kitchen God

Spring cleaning and offering sacrifices to the Kitchen God are the two main tasks of *hutong* residents before Spring Festival. To celebrate the Chinese new year in clean surroundings, people choose an appropriate day from the 15th

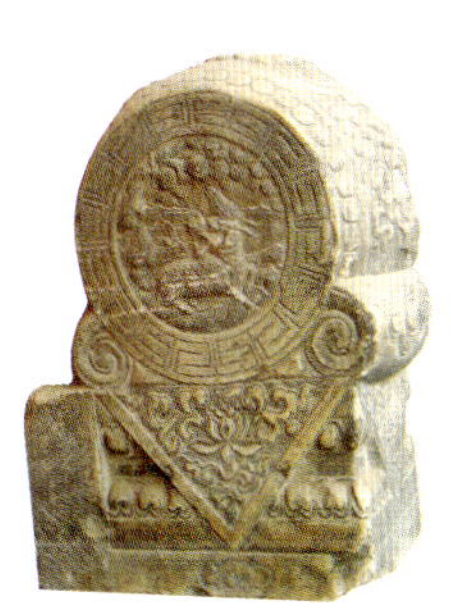

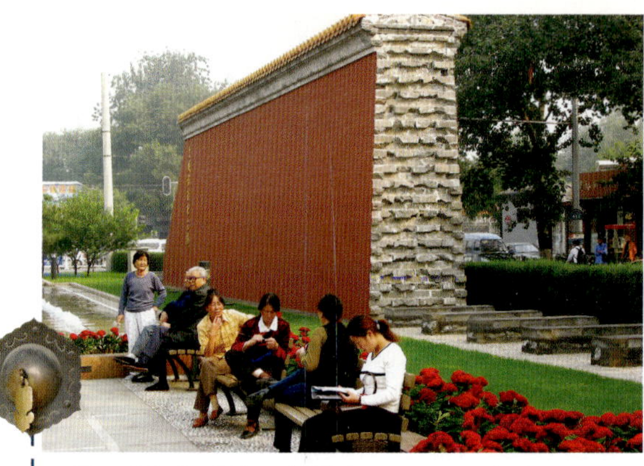

to the 23rd of the 12th lunar month to sweep the dirt from the walls and ceilings, clean the furniture and replace the old New Year pictures on the wall and paper cuts on the window with new ones. The custom of offering sacrifices to the kitchen god has its origins in the fire worship of ancient Chinese. More than 2,000 years ago, the Kitchen God (a god sent from heaven to each family to take charge of that family's kitchen affairs and control its fortune) became the god to whom Chinese people worshiped and made sacrifices. Every family had a shrine built on its brick kitchen range to the Kitchen God. It is said that, on the 23rd or 24th day of the last lunar month, each family's Kitchen God returns to heaven to

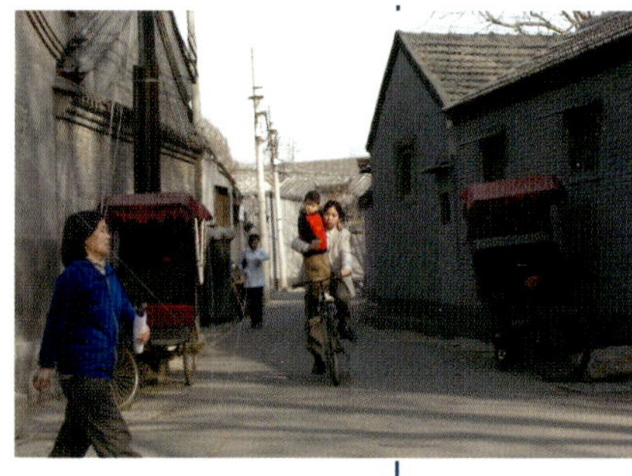

A rather dangerous way to ride a bicycle

A cobbler at work

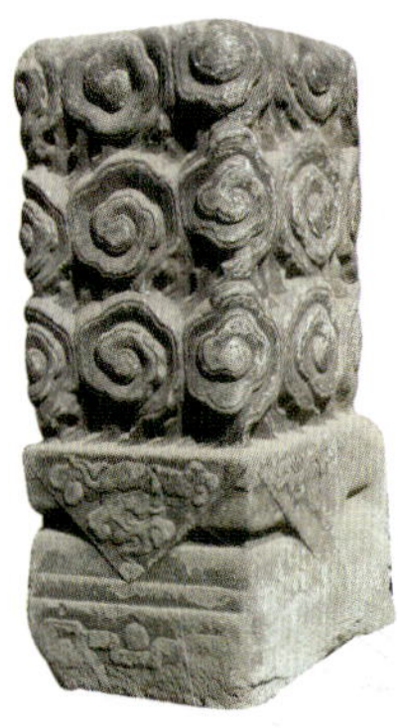

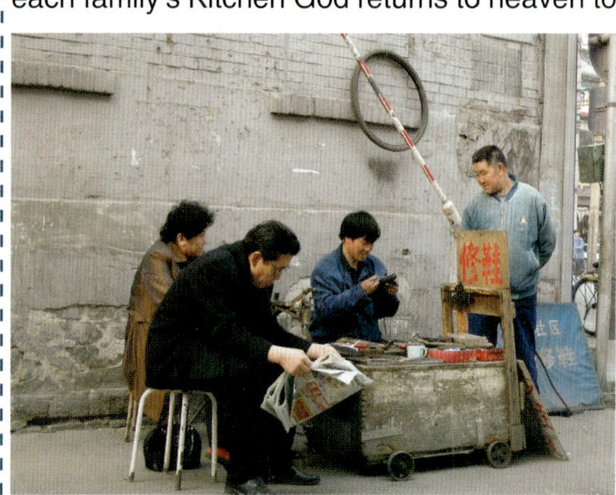

give the Jade Emperor (the ruler of heaven in Chinese mythology) a report on that family's activities during the previous year. On that day, people burn images of the Kitchen God to send him off to heaven and they put up new images. They also smear the god's mouth with maltose sugar so that he cannot speak ill of their family in front of the Jade Emperor.

Lunar New Year's Eve

Lunar New Year's Eve, the last day of the 12th month of the Chinese lunar year, is when *hutong* residents are busiest and happiest. They first put up Spring Festival scrolls and pictures of door gods in the hope of enjoying happiness and longevity, driving out evil spirits and getting rid of disease. They put out a variety of food as offerings, light candles, and make sacrifices to their ancestors and the gods. It was said that gods would descend to the world between the evening of New Year's Eve and early on New Year's Day, during which time people would burn joss sticks and pray for blessings on bended knee. According to custom, all the members of the family gather on New Year's Eve to enjoy a family reunion dinner, which is the most sumptuous of the year. The dinner includes fish, meat, chicken and various vegetables. *Jiaozi*

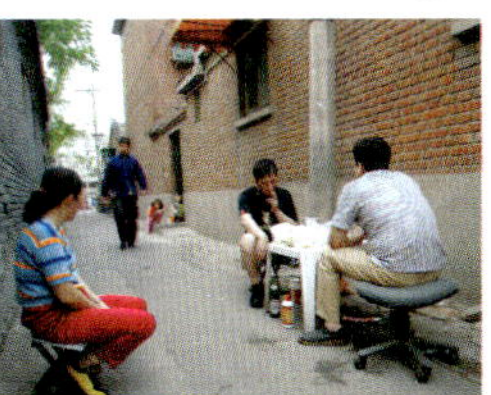

A man doing grinding work

Meeting friends in the hutong

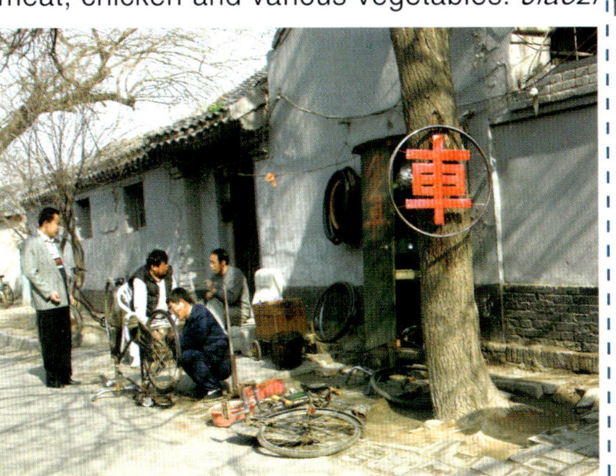

There are bicycle repairers everywhere.

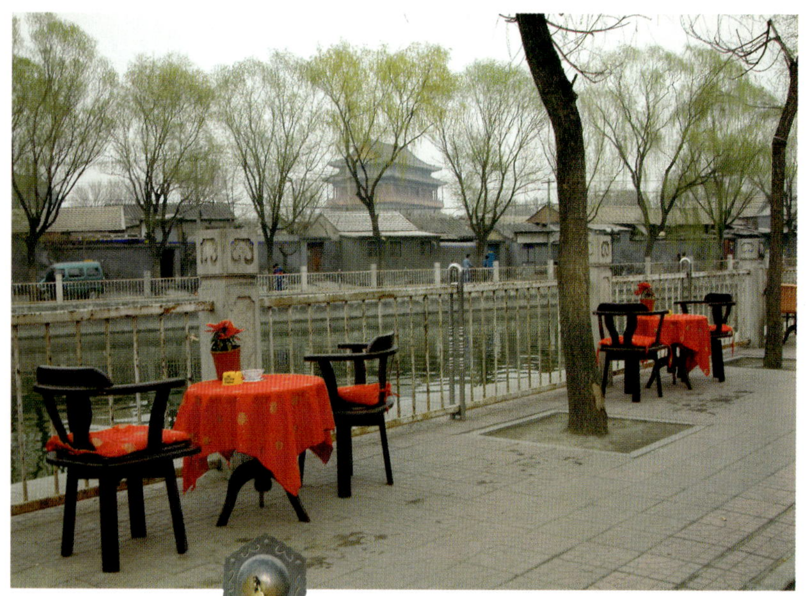

An open-air teahouse in the Houhai area

dumplings are a key New Year food. Families gather together and say auspicious words so that they will have good luck and a harmonious and happy family life. It is customary for people to stay up all night on New Year's Eve, a custom known as *shousui*, which means "cherishing time." Young people stay up all night or *shousui* in order to increase the lifespan of their parents. Adults play cards and mahjong, while children play with lanterns and let off firecrackers. At midnight, *jiaozi* dumplings are eaten again to welcome the god's returning descent. This marks the end of the New Year's Eve celebration.

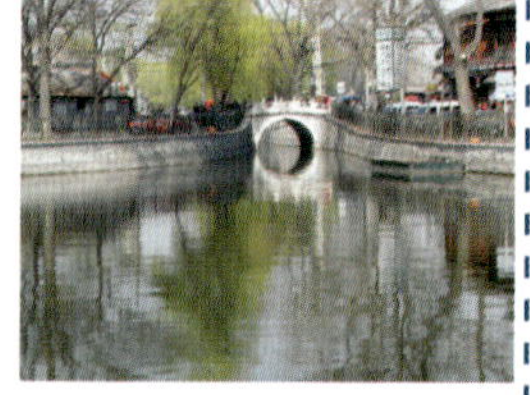

Yinding Qiao (Silver Ingot Bridge) in the Houhai area

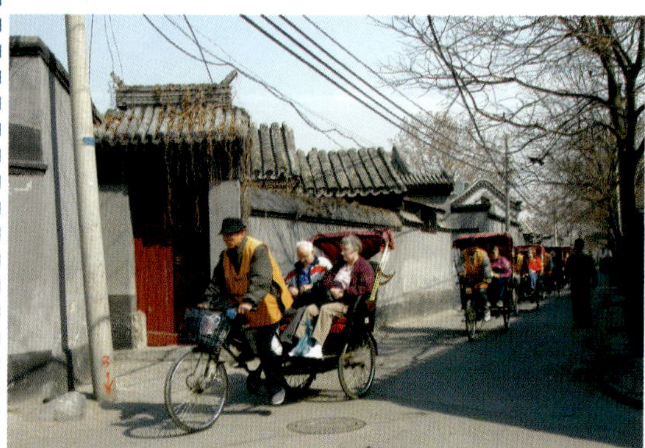

A tricycle tour of Beijing's *hutong*

Lantern Festival

The Lantern Festival takes place on the 15th day of the first lunar month. This is when every family eats *yuanxiao*, round dumplings made with glutinous-rice flour. Raisins, nuts, melon seeds, sugar, and so on are made into small balls for the dumpling fillings and these are then shaken in glutinous-rice flour until the fillings are securely wrapped up. The round dumpling shape symbolizes togetherness, happiness and harmony. In addition to having *yuanxiao*, another major activity is hanging up lanterns. In Beijing, the Lantern Festival actually lasts from the 13th day to the 17th day of the first lunar month. During this period, there used to be many lantern fairs, such as those in the Dengshikou (Lantern Market Entrance) area east of Donghuamen (Eastern Flower Gate), Di'anmen (Gate of Earthly Peace), Xinjiekou (New Street Entrance), and Xisi (West Four) Decorated Archway. People come from far and near and swarm into the lantern fairs to enjoy

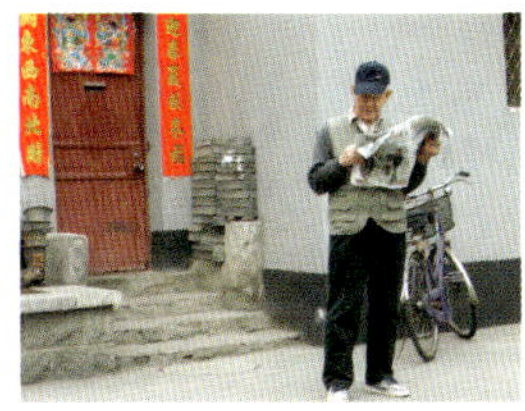

New things are always happening in Beijing.

Dongsi Shitiao (East Four Tenth Lane)

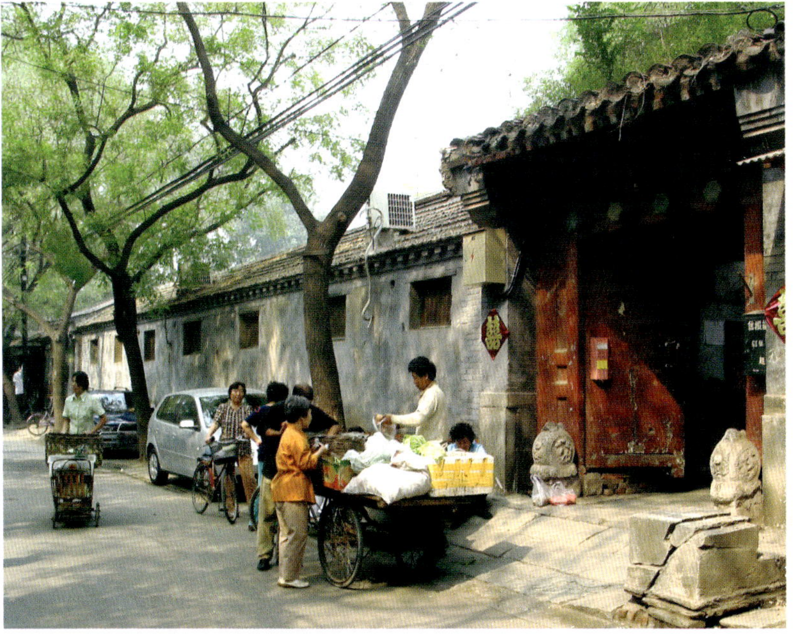

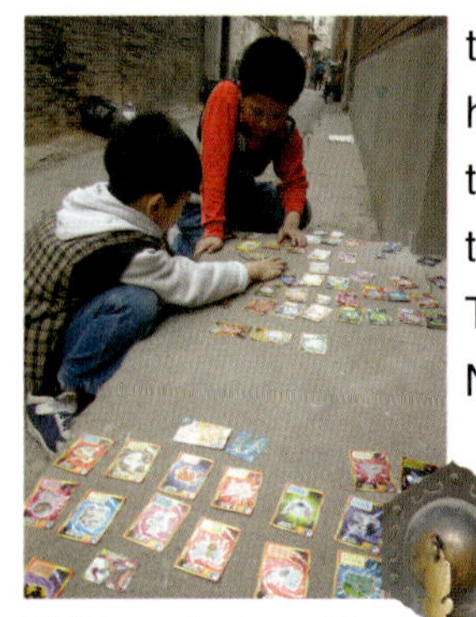
Children playing with picture cards

the lanterns and, of course, take some back home to add to the happy atmosphere. The Lantern Festival is a happy occasion, which seems to make people more generous and tolerant. The festival represents the end of the Chinese New Year celebrations.

Dragon Boat Festival

The Dragon Boat Festival takes place on the fifth day of the fifth lunar month, so it is also known as Double Fifth Day. During the Warring States Period, the Chu minister Qu Yuan (circa 340-277 BC) was deposed by the emperor after being framed by some treacherous officials and capitulators. He threw himself into the Miluo River in extreme sorrow and indignation on the fifth day of the fifth lunar month.

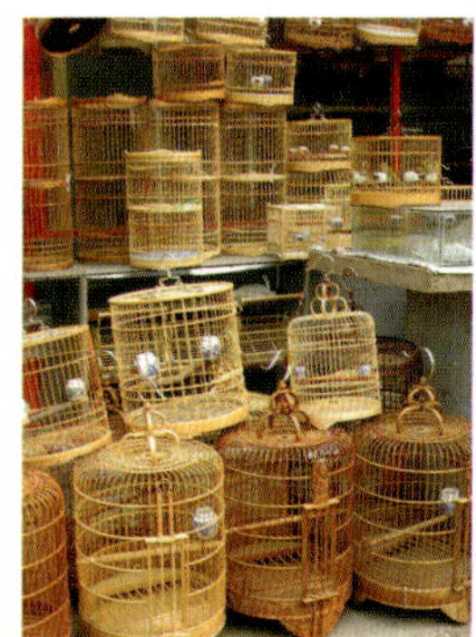
Cage birds are very popular in Beijing.

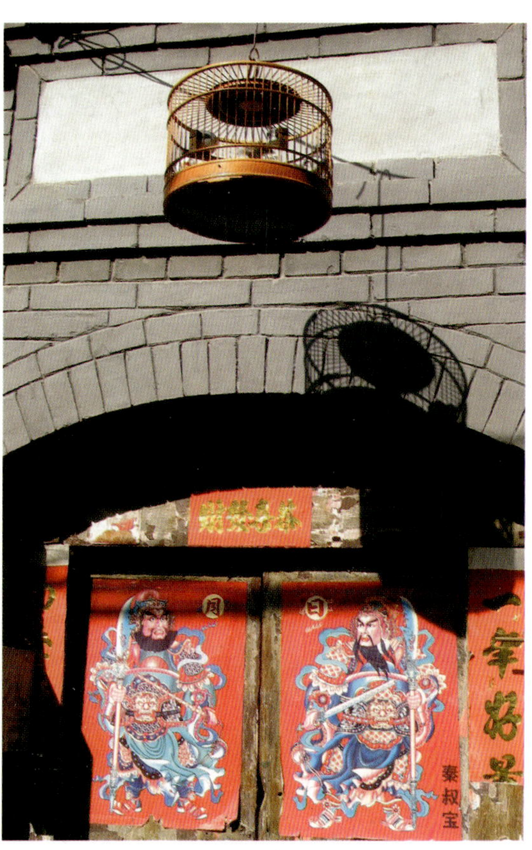

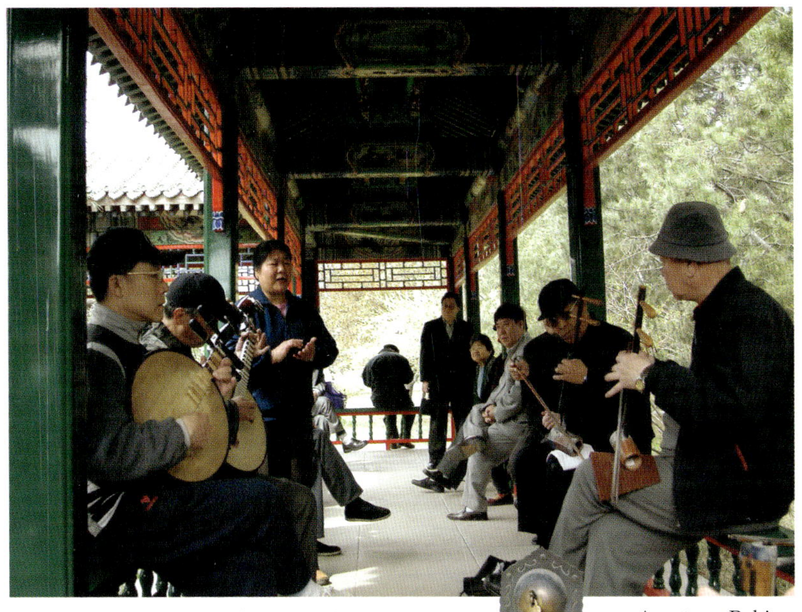
Amateur Peking opera performers

From that time to this, people commemorate Qu Yuan on the anniversary of his death: the fifth day of the fifth lunar month. According to legend, after Qu Yuan's death, people threw bamboo leaves filled with cooked rice into the water. The fish would therefore eat the rice rather than the heroic poet's body. This later became the custom of eating *zongzi* (the pyramid-shaped glutinous rice dumplings wrapped in bamboo or reed leaves). People also put flowers in the courtyards.

Another aspect of Double Fifth Day is the timing: At the beginning of summer, when diseases are likely to strike, people also wore talismans to fend off evil spirits. Little girls would decorate the ends of their pigtails or the fronts of their jackets with small pendants made of colorful threads and shaped like *zongzi*. Boys would have the character 王 (wáng, king) written on their forehead in realgar wine. They might hang up pictures of the Heavenly Master and Zhong Kui, a guardian against evil spirits, on the door of their homes, stick up red paper cuts

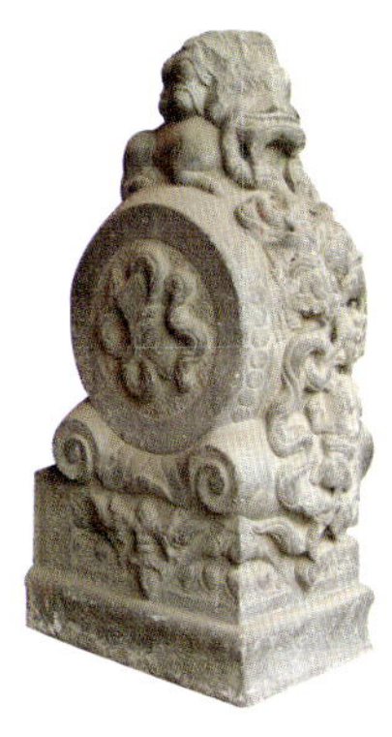

in the shape of snakes, scorpions, centipedes and toads and also attach some sweet flag leaves and mugwort outside their rooms and gates.

Mid-Autumn Festival

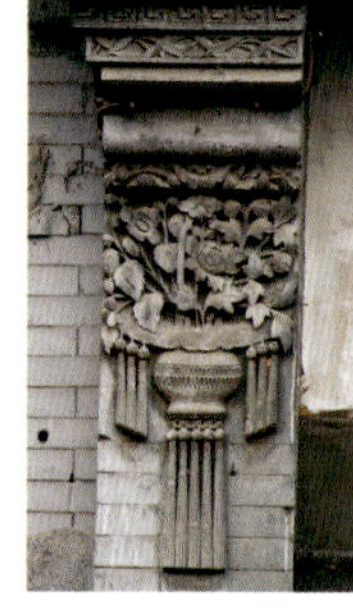

Falling on the 15th day of the eighth lunar month, Mid-Autumn Festival is the second most important festival for *hutong* residents. To prepare the traditional moon cakes, people mix together paste made from red beans or dates, assorted nuts and sugar to make the filling, cover this in flour and bake it. Chinese people would also celebrate Mid-Autumn Festival by worshiping the moon. They would place a table for burning incense in the courtyard and offer a sacrifice of fruit and moon cakes to the moon goddess Chang'e. It is said that this custom derives from the legend that a boy made a

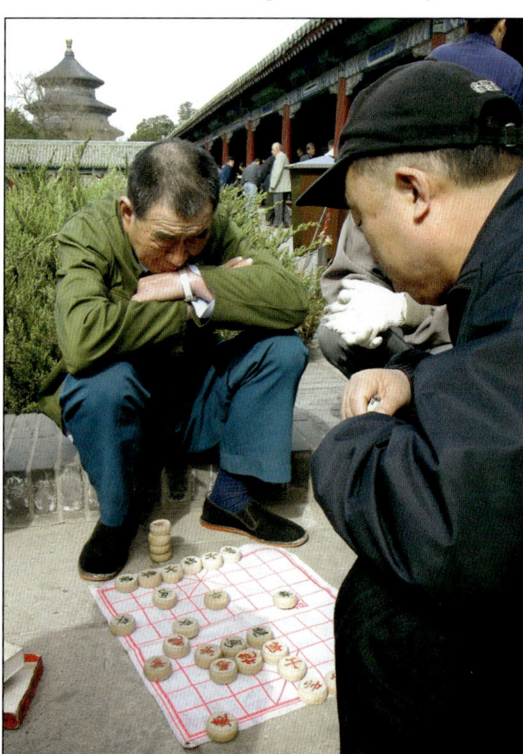

Two retired people play Chinese chess in the park.

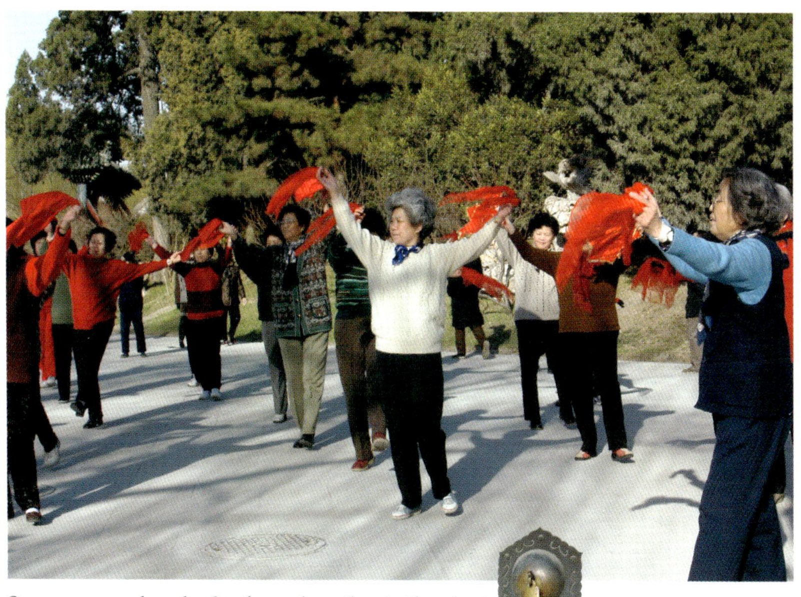

Scores or even hundreds of people gather in the street after dinner, wearing bright traditional clothes, waving red fans or silk scarves and swinging about cheerily, doing *yangge* dancing to the rhythm of drums and gongs. The dance is performed every day except in bad weather. *Yangge* dancing gives old people needed exercise and has almost become a must in their everyday lives.

sacrifice to Chang'e every Mid-Autumn Festival to thank her for her help. Clay rabbit toys known as *tuye* are popular during Mid-Autumn Festival. It is said that the clay rabbit design imitates Chang'e's pet rabbit, which pounds medicine on the moon. Children in particular love the clay rabbit.

As time has passed, great changes have taken place in quadrangle houses. Quadrangle houses that used to be inhabited by only one household are now inhabited by several families, who help each other and enjoy the intimate environment like one big family.

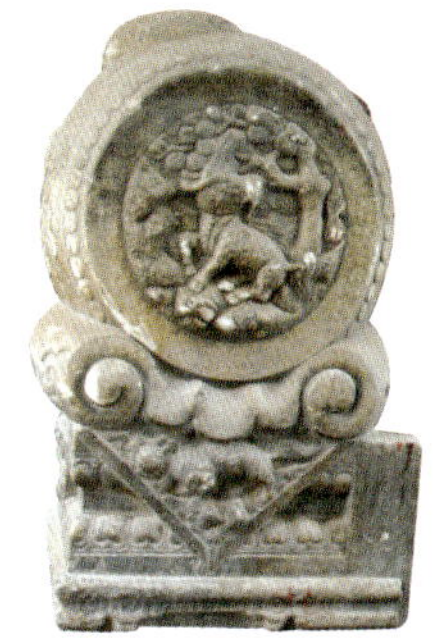

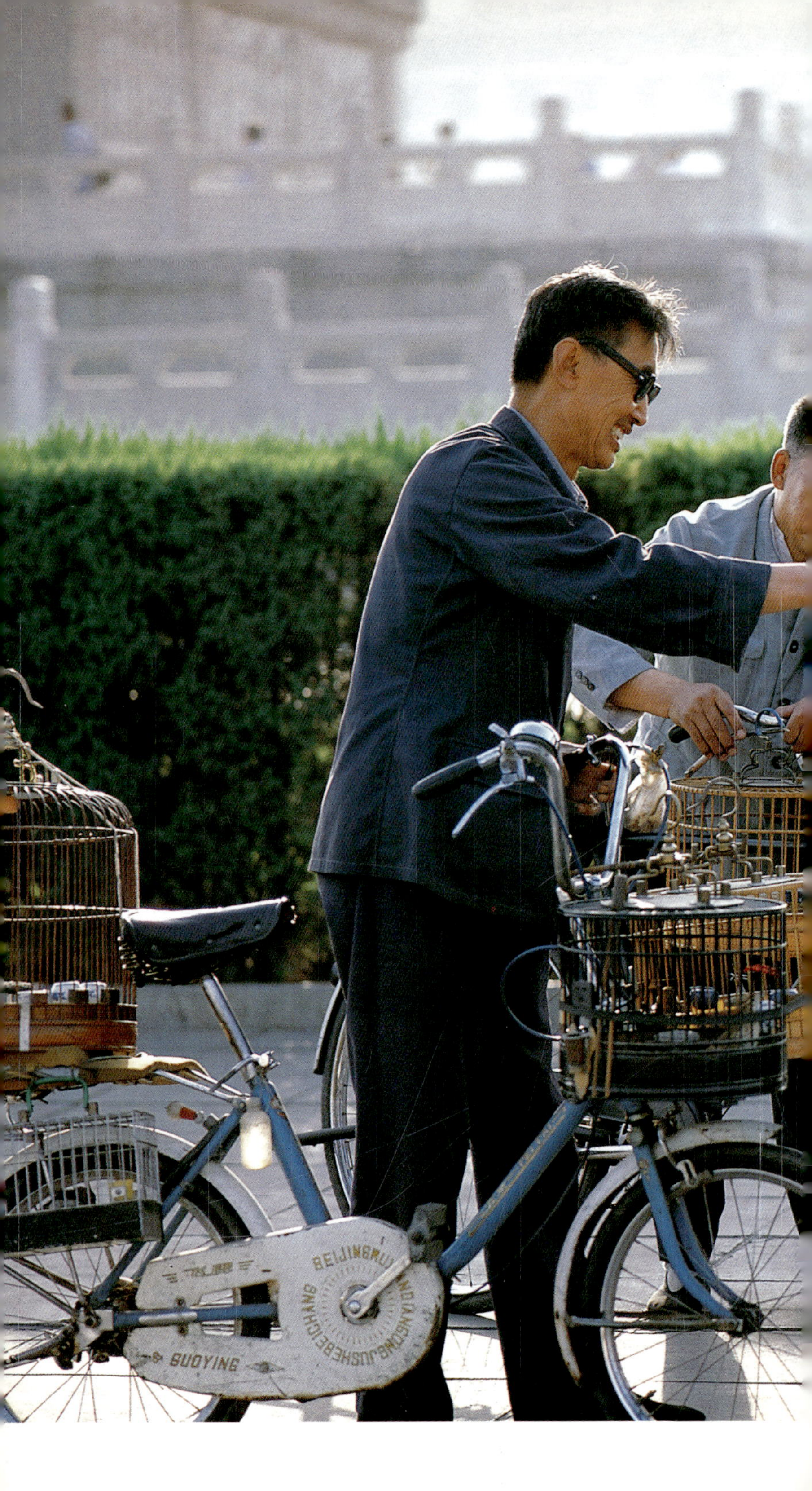

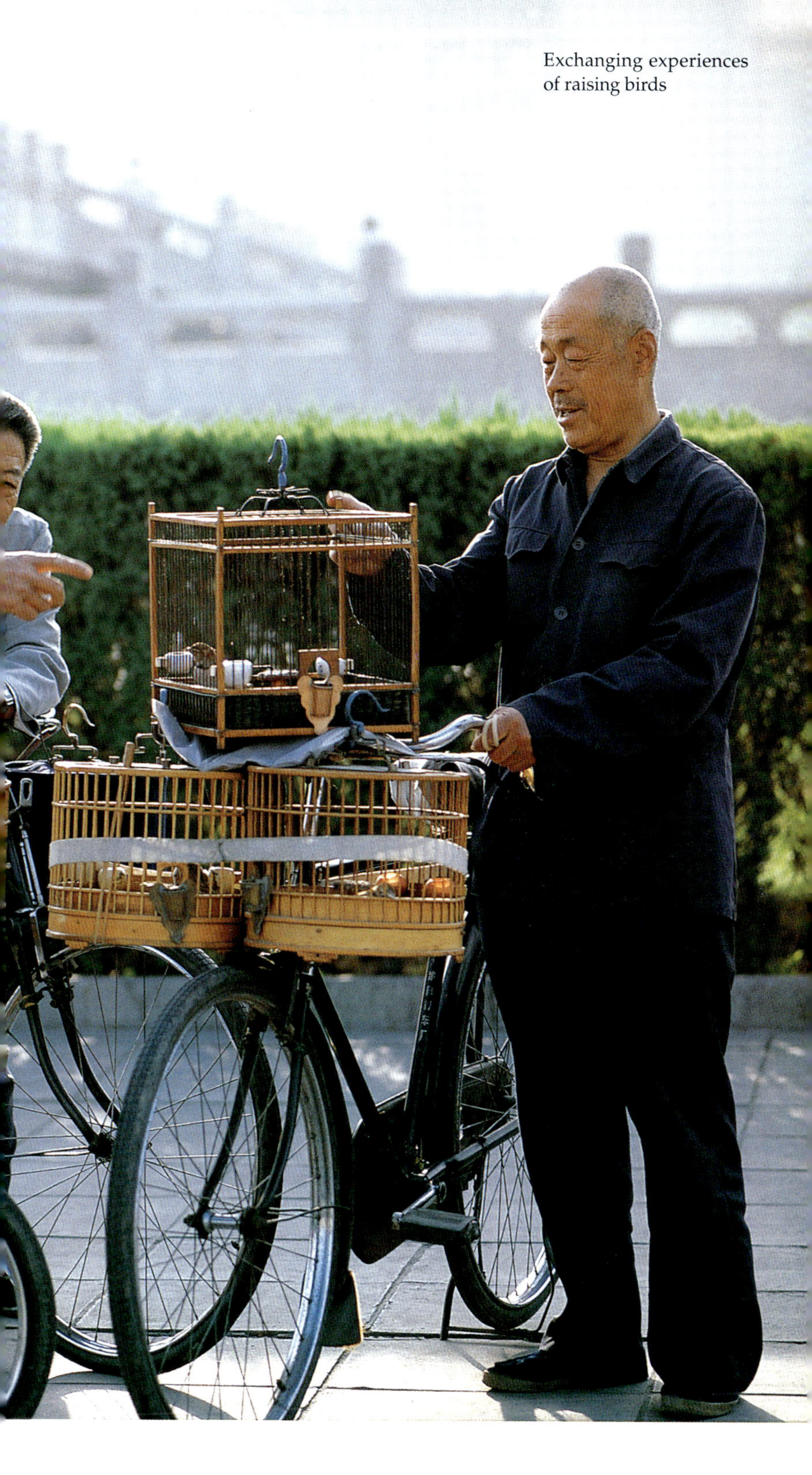
Exchanging experiences
of raising birds

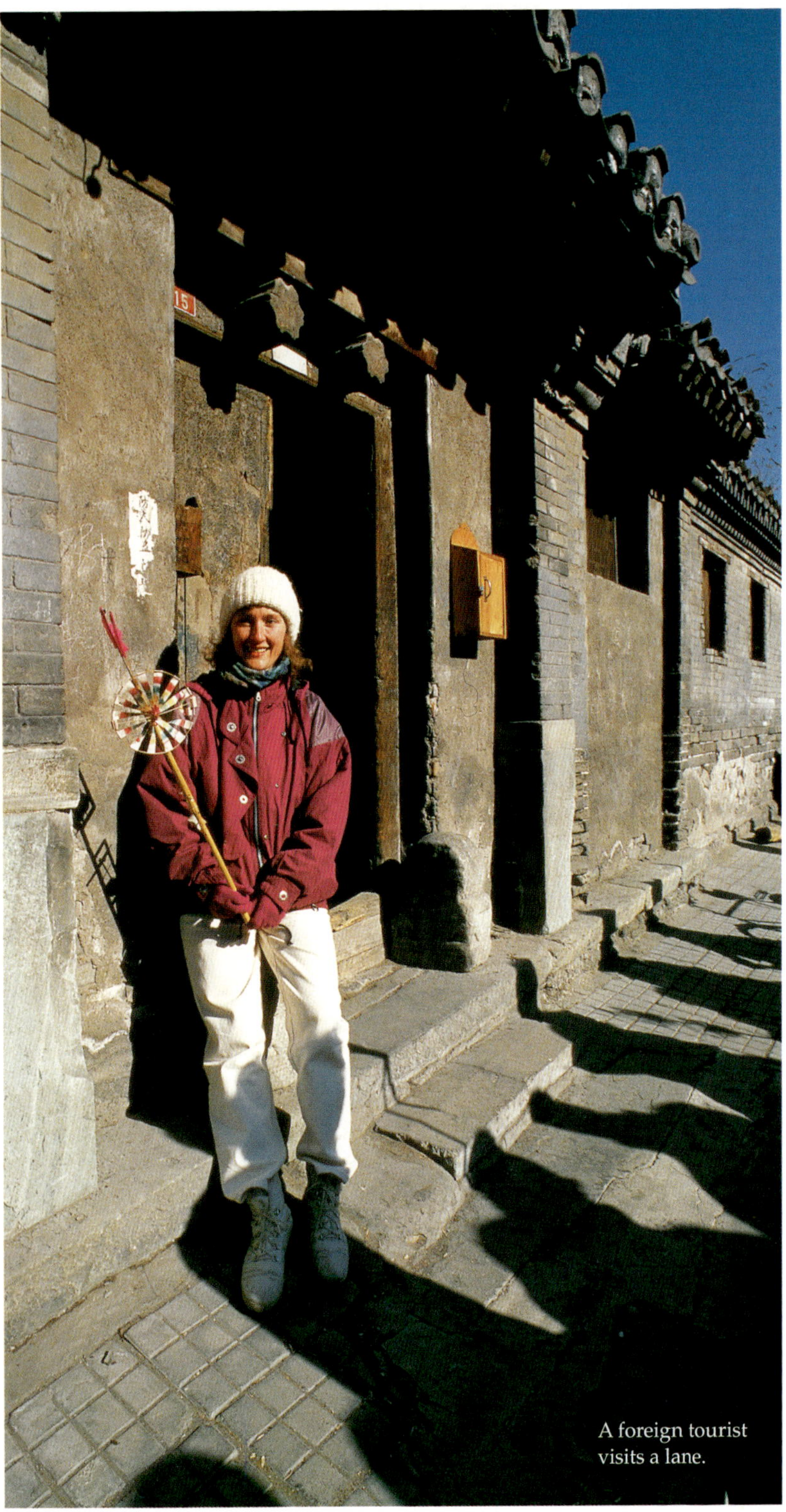

A foreign tourist
visits a lane.

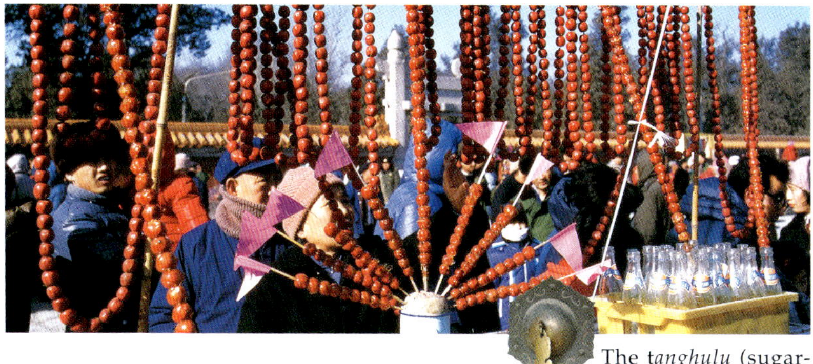

V. Temple Fairs

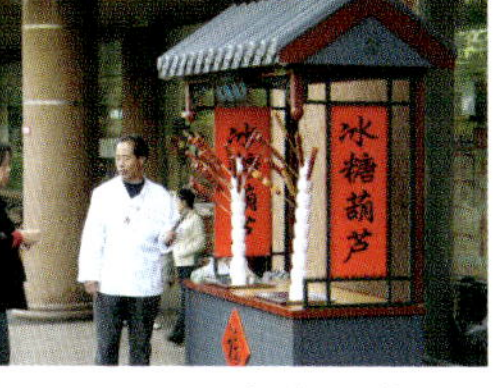

The *tanghulu* (sugar-coated haws on a stick) found at temple fairs are different from the usual kind.

Temple fairs are a traditional celebration at the lunar New Year. They have their origins in the Chinese religion of Taoism. Elaborate rituals and religious activities including the worship of gods, the burning of incense, folk art performances and festivals regularly took place around the temples. These later developed into a kind of carnival, which involved commercial activities in addition to religious activities and folk art performances.

A tanghulu seller in front of a market

At the fairs, there are lots of games to play, food to eat, household goods to buy, and performances to enjoy, such as cross-talk comedy, storytelling and vaudeville-style acts, and there are crowds of people. As an indispensable part of traditional folk customs, temple fairs play an important role in traditional Chinese culture.

Eating baked sweet potatoes

Today, instead of disappearing from the scene, temple fairs have maintained their traditional style while constantly adding modern content.

The most influential temple fairs in Beijing are the Baiyunguan (White Cloud Temple), Dazhongsi (Big Bell Temple), Longtan (Dragon Pool) and Ditan (Temple of the Earth) temple fairs. The

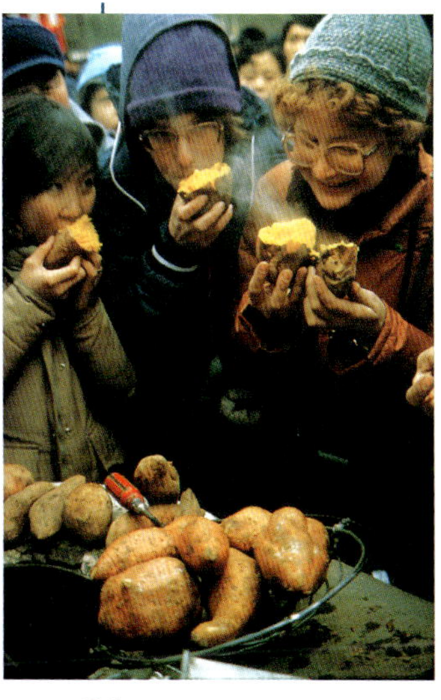

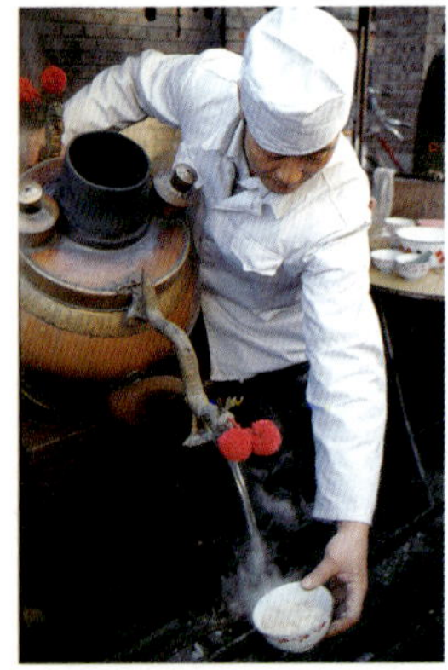

Pouring out *chatang* (paste or custard made of millet or sorghum flour)

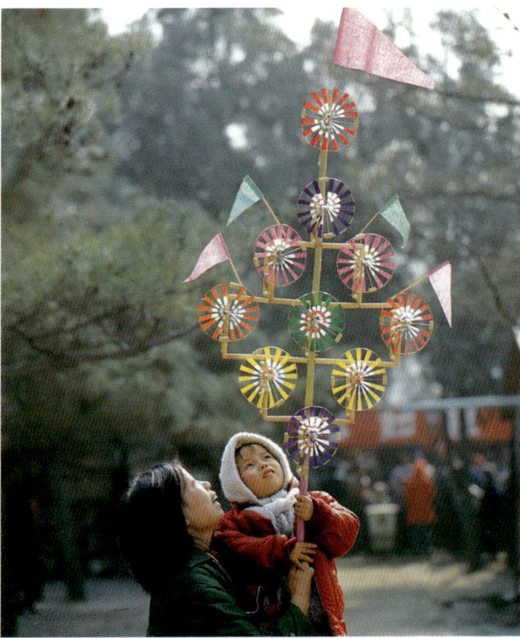

Dough figurines

fairs are held for a week during Spring Festival time and attract millions of visitors.

Baiyunguan is Beijing's largest Taoist temple and the headquarters of the Chinese Taoist Association, while Ditan is where ceremonies were held to honor and worship the god of the earth.

Ditan (Temple of the Earth) Fair

Located near Andingmen (Stability Gate), Ditan was originally where emperors of the Ming and Qing dynasties worshipped the god of earth.

Every summer solstice (June 22 according to the Gregorian calendar), the emperor would come to Ditan to command the ceremony in person.

At the Ditan temple fair, there are puppet shows, demonstrations by street performers from the Tianqiao area, acrobatics and displays of folk art and customs.

The Ditan ceremony is stamped with Chinese cultural characteristics. The ancients made

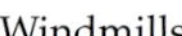

Windmills

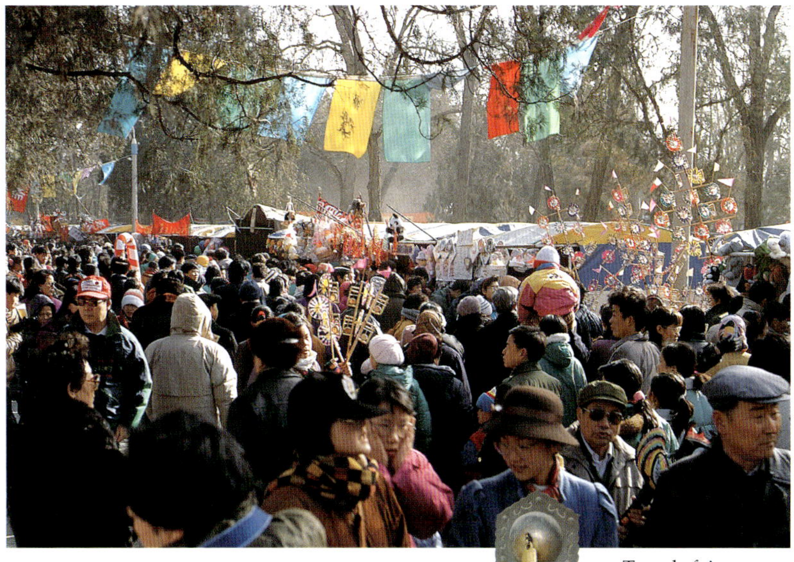

Temple fairs attract countless people every year.

sacrifices to heaven, earth, the mountains and rivers to demonstrate their worship of nature. The Ditan temple is China's biggest temple for worshiping the god of earth. Its altar is the main part of its architecture and is also China's biggest rectangular altar. The music and dances performed during the sacred ceremony are national treasures. The ceremony has profound connotations. In particular, the so-called sacrifices of the five mountains, five towns, four seas and four rivers are symbols of China's great expanse, fertility and unity.

Baiyunguan (White Cloud Temple) Fair

Baiyunguan (White Cloud Temple) is the largest Taoist temple in Beijing. At the Baiyunguan fair, there are various kinds of folk entertainment, such as stilt walking, lion dances and "rowboat" dances, but the most popular traditional amusement among local people is the game of hitting the "golden coin" hole.

At the Baiyunguan entrance, there is a bridge with no water underneath, called Wofeng (Leeward) Bridge. Under the bridge sits a

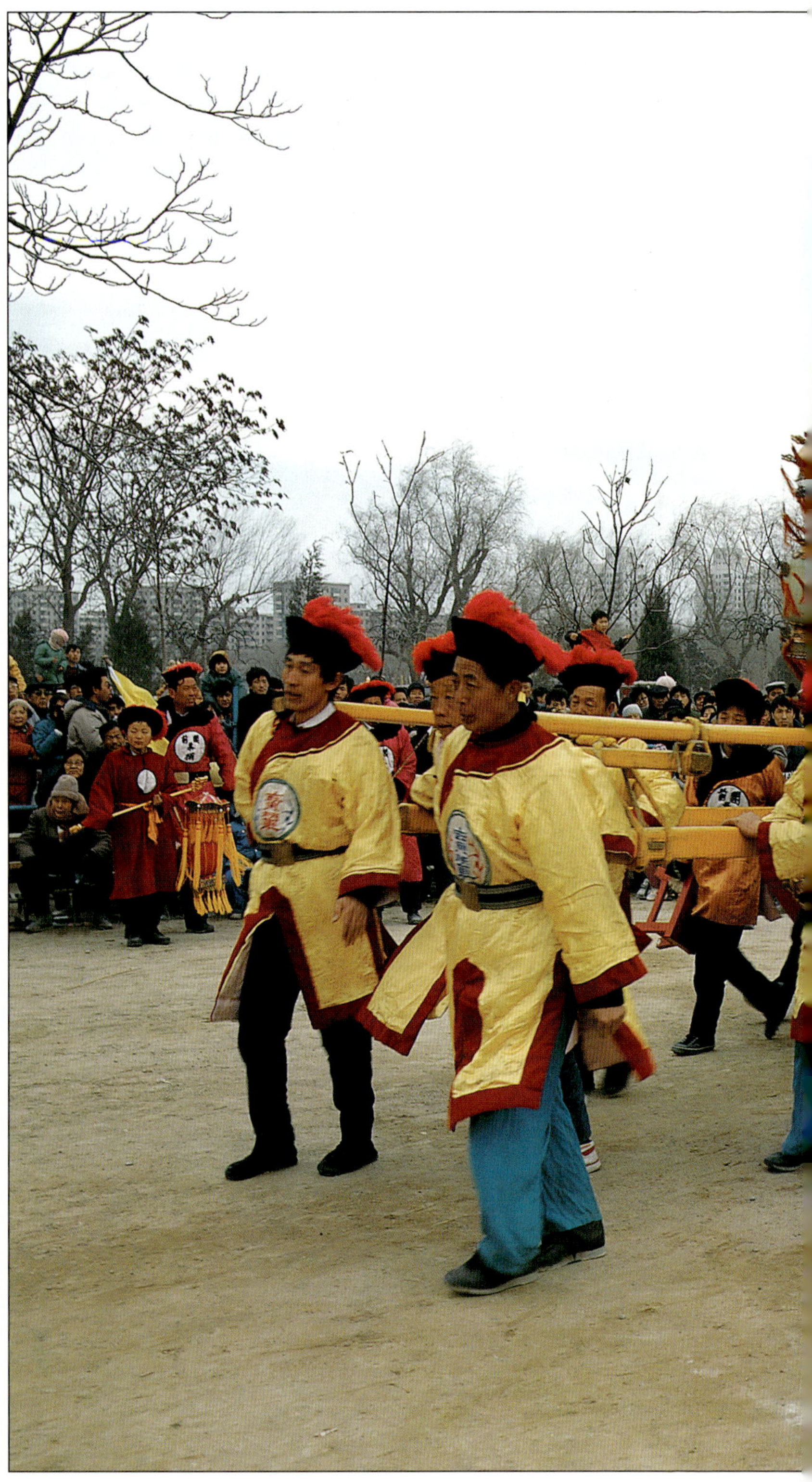

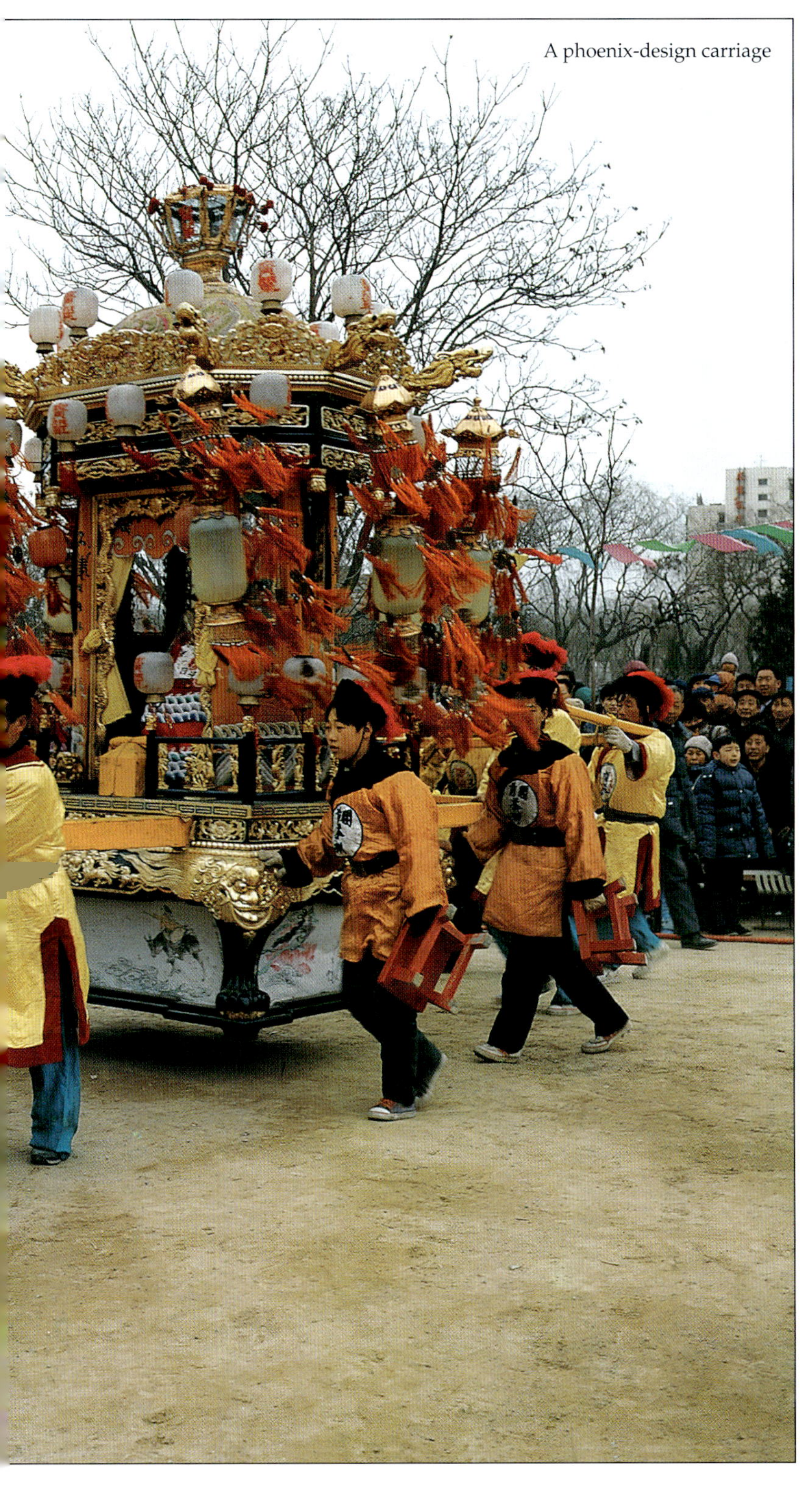

A phoenix-design carriage

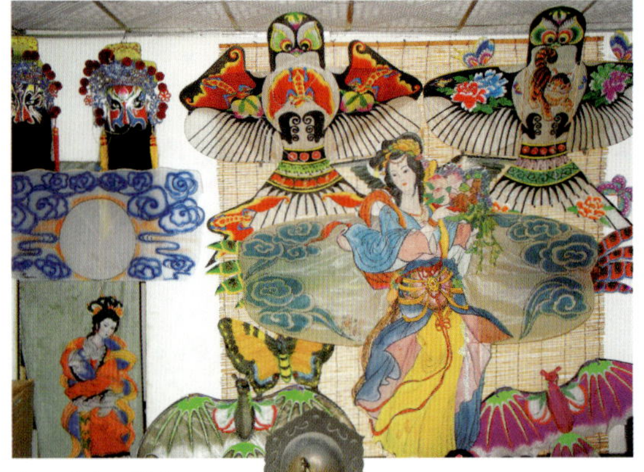

A variety of kites

Taoist with white hair and a youthful complexion, wearing a heavy Taoist robe and with his eyes closed. Two big coins, made of chipboard, hang down, one in front of his head and the other behind. There are bells hanging inside the holes in the big coins. Visitors exchange real money for temple coins by the bridge and throw these at the "golden coin" holes. It is said that anyone who hits a bell in one of the holes will have good luck and be safe and sound in the new year.

Longtan (Dragon Pool) Temple Fair

The Longtan temple fair is held in Longtan Park near Chongwenmen (Gate of Literary Virtue). The temple fair is a gathering of excellent Chinese and foreign folk art. The performances include one with lucky *hada* silk scarves performed by Tibetans from Qinghai Province, the Huangguoshu (yellow fruit tree) folk dance

Two performers doing cross-talk comedy (xiangsheng)

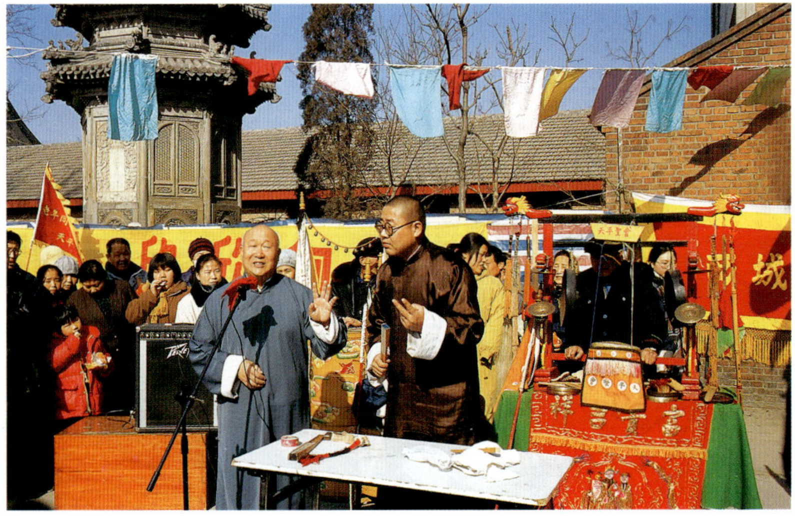

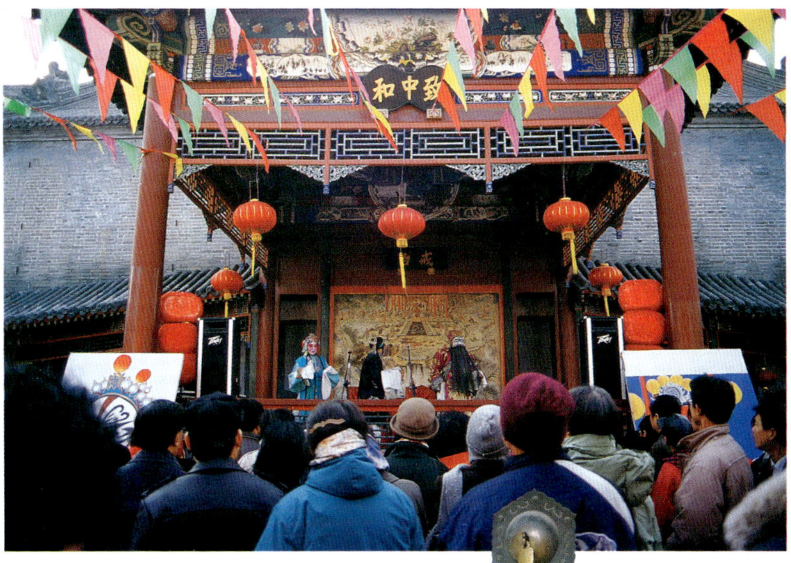

by the Bouyei ethnic from Guizhou Province, the seashore drum dance from Zhejiang Province, and a Hashima drumming performance from Japan.

There are traditional snacks from Beijing's age-old restaurants at the Longtan temple fair. Also available are various kinds of traditional Tianqiao area folk performances such as ballad singing, storytelling with musical accompaniment, comic dialogue, and acrobatics.

National sports champions assigned by the State Physical Culture Administration put on displays of games and fighting at the Longtan temple fair. Champions play visitors at the game of go, Chinese chess, international chess, checkers and gobang (five-in-a-row). In the fighting displays, the national judo, wrestling and kickboxing teams demonstrate their skills and invites challenges from the audience.

Honglou (Red Mansions) Temple Fair in Grand View Garden

Grand View Garden (Daguanyuan) is

A Peking opera performance at a temple fair

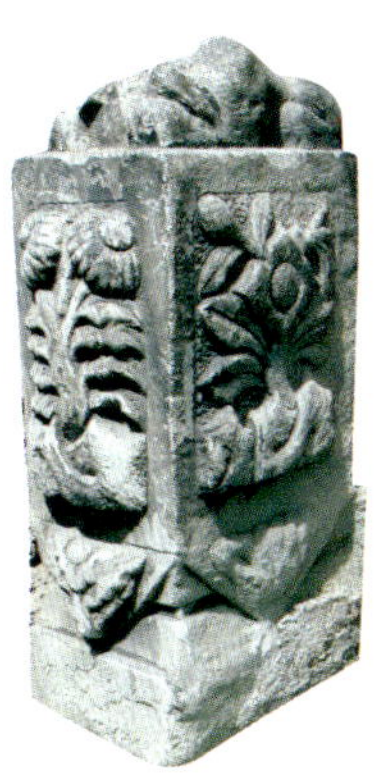

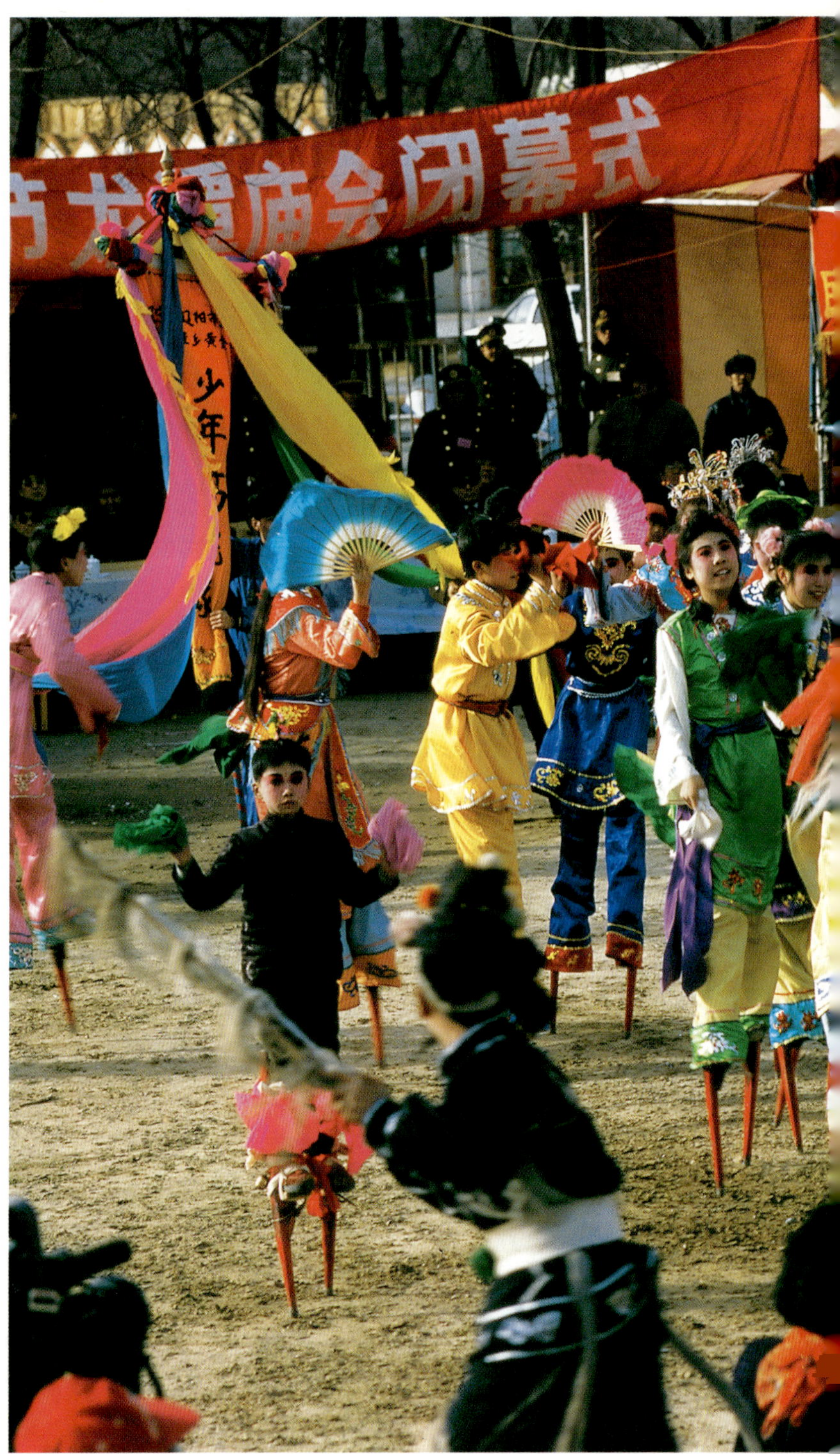

Stilt-walkers at the Longtan
(Dragon Pool) Temple Fair

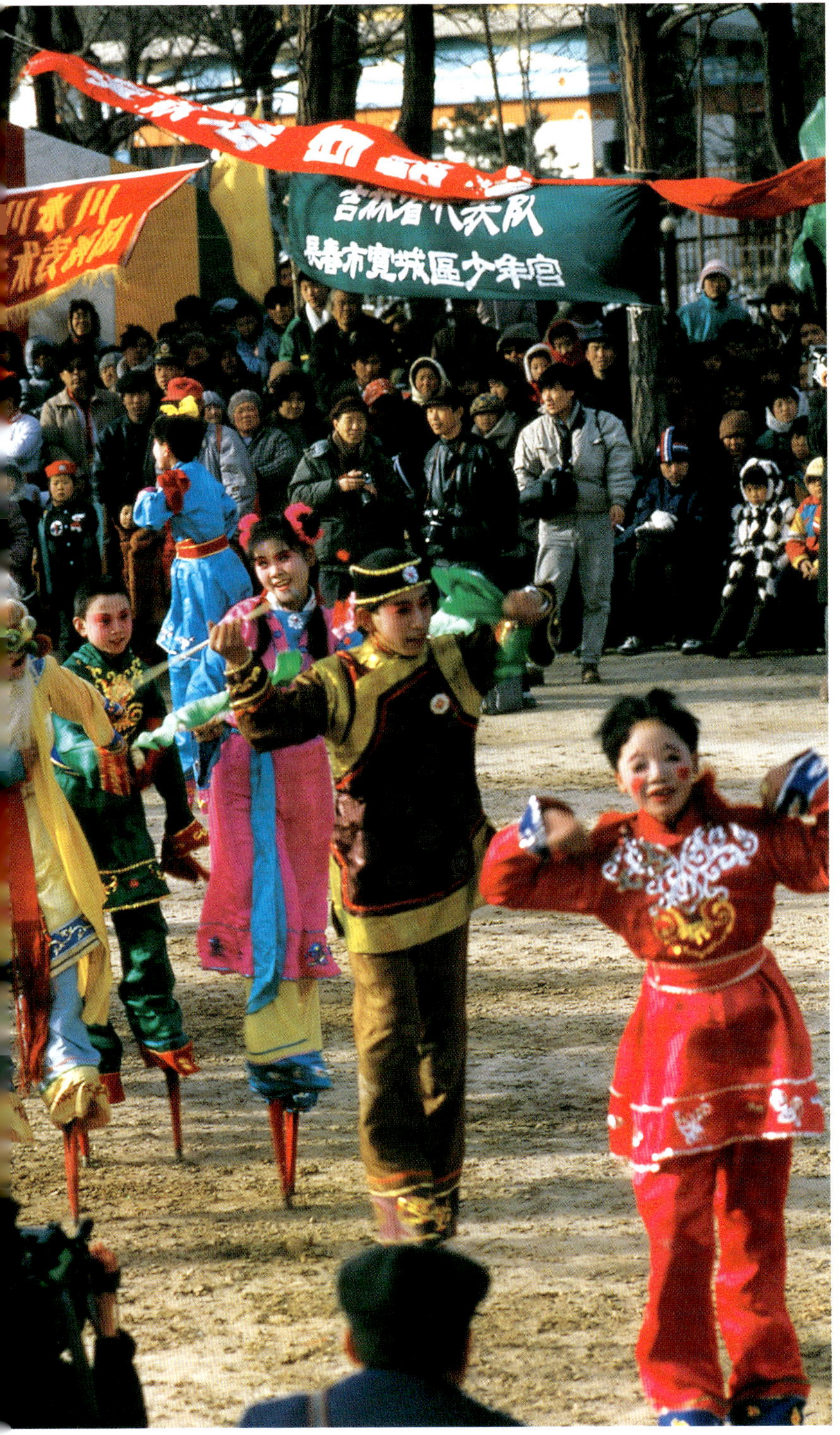

吉林省长春队
长春市宽城區少年宫

reminiscent of a luxurious garden in the Ming or Qing Dynasty style. In the Chinese classic novel *A Dream of Red Mansions* (*Hongloumeng*), Grand View Garden is the site of the mansion belonging to the Jia family, noble officials during the Ming Dynasty. The layout here is exactly like that described in the novel. The Honglou temple fair is mixture of folk customs and the culture of *A Dream of Red Mansions*. At the fair, visitors can see typical traditional Tianqiao area folk performances and the making of folk craft works. Games of chess and all kinds of performances take place

A stone drum in front of a prince's mansion

A lion dance

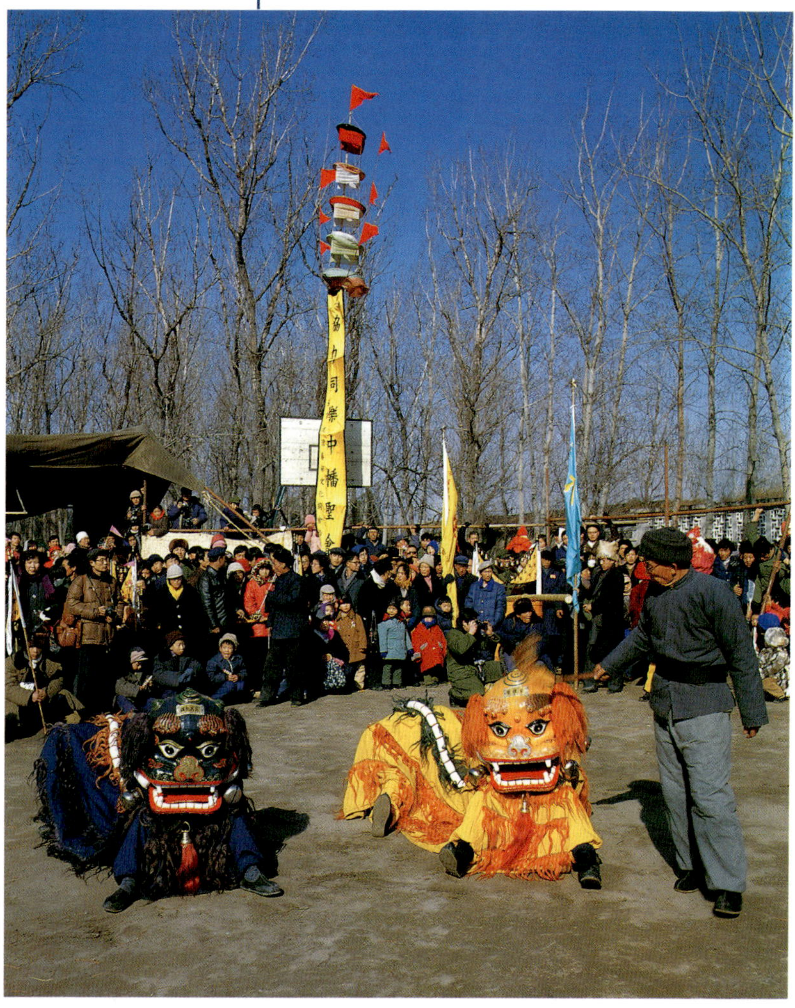

100

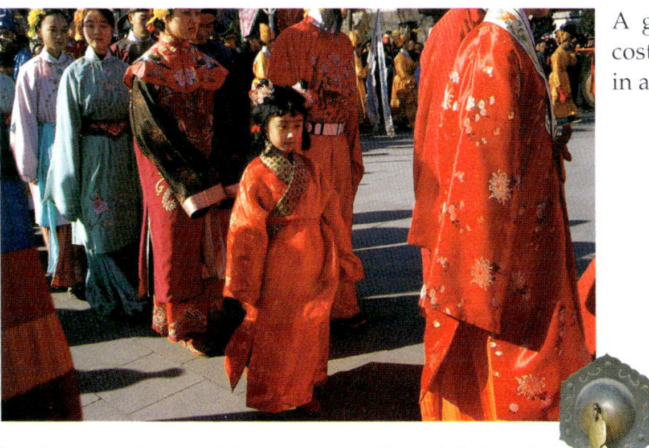

A girl in ancient costume takes part in a performance.

in the garden, with a corner for children's entertainment. "Homecoming of the Imperial Concubine," a scene from *A Dream of Red Mansions* is also performed, telling the story of the Jia family's eldest daughter. The temple's Grand View Garden was built specially for these occasions. The appearance of the imperial concubine in her phoenix crown and gorgeous gown under the high Homecoming Memorial Arch, gracefully greeting the audience, is a highlight of the Honglou temple fair's garden performances.

The "land boat" dance

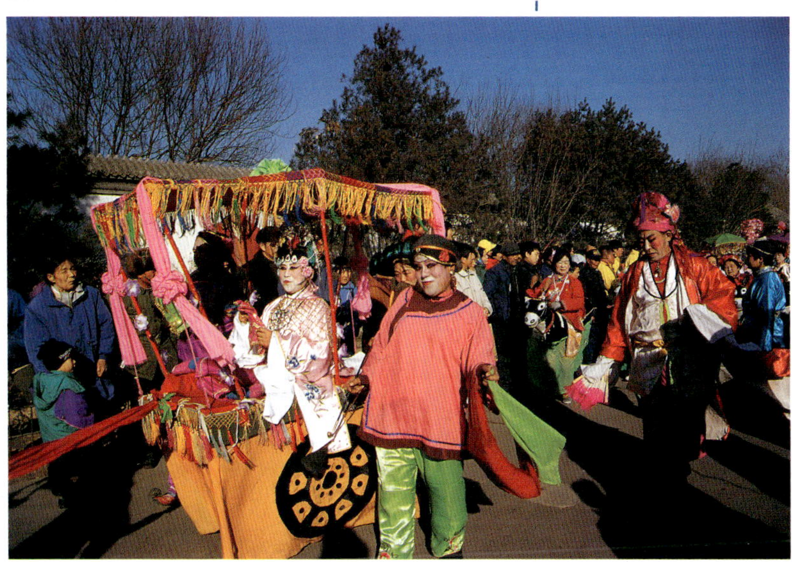

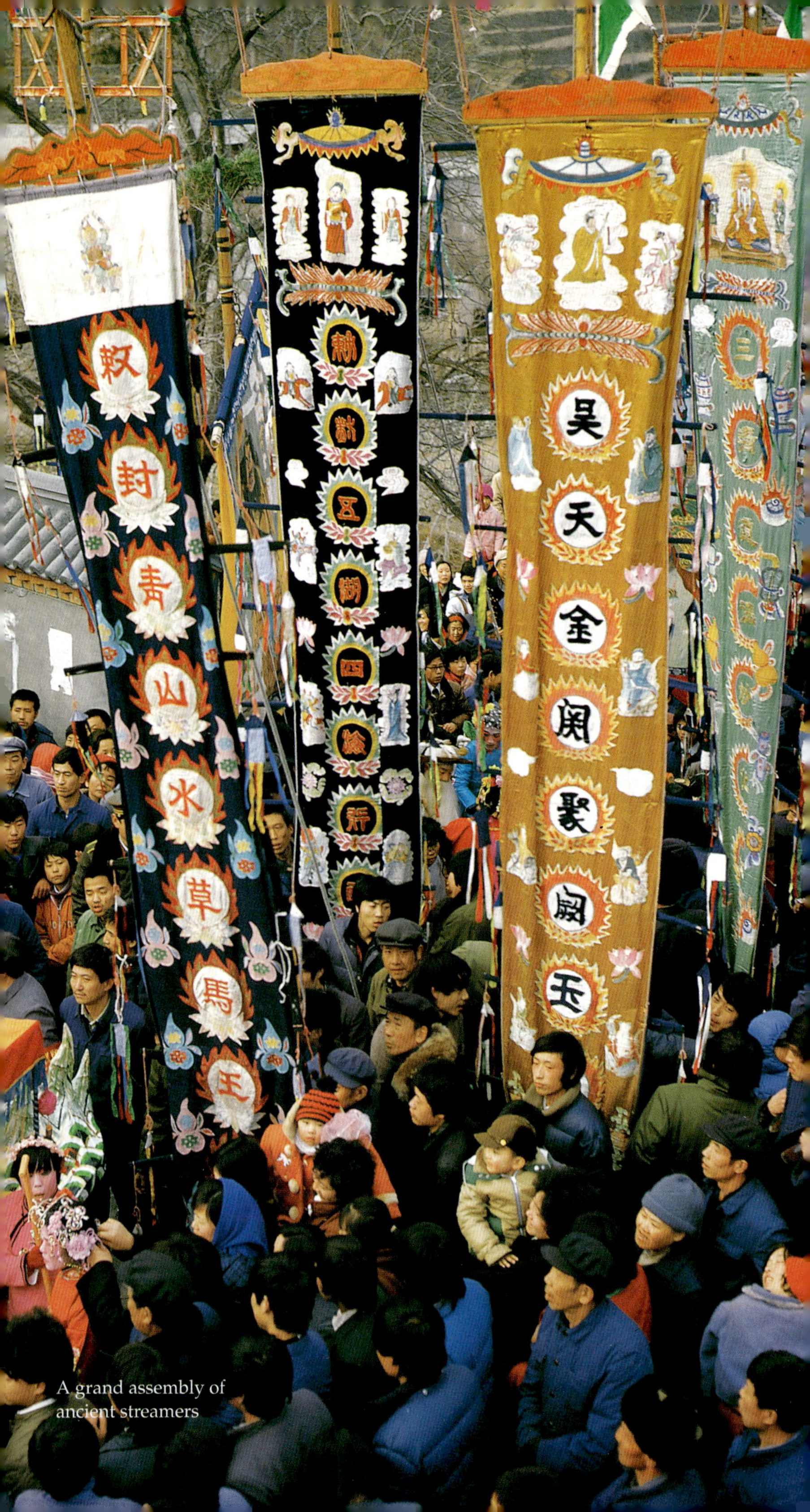

A grand assembly of ancient streamers

Traditional Beijing Temple Fairs

(Of the major traditional temple fairs listed below, only those at Baiyunguan and Miaofengshan still take place today. The others are listed for historical interest.)

Name	Religion	Location	Lunar date	Activities
Baiyunguan (White Cloud Temple)	Taoism	Baiyun Lu (White Cloud Road), West of Xibianmen (Western Informal Gate), Xicheng District	1st to 19th of the first month, 23rd and 24th of the sixth month	Celestial Gods Descent Day (8th day of the first month), Jade Emperor's birthday (9th day of the first month), lantern fair, scripture-sunning fair on the 18th and 19th of the sixth month, entertainment
Bixia Yuanjunci Beiding (North Temple to Princess Aurora)	Taoism	North of Deshengmen	1st to 15th of the fourth month	Food market
Bixia Yuanjunci Dongding (East Templc to Princess Aurora)	Taoism	East of Dongzhimen	1st to 18th of the fourth month	Food market
Bixia Yuanjunci Nanding (South Temple to Princess Aurora)	Taoism	Nanyuan Township, Fengtai District	1st to 15th of the fifth month	Worship of Princess Aurora, large pilgrims' fair, horse racing
Bixia Yuanjunci Beiding (North Temple to Princess Aurora)	Taoism	North of Deshengmen	1st to 15th of the fourth month	Food market
Bixia Yuanjunci Xiding (West Temple to Princess Aurora)	Taoism	Sijiqing Township, Haidian District	1st to 15th of the fourth month	Worship of Princess Aurora, large pilgrims' fair
Bixia Yuanjunsi (Temple to Princess Aurora)	Taoism	Tongxian County	15th to 18th of the fourth month	Worship of Princess Aurora, large pilgrims' fair
Dacun	Taoism	Dacun Township,	8th of the fourth	Performances to give

Name	Religion	Location	Lunar date	Activities
Niangniangmiao (Big Village Goddess Temple)		Mentougou District	month	thanks to the gods, stalls, entertainment
Dongba Niangniangmiao (Dongba Goddess Temple)	Taoism	Dongba, Chaoyang District	1st to 7th of the fifth month	Performances to give thanks to the gods, stalls, entertainment
Guandimiao (Temple to Lord Guan), outside Zuo'anmen	Buddhism	Shilihe, outside Guang'anmen	13th of the fifth month, 24th of the sixth month	Worship, performances to give thanks to Buddha, food market, sacrifices to Lord Guan on his birthday
Houheisi (Back Dark-Roofed Temple)	Tibetan Buddhism	Outside Deshengmen (Moral Victory Gate)	15th and 23rd of the first month	Dancing to drive out demons, entertainment, stalls
Huashenmiao (Temple to the Flower Goddess)	Taoism	North of Jijiamiao Village in the east of Fengtai Town	12th of the second month, 29th of the third month	Flower growers offer sacrifices and give performances to the flower goddess
Jilelin (Ecstatic Forest Temple)	Buddhism	Andingmenwai Dajie (Outer Street of the Stability Gate)	7th of the fifth month	Stonemasons, carpenters and builders offer sacrifices to Lu Ban, the master carpenter
Jietaisi (Temple of Ordination Altar)	Buddhism	On Ma'anshan (Saddle Hill), Fengtai District	1st to 15th of the fourth month, 6th of the sixth month	Sacrifices to Sakyamuni on his birthday (8th day of the fourth month), scripture-sunning fair, entertainment, stalls
Jingzhongmiao (Loyalty Temple)	Taoism	Dongzhimennei Dajie (Straight East Gate Inner Street)	1st, 13th to 17th of the first month	Worship, lantern fair, entertainment, stalls
Jingzhongmiao (Loyalty Temple)	Taoism	Shandongkou outside Qianmen (Front Gate)	1st, 13th to 17th of the first month	Worship, lantern fair, entertainment, stalls
Miaofengshan (Divine Peak Mountain)	Taoism	Mentougou District	1st to 15th of the fourth month, 15th of the seventh month	Worship of Princess Aurora, large pilgrims' fair, prayers and burning of paper clothes and money for the dead during the Zhongyuan Festival (15th day of the seventh month)
Pantaogong (Peach of Immortality Palace)	Taoism	West of Dongbianmen (Eastern Informal Gate)	1st to 15th of the third month	Worship of the Heavenly Queen Mother, pilgrims' flower fair, entertainment
Sanzhongsi	Taoism	East of	2nd of the first month	Worship, entertainment,

Name	Religion	Location	Lunar date	Activities
(Temple to the Three Loyal Heroes –Zhuge Liang, Yue Fei and Wen Tianxiang)		Dongbianmen (Eastern Informal Gate)		stalls
Shanguosi (Good Karma Temple)	Buddhism	North of Guang'anmen (Gate of Pervasive Peace)	6th of the sixth month	Scripture sunning fair (where scriptures made damp in winter are left to dry in the sun)
Taiyanggong (Sun Palace)	Buddhism	Zuo'anmennei Dajie (Left Gate of Peace Inner Street)	1st to 15th of the second month	Worship of the sun god, market
Tanzhesi (Temple of the Pool and Wild Mulberry)	Tibetan Buddhism	Mentougou District	1st to 15th of the third month	Worship, entertainment, stalls
Tianxiangong (Goddess Palace)	Buddhism	Nangangzi, outside Chongwenmen (Gate of Literary Virtue)	15th to 18th of the fourth month	Worship of Princess Aurora, pilgrims' fair
Tianxianmiao (Goddess Temple)	Taoism	Gaoliangqiao (Broomcorn Bridge), west of Xizhimen	8th of the fourth month	Worship of Princess Aurora
Wanshousi (Longevity Temple)	Buddhism	Northwest of Xizhimen (Straight West Gate)	1st to 15th of the fourth month	Sacrifices to Sakyamuni on his birthday (the 8th day of the fourth month), the giving of beans as an act of friendship, entertainment, stalls
Wofosi (Reclining Buddha Temple)	Tibetan Buddhism	West of Dongbianmen (Eastern Informal Gate)	28th to 30th of the third month, 1st to 5th of the fifth month	Worship, entertainment, stalls
Wofosi (Temple of Reclining Buddha)	Buddhism	Outside Chongwenmen (Gate of Literary Virtue)	1st to 15th of the fifth month	Worship, entertainment, stalls
Xihuangsi (West Yellow Temple)	Taoism	West of Andingmen (Stability Gate)	15th of the first month	Dancing to drive out demons, religious rituals, contests to choose the best-decorated horses and carriages
Xiangyansi (Incense Rock Temple)	Buddhism	Yongfengxiang, Haidian District	5th of the fourth month	Performances to give thanks to Buddha, entertainment, stalls

Name	Religion	Location	Lunar date	Activities
Yajishan	Taoism	Pinggu County	1st to 15th of the fourth month	Worship of Princess Aurora, large pilgrims' fair
Yaoshenmiao (Temple to the Coal Pit God)	Taoism	Mentougou District	17th of the 12th month	Miners offer sacrifices to the Coal Pit God
Yonghegong (Lama Temple)	Buddhism	North of Beixinqiao (North New Bridge), by Yonghegong subway station	30th of the first month, 1st of the second month, 13th of the fifth month	Dancing to drive out demons, entertainment, stalls Worship
Zhenwumiao (Temple of Genuine Prowess)	Buddhism	Dongba, Chaoyang District	3rd of the third month	

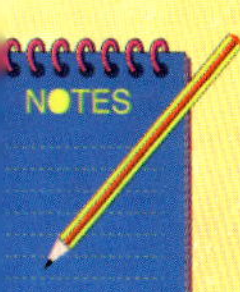

Travel notes

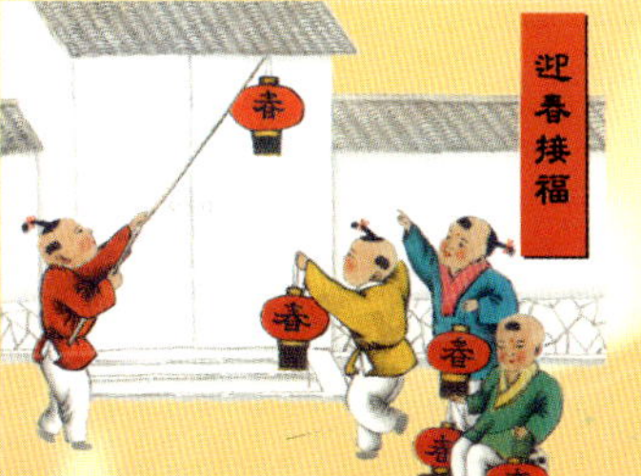

图书在版编目（CIP）数据

北京胡同·名人故居/肖晓明策划．李连霞撰文．
－北京：外文出版社，2003.12
（漫游北京）

ISBN 7-119-03346-8

Ⅰ．北… Ⅱ．①肖… ②李… Ⅲ．①城市道路－简介－北京市－英文
②名人故居－简介－北京市－英文 Ⅳ．k921：k878.2

中国版本图书馆 CIP 数据核字(2003)第 055066 号

策　　　　划：肖晓明

执 行 编 辑：兰佩瑾
撰　　　　文：李连霞
摄　　　　影：王建华　　王文波　　高明义　　严向群　　兰佩瑾等
翻　　　　译：严　晶
封 面 设 计：吴　涛
版 式 设 计：元　青等
责 任 编 辑：兰佩瑾

北京胡同·名人故居

© 外文出版社
外文出版社出版
（中国北京百万庄大街 24 号）
邮政编码：100037
外文出版社网页: http://www.flp.com.cn
外文出版社电子邮件地址: info@flp.com.cn
sales@flp.com.cn
北京大容彩色印刷有限公司印刷
中国国际图书贸易总公司发行
（中国北京车公庄西路 35 号）
北京邮政信箱第 399 号 邮政编码 100044 作
2005 年 1 月(长 24 开)第 1 版
2005 年第 1 版第 1 次印刷
（英）
ISBN 7-119-03346-8/J·1653（外）
004500（平）
85-E-563P